RESPONSE TO THE END OF HISTORY
Eschatology and Situation in Luke-Acts

SOCIETY
OF BIBLICAL
LITERATURE

DISSERTATION SERIES

J. J. M. Roberts, Old Testament Editor
Charles Talbert, New Testament Editor

Number 92

RESPONSE TO THE END OF HISTORY

by
John T. Carroll

John T. Carroll

RESPONSE TO THE END OF HISTORY
Eschatology and Situation in Luke-Acts

Scholars Press
Atlanta, Georgia

RESPONSE TO THE END OF HISTORY
Eschatology and Situation in Luke-Acts

John T. Carroll

Ph.D., 1986
Princeton Theological Seminary

Advisor:
David R. Adams

Library of Congress Cataloging-in-Publication Data

Carroll, John T., 1954–
  Response to the end of history.

  (Dissertation series ; no. 92)

  1. Eschatology—biblical teaching. 2. Bible.
N.T. Luke—Criticism, interpretation, etc. 3. Bible.
N.T. Acts—Criticism, interpretation, etc. I. Title.
II. Series: Dissertation series (Society of Biblical
Literature) ; no. 92.
BS2545.7C37 1988   236   87-12699
ISBN 1-55540-148-1
ISBN 1-55540-149-X

Printed in the United States of America

Contents

Preface

Study of Luke's expectation of the end of history has provided me both challenge and joy over the past three years, and now I come to the end of this research project. I do so all too aware that questions left unanswered and broader implications left unpursued still beckon. The task of extending my study of this dimension of early Christian experience to writings outside Luke-Acts is one which I plan to engage over a lifetime. Successful completion of a work of such magnitude carries with it the accumulation of an enormous debt of gratitude. The survey of recent scholarship (chapter 1) and the ensuing exegetical discussion both reflect my indebtedness to a host of scholars; even where I have disagreed with their methods and findings, I have learned from their work.

I thank the members of my dissertation committee, Dr. David R. Adams, Professor Paul W. Meyer, and Dr. Martinus C. de Boer, for their sage counsel, valuable criticisms, and encouragement at every turn. Although I cannot pretend to have mastered the art of exegesis, what proficiency I have acquired is due in large measure to the excellent models from whom I have learned: David Adams, Paul Meyer, and J. Christiaan Beker. I thank each of them. To David Adams a special debt of gratitude is owed, for he not only prompted me to this particular research project but also contributed his gift of critical acumen each step of the way.

I include a word of thanks to my parents, James R. and Mildred L. Carroll, whose love and example have left such a deep imprint on me, this dissertation being no exception. Above all, I thank my wife, Cindy Walker, and my son, Andrew Walker Carroll, for their constant love and support throughout the process of research and writing. They have inspired me, tolerated me, believed in me, and rescued me from a one-dimensional existence. It is to Cindy that I dedicate this study.

1

Research on Eschatology and Situation in Luke-Acts: Survey and Method

The subject of Lukan eschatology has maintained a prominent position in Lukan studies throughout the past three decades. This period has witnessed an accumulation of hypotheses but little agreement in method or results. The nature of Luke's future expectation remains an open question.

Because of the number and diversity of proposals regarding Luke's eschatological perspective, the study begins with an extensive (though not exhaustive) survey of recent research. By means of a typology of views on Lukan eschatology, I aim to clarify the issues involved. Chapter 1 concludes with a discussion of methodological issues; here I outline the method that has guided the present examination of Luke's eschatological expectation.

A. SURVEY OF RESEARCH

The appearance in 1953 of H. Conzelmann's monograph *Die Mitte der Zeit*,[1] it is generally recognized,[2] represented a watershed in the study of Luke-Acts. That pioneering redaction-critical probe of Luke-Acts (primarily of Luke[3]) served as a catalyst for renewed interest in Lukan theology and, specifically, in the eschatological perspective of Luke-Acts. Conzelmann's portrait of "uneschatological Luke" has exerted far-reaching influence, with E. Grässer[4] and E.

---

[1] English translation: *The Theology of St. Luke,* tr. G. Buswell (New York: Harper & Row, 1961).

[2] See, e.g., C. H. Talbert, "The Redaction Critical Quest for Luke the Theologian," in *Jesus and Man's Hope,* ed. D. G. Buttrick (Pittsburgh, 1970) 171–222, 171; and especially "Shifting Sands: The Recent Study of the Gospel of Luke," *Int* 30 (1976) 381–95, 382–83; S. G. Wilson, "Lukan Eschatology," *NTS* 15 (1969–70) 330–47, 330; B. R. Gaventa, "The Eschatology of Luke-Acts Revisited," *Encounter* 43 (1982) 27–42.

[3] P. Borgen redressed this imbalance in Conzelmann's inquiry, by focusing attention more closely on the narrative of Acts, in "Eschatology and Heilsgeschichte in Luke-Acts" (Madison, NJ: Drew University Ph.D. dissertation, 1956).

[4] See especially *Das Problem der Parusieverzögerung in den synoptischen Evangelien und in der Apostelgeschichte* (Berlin: Töpelmann, 1957); and more recently "Die Parusieerwartung in der Apostelgeschichte," in *Les Actes des Apôtres: traditions, rédaction, théologie,* ed. J. Kremer (Leuven: University, 1979) 99–127.

Haenchen[5] giving added impetus to this appraisal of Luke's enterprise. Far from forging a consensus, however, Conzelmann's reading of Luke-Acts has provoked a continuing debate, the yield being a chorus of discordant voices united only in their disagreement with the Professor from Göttingen.

The aim of this section is to sketch the larger contours of recent work on Lukan eschatology, and to do so from the vantage point afforded by a particular hypothesis.[6] My hypothesis is that the disarray in approaches to Lukan eschatology has resulted, in great measure, from a failure to consider the correlation between Luke's eschatological perspective and the situation to which his eschatological message was addressed.

This survey of research will therefore focus on the manner in which significant investigations of Lukan theology have—whether explicitly or not—located Luke's eschatological view in a specific social and historical setting. In order to give some order to a field which resists systematization, I will place the studies to be discussed under certain headings, where common emphases permit.[7] The present inquiry seeks not simply to add another voice to the chorus but also to illumine reasons for the prevailing confusion.

---

[5] *The Acts of the Apostles,* tr. B. Noble and G. Shinn, rev. R. McL. Wilson (Philadelphia: Westminster, 1971).

[6] Useful sketches of recent research may be found in F. Bovon, *Luc le théologien: vingt-cinq ans de recherches (1950–1975)* (Neuchatel/Paris: Delachaux & Niestlé, 1978) 11–84; E. Grässer, "Acta-Forschung seit 1960," *TRu* 42 (1977) 1–68, 63–66; E. Plümacher, "Acta-Forschung 1974–1982," *TRu* 48 (1983) 1–56, 35–45; J. Zmijewski, *Die Eschatologiereden des Lukas-Evangeliums* (Bonn: Peter Hanstein, 1972) 1–37; H. Farrell, "The Eschatological Perspective of Luke-Acts" (Boston: Boston University Ph.D. dissertation, 1972) 6–15; Gaventa, "Revisited," 27–33; R. Maddox, *The Purpose of Luke-Acts* (Edinburgh: T. & T. Clark, 1982) 100–02; and E. Richard, "Luke—Writer, Theologian, Historian: Research and Orientation of the 1970's," *BTB* 13 (1983) 3–15, 5.

[7] This thematic arrangement—necessary because of the magnitude and complexity of research in the field—has the disadvantage of blurring lines of development of scholarship on this question. In particular, the prominent role played by parousia delay in the analysis of Lukan eschatology should be seen in the light of the wider approaches to New Testament eschatology advanced by J. Weiss (e.g., *Die Predigt Jesu vom Reiche Gottes* [Göttingen: Vandenhoeck and Ruprecht, 1892]; ET: *Jesus' Proclamation of the Kingdom of God* [Philadelphia: Fortress, 1971]); A. Schweitzer (e.g., *Von Reimarus zu Wrede* [Tübingen: J. C. B. Mohr, 1906]; ET: *The Quest of the Historical Jesus* [New York: Macmillan, 1968]); M. Werner (e.g., *Die Entstehung des christlichen Dogmas problemgeschichtlich dargestellt* [Bern: Paul Haupt, 1941]; ET: *The Formation of Christian Doctrine* [London: Adam & Charles Black, 1957]); and R. Bultmann (e.g., *Theology of the New Testament* [2 vol.; London: SCM, 1955] 2.114–18, 137–38). Nevertheless, it is legitimate to begin the present sketch of scholarship with Conzelmann because, although he is simply elaborating the Bultmann line, Conzelmann's application of redaction critical methodology to Luke-Acts did alter the climate of Lukan scholarship, in the process casting the spotlight on eschatology in a manner unprecedented in earlier study.

1. "Un-eschatological Luke": The Eschaton Recedes
in Time and in Significance in Luke-Acts

Although it was Conzelmann who first forged this exegetical approach into a cogent synthesis, he had antecedents, all within the Bultmann camp. R. *Bultmann* himself set the agenda: in his view, the author of Luke-Acts perceived Christianity as "an entity of world history." That Luke wrote

> an account of the origin and earliest history of the Christian Church — in which the eschatological Congregation, of course, would have no interest — shows how far removed he is from its own way of thinking. The fact that he wrote Acts as a sequel to his Gospel completes the confirmation that he has surrendered the original kerygmatic sense of the Jesus-tradition . . . and has historized it.[8]

Bultmann's student P. *Vielhauer* actually launched (in print) this line of argument with his essay "Zum 'Paulinismus' der Apostelgeschichte" (1950),[9] in which he argued "how uneschatologically Luke thinks is apparent not only from the content, but especially from the fact of Acts."[10] Imminent eschatological expectation and the decision to leave to posterity an account of Christian origins are, according to this view, mutually exclusive. E. *Käsemann* seconded this approach to Luke with characteristic boldness:

> You do not write the history of the Church, if you are expecting the end of the world to come any day. Acts thus shows clearly that, while apocalyptic hope may still belong to the stock-in-trade of Christian doctrine, yet for Luke himself it no longer possesses any vital interest![11]

The exegetical undergirding of this picture of Luke, however, awaited the contribution of *Conzelmann*.[12] Luke's treatment of his Markan source, Conzelmann argued, betrays a coherent and consistent plan: imminent eschatological expectation gives way to a structured salvation-history. Luke detaches historical events from the eschaton, which he expects only in the remote future. In Conzelmann's judgment, it is "obvious" that the phenomenon of parousia delay has prompted Luke to these reflections.[13] Here is the situational correlate of Lukan eschatology: Luke incorporates the delayed parousia into salvation-history in what amounts

[8] *Theology of the New Testament,* vol. 2, tr. K. Grobel (London: SCM, 1955) 116–17. The German edition of Bultmann's *Theologie* was issued in three volumes (1948, 1951, 1953). This quotation comes from volume three (1953).

[9] *EvT* 10 (1950–51) 1–15; English translation by W. C. Robinson and V. P. Furnish in *Studies in Luke-Acts,* ed. L. E. Keck and J. L. Martyn (Nashville: Abingdon, 1966) 33–50.

[10] Ibid., 47.

[11] "The Problem of the Historical Jesus," in *Essays on New Testament Themes* (London: SCM, 1964) 15–47, 28.

[12] His *St. Luke* was anticipated by the essay "Zur Lukasanalyse," *ZTK* 49 (1952) 16–33; and see the extension of his program in *Die Apostelgeschichte* (Tübingen: J. C. B. Mohr, 1963).

[13] *St. Luke,* 97.

to an "anti-apocalyptic" struggle.[14] Corresponding to this interest in history is an enhanced concern for Christian life in the present, particularly for the behavior of the Christian under persecution.[15] In Luke's hands, the Spirit becomes a substitute for imminent eschatological faith, indeed a "solution of the problem of the Parousia."[16]

Even apart from the objection often raised by Conzelmann's detractors, that parousia delay plays an exaggerated role in his reconstruction,[17] this reading of Luke-Acts fails to account for important passages, especially those which maintain an imminent hope and those which narrate the birth and infancy of Jesus.

E. *Grässer* extended Conzelmann's thesis in a thorough analysis of the motif of the non-arrival of the parousia in the synoptics and Acts.[18] Grässer portrays Jesus as holding consistently to an imminent expectation: "Die Verkündigung des nahen Endes beherrscht Jesu Botschaft von ihren Anfang bis zu ihrem Ende!"[19] While no trace of parousia delay may be detected in Jesus' own proclamation of the kingdom, delay of the parousia surfaces practically everywhere in the synoptic tradition and exerts a formative influence in the very composition of the synoptic gospels.[20] By the time of Luke, the non-appearance of the parousia had become a pressing problem. Luke sets out to resolve it by recasting his sources to suppress the imminent hope. Luke, writing after 70 C.E., brings the apocalyptic instruction of Mark 13 "up to date": past events (from Luke's vantage point) are secularized as purely political events and separated by a long interval from future eschatological events. Moreover, Luke emphasizes paraenesis much more strongly even than Mark and Matthew.[21] For example, if the Matthean parables focus attention on the kingdom as the promised divine goal, Luke's parables concentrate on the Christian life, the human way leading

---

[14]   Ibid., 123.

[15]   Ibid., 232; cf. "Lukasanalyse," 61.

[16]   See *Apostelgeschichte,* 22: "Der Geist ist das Charakteristikum der neuen Epoche der Heilsgeschichte: die Naherwartung der Parusie ist durch die Verheissung des Geistes ersetzt"; and *St. Luke,* 136.

[17]   See, e.g., D. E. Aune, "The Significance of the Delay of the Parousia for Early Christianity," in *Current Issues in Biblical and Patristic Interpretation,* ed. G. F. Hawthorne (Grand Rapids: Eerdmans, 1975) 87–109; E. E. Ellis, *Eschatology in Luke* (Philadelphia: Fortress, 1972) 17–18; H.-W. Bartsch, *Wachtet aber zu jeder Zeit: Entwurf einer Auslegung des Lukasevangeliums* (Hamburg-Bergstedt: H. Reich, 1963) 107–08; Talbert, "Redaction," 173; D. Flusser, "Salvation Present and Future," in *Types of Redemption,* ed. R. J. Zwi Werblowski and C. J. Bleeker (Leiden: Brill, 1970) 45–61; G. Braumann, "Das Mittel der Zeit: Erwägungen zur Theologie des Lukasevangeliums," *ZNW* 54 (1963) 117–45, 140, 145; Maddox, *Purpose,* 105–15; J. Ernst, *Herr der Geschichte* (Stuttgart: Katholisches Bibelwerk, 1978) 41–42; S. S. Smalley, "The Delay of the Parousia," *JBL* 83 (1964) 41–54.

[18]   *Problem;* cf. "Parusieerwartung."

[19]   *Problem,* 75.

[20]   Ibid., 77.

[21]   Ibid., 170.

over a span of time to the kingdom.[22] Grässer contends that the distinctive
eschatological perspective of the author, not a distinctive tradition stemming
from a particular community, underlies this difference.[23]

What is constitutive of Luke's eschatological vision is no longer the imminence of the End but the duration of God's plan. The imminent parousia drops
out, and *Heilsgeschichte* takes over, with the Spirit replacing the eschaton.[24]
Although parousia delay became a problem in the earliest tradition-forming
Christian community, only Luke responds at the level of sustained reflection,
moving beyond temporary "fixes" of the eschatological outline to a lasting
solution cut loose from any connection of the End to a given point in time.[25]
Luke's ingenious answer to the parousia problematic was a "bringing up to date"
which rendered unnecessary any further revisions! In the end, Grässer places his
seal of approval on the formulation of Vielhauer: Luke replaces the primitive
apocalyptic hope with a salvation-history scheme of promise and fulfillment,
and eschatology finds its proper place on the margins of this history.[26]

E. *Haenchen* championed the Conzelmann cause in his magisterial Acts
commentary. Haenchen's discussion of Acts 1:9-12 is illustrative. Here Luke is
said to depict the disciples as a model of a specific attitude prevalent in his own
day, namely, "belief in the imminence of the last days."[27] The heaven directed
stare of v 11 is forbidden "because it expresses the imminent expectation."[28]
According to Haenchen, therefore, Luke's situation included the presence of
Christians who still advocated imminent parousia hope, a position to which
Luke was unalterably opposed. Against this view Luke advocated a "new form
of the Christian hope, which renounces all dating of the Parousia."[29] The author
of this edifying church history "no longer watches passionately, like Paul, for the
imminent turn of the ages, but he lives in the certainty that even in this our time
God's goodness is new every morning."[30]

The scholars so far considered[31] agree that Luke no longer held to the imminent hope which characterized his inherited tradition. They are of one mind as
well in identifying the broader setting in which this distinctive eschatological
point of view emerged, namely, that period toward the close of the first century

[22] Ibid., 197.

[23] Ibid.

[24] Ibid., 170, 206-07.

[25] Ibid., 219-20, 170, 178.

[26] *Problem,* 215 (quoting Vielhauer's essay "Zum 'Paulinismus' "). Grässer once points
to Luke's interest in the *Vollendung* of the individual (e.g., Acts 10:42 and the emphasis
in Acts on the resurrection); however, the observation remains undeveloped.

[27] Haenchen, *Acts,* 151.

[28] Ibid., 150.

[29] Ibid., 152.

[30] Ibid., 132.

[31] The most recent re-statement of this position comes from the pen of G. Klein
("Eschatologie" [IV, Neues Testament], *TRE* 10 [1982] 270-99, 292-94).

C.E. when (they contend) the failure of the expected eschaton to materialize posed an acute problem for Christian faith. The most specific description of Luke's setting that is offered in these studies appears in the hint of Haenchen that Luke encountered in his community resurgent apocalyptic enthusiasm. While the presence in Luke-Acts of a delay motif is undeniable, the question remains whether the precise situational correlate discerned by the Conzelmann camp best accounts for all the evidence in the Lukan writings.

We also need to consider five further studies of Lukan eschatology heavily influenced by Conzelmann and united in the judgment that Luke pushes the eschaton to the distant future.[32] First, P. *Borgen*, in his Ph.D. dissertation, pursued the inquiry into Acts (Conzelmann based his findings largely upon the gospel), and, while perceiving less of a wedge between eschatology and salvation-history, nonetheless arrived at a similar conclusion regarding the timing of the eschatological fulfillment.[33] When the church's mission to the end of the earth is completed, the true Israel of the past together with Gentile Christians will gather in the kingdom at the eschaton:

> In this way the author included his contemporary situation of Gentile mission in the plan of God, although he could not retain the perspective of an eschatological imminence. By his interpretation of *Heilsgeschichte* he gave a theological basis for the continuity and discontinuity and the equality between his own Gentile Church and the Jewish Church before the transition.[34]

Borgen accepts Conzelmann's thesis that the Lukan salvation history was a response to the delayed parousia;[35] however, he differs from Conzelmann in regarding the burning question of "When?" as still a live issue among Luke's readers.[36] The author of Luke-Acts aims his polemic not at apocalyptic specula-tion but at a problematic imminent expectation evoked by certain events. In Luke's sight, the mistake is linking imminent expectation to the wrong events: these represent signs of the unfolding salvation-history, not of the End.[37] Unlike the other scholars surveyed already, Borgen hazards a concrete suggestion concerning Luke's setting. He proposes a school-setting for Luke-Acts, that is, a school for missionary teaching and preaching.[38] Borgen argues, on the basis of Luke 1:1–4, that "Theophilus must have received instruction at the school, and Luke-Acts contains the instruction which he received, the certainty of which he had begun to doubt (because of the delay of the parousia)."[39]

---

[32] Despite the debt to Conzelmann, these scholars stand at some remove from the Bultmann program epitomized by Conzelmann — hence separate treatment here.

[33] "Heilsgeschichte."

[34] Ibid., 272.

[35] Ibid., xiii.

[36] Ibid., 4, 8.

[37] Ibid., 15–17.

[38] Ibid., 82.

[39] Ibid., 130 n. 26.

J.-D. *Kaestli* devoted a brief monograph to the subject of Luke's eschatology.[40] Kaestli agrees with Conzelmann that the eschaton retreats in Luke-Acts; like Borgen, however, he refuses to attach to the Lukan perspective the negative valuation customary in Bultmannian circles.[41] In Kaestli's view, Luke's eschatological perspective is no longer based on the proximity of the kingdom of God; it loses its cosmic viewpoint and takes on an individual accent.[42] Illustrative is Kaestli's handling of Luke 9:27 ("But truly I tell you, there are some of those standing here who will not taste death until they see the kingdom of God"):

A l'idée d'avènement du Royaume, Luc substitue une conception intemporelle. Il apporte une correction décisive à l'attente de la parousie. Tout en maintenant son orientation future, il la détache de toute considération de temps. La solution ainsi élaborée ne risque donc plus d'être mise en question par la continuation de l'histoire.[43]

Examination of pertinent passages in Luke-Acts[44] yields the clear finding that "la fièvre apocalyptique qui marquait la tradition antérieure est systématiquement atténeuée ou effacée" by Luke.[45] Kaestli reconstructs three elements of the setting in which Luke developed his eschatological orientation: (1) with the passage of time, the founding events were becoming further removed into the past; (2) apocalyptic expectations had not been realized; and (3) gnostic mythologizing of Jesus was stepping into prominence.[46] To the general observations of setting already made by Conzelmann, Kaestli adds the more specific reference to Gnosis (not, however, sketched with the specificity in the studies of C. H. Talbert and H.-W. Bartsch, which will be considered later in the chapter).

The dissertation of J. *Zmijewski* should receive preliminary attention at this

---

[40] *L'Eschatologie dans l'Oeuvre de Luc* (Genève: Labor et Fides, 1969).

[41] According to Kaestli, Luke must be evaluated in accordance with his own situation: his historicizing activity is appropriate given his historical setting (ibid., 92). Others refuse to join the ranks of Luke's detractors: see Borgen, "From Paul to Luke. Observations toward Clarification of the Theology of Luke-Acts," *CBQ* 31 (1969) 168–82; W. G. Kümmel, "Luc en accusation dans la theologie contemporaine," in *L'Evangile de Luc: Problèmes littéraires et théologiques,* ed. F. Neirynck (Bibliotheca Ephemeridum Theologicarum Lovaniensium XXXII, 1973) 93–109; W. C. van Unnik, "Luke-Acts, a Storm Center in Contemporary Scholarship," in *Studies in Luke-Acts,* ed. L. E. Keck and J. L. Martyn, 15–32; U. Wilckens, "Interpreting Luke-Acts in a Period of Existentialist Theology," in *Studies in Luke-Acts,* ed. L. E. Keck and J. L. Martyn, 60–83.

[42] *Eschatologie,* 71.

[43] Ibid., 18.

[44] Luke 9:27; 12:49–59; 16:16; 17:20–18:8; 19:11–27; 21:5–36; 22:14–38; Acts 1:6–11; 2:17; 3:20–21; 10:42–43; 17:30–31.

[45] Ibid., 97.

[46] Ibid., 92.

point,[47] although his analysis is confined to the discourses of Luke 17 and 21 and so will figure in the discussion of those passages. Zmijewski's ponderous effort is marked nevertheless by an energetic insistence upon the inter-connectedness of history and eschatology in Luke. Against Conzelmann, Zmijewski denies that Luke separates eschatology from history or replaces eschatology with history. Instead, Luke "historicizes" by demonstrating the eschatological character of history itself. He does this by pointing to the material ("sachlichen") — *not* temporal ("zeitlichen") — connection between historical events such as the destruction of Jerusalem and the end of the world.[48] History itself has an eschatological quality for Luke, because it is part of a salvation history that moves toward the End, and because in Jesus "ist . . . die für die Endzeit verheissene eschatologische Gottesherrschaft bereits gegenwärtig und in seinem Wort und Werk wirksam geworden."[49] Yet, despite the disagreement with Conzelmann over the relation of history to eschatology, Zmijewski does assent to Conzelmann's verdict that the eschaton recedes in time in Luke-Acts. The endtime continues to lie at a "more or less great distance."[50]

As for the setting in which this eschatological perspective arose, Zmijewski diverges from Conzelmann in one crucial respect. He contends that Luke's motive was *not* to correct a misguided imminent expectation. Luke's enterprise was not prompted by disappointed imminent hopes, but by reflection upon traditions present in his sources.[51] Zmijewski furthermore emphasizes the tendency of Luke to draw the practical, paraenetic consequences of his eschatological convictions. However, all concreteness evaporates when the point is developed: Luke does not have any particular situation in view; instead he aims to give guidance for "every possible situation" in which Christians may be brought into danger or persecution. All such situations are posed between two "moments," on the one hand, the extent of the time until the End, and on the other hand, the suddenness of the parousia itself.[52]

Another discussion of our theme that begins as a sustained conversation with Conzelmann is W. C. *Robinson's Der Weg des Herrn.*[53] Robinson is especially critical of the way in which John the Baptist figures into Conzelmann's

---

[47] *Die Eschatologiereden des Lukas-Evangeliums* (Bonn: Peter Hanstein, 1972); cf. the synopsis (which touches upon only a few of the themes developed in the larger study) in "Die Eschatologiereden Lk 21 und Lk 17," *BibLeb* 14 (1973) 30–40.

[48] *Eschatologiereden*, 98.

[49] Ibid., 559; see p. 312 for a typical statement of the eschatological tenor of Luke's salvation history.

[50] Ibid., 98.

[51] Ibid., 313, 565–66. One of Zmijewski's special interests is to show the continuity between Luke and pre-Lukan eschatology (particularly Mark).

[52] Ibid., 323.

[53] Hamburg: Herbert Reich, 1964. English translation, *The Way of the Lord,* published privately in the United States, 1962.

periodization of salvation history.[54] Robinson comes closer to Conzelmann, however, in his interpretation of Luke's eschatology. Luke transforms the problem of *Naherwartung* and delay into a practical problem of world mission. In other words, we witness in Luke the transformation of eschatology into historical geography: "Luke 'geographizes' eschatology."[55] The future kingdom does retain a place in Luke's thought — that is the goal toward which the historical geography aims — but the future kingdom is no longer regarded as imminent, nor is it emphasized.[56] Inasmuch as Robinson's treatise is executed almost entirely on the level of exegetical-theological inquiry, matters of setting play little part in the discussion. Robinson does indicate, though, that Luke was not so much interested in addressing the problem of parousia delay as in showing the continuity in history.[57]

The final study to be discussed under this first heading is that of G. *Braumann.*[58] Like Conzelmann, he discovers a parousia pushed into the distant future in Luke-Acts.[59] While granting, however, that the delay motif plays an important role in the Lukan writings, Braumann identifies as the main focus in Luke-Acts not the theoretical problem of parousia delay but rather the practical problem of persecution. Because Luke no longer affirms an imminent eschaton, he cannot console a persecuted community by focusing its attention on a deliverance close at hand.[60] Instead, he enables his readers to find comfort in their solidarity in suffering with the prophets, with John the Baptist, and with Jesus. It is in service of this practical, paraenetic aim that Luke develops his salvation history. Recourse to historical epochs, accompanied by a distant expectation of the eschaton, gives Luke the answer he seeks for doubts that have arisen under the pressure of persecution. Despite the apparently disconfirming evidence of present persecution, encountered during the history that has opened up while the parousia lingers, the church finds assurance that it — not the Judaism that has repudiated the church's witness — represents the true people of God.[61] Braumann, unlike most of the scholars treated so far, emphasizes a concrete setting for Luke's eschatology. The general rubric of parousia delay finds its place in this reconstruction, too, but only as presupposition. It is, of course, debatable whether Braumann's depiction of a persecuted church represents Luke's situation accurately.

---

[54] *Weg,* 16–21. Robinson objects to Conzelmann's de-eschatologizing of John the Baptist. Luke does not eliminate Mark 9:9–13 because it portrays the Baptist in eschatological terms but because it describes as past a restoration that Luke expected in the future (pp. 18–19).

[55] Ibid., 36, 38.

[56] Ibid., 66.

[57] Ibid., 45.

[58] "Mittel." See also his article, "Die lukanische Interpretation der Zerstörung Jerusalems," *NovT* 6 (1963) 120–27.

[59] E.g., "Mittel," 145.

[60] Ibid., 141.

[61] Ibid., 144, 137–40.

2. Consistent Imminent Eschatology in Luke-Acts

At the other end of the spectrum stand several studies which insist on the presence of a living imminent hope in the Lukan writings. F. O. *Francis,* in an essay published in 1969,[62] argues that Conzelmann's model of Lukan eschatology was not arrived at inductively:

> The study of Luke-Acts, and in particular the problem of Luke's eschatology, has been truncated by a restrictive foreknowledge of what the two-volume work can mean. . . . One need only list the numerous passages in Luke's volumes that reflect another eschatological point of view. Such passages are shunted aside either in silence or as being insignificant remnants of earlier pre-Lukan tradition.[63]

To this de-eschatologized Luke, Francis opposes an interpretation of Luke's eschatology that assigns a normative role to Acts 2:16–21. The last days do not recede to a distant horizon in the Lukan writings; rather, the eschatological consummation will come speedily, though not immediately.[64] Only the cosmic upheaval remains beyond the time of Luke's composition.[65] Francis, taking a clue from Acts 2 (where Joel 3:1–5 LXX is quoted to interpret the era launched by Pentecost), reads the discourse of Luke 21 as an eschatological meditation on Joel.[66] (Indeed, Francis emphasizes the crucial function of scripture in Lukan eschatology.[67]) If Conzelmann's approach severed history and eschatology, Francis sees Luke as underscoring the paradox of history and eschatology: "the profound achievement of Luke-Acts is its synthesis of orderly historical narrative . . . with its view of the eschatological truth of the church's teaching. . . ."[68] Francis does not identify the setting that prompted this synthesis, an omission all the more striking in the light of his assertion that

> The two-volume work constitutes an important recognition of the full range of our humanity in its attention to the broad, complex social and temporal matrix in which we live.[69]

Just what that matrix was for Luke Francis does not venture to say.

The slogan "not immediate but imminent," which surfaces in the study by

---

[62] "Eschatology and History in Luke-Acts," *JAAR* 37 (1969) 49–63.

[63] Ibid., 54.

[64] Ibid., 55, 58–59.

[65] Ibid., 58 n. 42.

[66] Ibid., 55–57. Francis suggests (p. 56) "that Luke's programmatic, eschatological use of the Joel prophecy provides the thematic structure and eschatological perspective for this entire threefold section [vv 12–19, 20–24, 25–26] in Luke 21."

[67] Ibid., 61.

[68] Ibid., 61. According to Francis, Luke finds "eschatological tension in the midst of history" (p. 62): "The end is not solely nor primarily out ahead of Luke; rather, he participates in the end that already infuses history."

[69] Ibid., 63.

Francis,[70] becomes a battle cry in the work of A. J. *Mattill*.[71] With unsurpassed zeal, Mattill advances the view that imminent hope governed Luke's eschatological perspective. He goes so far as to suggest that Luke's purpose in writing was to effect the imminent End.[72] He casts the author in the role of apocalyptic activist, the very part Luke refuses according to Haenchen's analysis. Mattill does give minimal attention to the question of Luke's setting, but here he does not go beyond the suggestions made by S. G. Wilson (to be discussed in the next section). That is, Luke—though an apocalyptic activist—operates as a pastoral theologian, and he must do so on two fronts. Troubled by over-heated apocalyptists, Luke introduces the delay motif into several passages. Yet, cognizant of those who doubt that the parousia will materialize at all, he includes the imminence motif.[73] Mattill never integrates this borrowed sketch of Luke's concrete setting into his portrayal of Luke the apocalyptist. It suggests, however, a correlation of eschatology and situation which must receive careful scrutiny in the course of the present study, because it has the merit of explaining both sets of materials in Luke-Acts (delay and imminence motifs).

In a seldom noted two-part article published in 1958, R. H. *Smith* had already presented a reading of Luke (focused upon Acts) that emphasized his imminent perspective.[74] Using the un-eschatological Luke of Conzelmann and company as a foil, Smith argues that history and eschatology in Luke-Acts are inseparable: "Luke interprets the history of which he writes eschatologically, and he sees eschatology unfolding historically."[75] According to Smith, the church's universal mission, far from being a replacement for eschatology, is in fact "a piece of eschatology," a sign of the End.[76] At the same time, Smith concedes that a delay motif is present:

[70] Ibid., 58–59.

[71] See especially "Naherwartung, Fernerwartung, and the Purpose of Luke-Acts: Weymouth Reconsidered," *CBQ* 34 (1972) 276–93; and most recently *Luke and the Last Things* (Dillsboro: Western North Carolina, 1979).

[72] *Last*, 232–33. Luke "wanted to promote the Pauline mission in particular and the world mission as a whole, for the proclamation of 'repentance and remission of sins . . . unto all nations' (Luke 24:47) was one of the preconditions of the imminent end. The Son of Man could not return in fiery glory (Luke 12:49) until that mission had been completed . . ." (p. 233). Luke, then, "writes to expedite the world mission and thereby to help fulfill the eschatological program" (p. 233). Luke's "ultimate weapon" in the final holy war was his pen (p. 232).

[73] Ibid., 69, 234.

[74] "The Eschatology of Acts and Contemporary Exegesis," *CTM* 29 (1958) 641–63; "History and Eschatology in Luke-Acts," *CTM* 29 (1958) 881–901. Smith's study is overlooked in the most recent discussion of eschatology in Acts (R. Schnackenburg, "Die lukanische Eschatologie im Lichte von Aussagen der Apostelgeschichte," in *Glaube und Eschatologie*, ed. E. Grässer and O. Merk [Tübingen: J. C. B. Mohr, 1985] 249–65, especially 250).

[75] "History," 882.

[76] Ibid., 891–92.

> Although Luke-Acts declares that these are the last days, that the beginning of the
> end has come, it likewise knows that the end of the end is yet to come.[77]

Still, with the arrival of Paul and the gospel at Rome in the conclusion of Acts,
the promise of Jesus (Acts 1:8) is now fulfilled, and "the condition of the coming
of the Kingdom set by Christ (Acts 1:8) has been met. . . . Far from relinquishing
hope in a near end, Luke's second volume seeks to nurture that hope."[78] In short,
Luke-Acts represents "history in expectation of God's last and universal act."[79]
Although Smith devotes little attention to the problem of Luke's setting, he
summarizes with approval the position of H. J. Cadbury (to be discussed below),
namely, that it is not the parousia delay itself but rather practical considerations
which inform Luke's eschatological perspective. Luke counters an over-expectant
attitude through incorporation of the delay theme.[80] Nevertheless, Smith fails to
connect his basic thesis, that imminent hope prevails in Luke-Acts, with such
questions of setting.

R. H. *Hiers,* too, discovers consistent imminent eschatology in Luke-Acts.[81]
Hiers contends that, granted Luke's historical context, his treatment of the theme
of the parousia is readily comprehensible. On the one hand, Luke demonstrates
that Jesus had not mistakenly believed or announced an imminent parousia. On
the other hand, he holds before his own contemporaries the hope/warning that
the kingdom of God may come soon.[82] According to Hiers, Luke constructs his
narrative in such a way as to show that the divine plan did not call for the events
of the parousia during the lifetime of Jesus or the earliest community. Imminent
expectation, inappropriate during this phase of God's plan, does, however,
become fitting at the time of the mission to the Gentiles. At the end of Acts (the
symbolic realization of the promise of Christianity's spread), all that remains is
the coming of the kingdom.[83] Hiers' position is almost identical to that of Smith.
Hiers, however, gives even less space than Smith to Luke's circumstance, except
that, like Conzelmann, he presupposes a situation in which the expected
parousia had been noticeably delayed. It is especially interesting that Conzelmann and Hiers identify the same situational correlate, yet link it to diametri-
cally opposed readings of Luke's eschatological point of view.

[77] Ibid., 895.

[78] Ibid., 897–98.

[79] Ibid., 901.

[80] "Contemporary," 663; here Smith draws upon the discussion of Cadbury in "Acts and
Eschatology," in *The Background of the New Testament and Its Eschatology,* ed. D. Daube
and W. D. Davies (Cambridge: University, 1964) 300–21.

[81] "The Problem of the Delay of the Parousia in Luke-Acts," *NTS* 20 (1974) 145–55. Cf.
Hiers' discussion of the significance of eschatology in the gospels, in "Eschatology and
Methodology," *JBL* 85 (1966) 170–84.

[82] "Problem," 146.

[83] "Problem," 148, 150, 155.

3. Dichromatic Approaches to Lukan Eschatology:
Two-Strand, Two-Document, and Two-Stage Eschatologies

A variety of solutions to the problem of eschatology in Luke-Acts take an intermediate position on the continuum reaching from un-eschatological Luke to Luke the apocalyptic activist. The studies summarized under this category are diverse, yet agree in resorting to dichromatic approaches to the subject.

S. G. *Wilson* actually offers a two-strand *and* two-document version of Luke's eschatology.[84] The latter facet of Wilson's approach may be noted first. The second volume of Luke, in Wilson's judgment, betrays a significantly different eschatological position from that of the gospel. All tension between delay and imminence evaporates in Acts, where there is no imminent hope. From this observation, Wilson concludes that it is likely that Luke wrote Acts much later than the gospel, and that his eschatological convictions had altered in the interim.[85] Within the gospel itself, Wilson discerns two distinct strands of eschatological material. A delay strand comes to expression in such passages as Luke 9:27; 19:11, 41–42; 21:20–24; and 22:69.[86] However, imminent expectation governs another set of passages not taken with full seriousness by Conzelmann (Luke 10:9–11; 12:38–40, 41–48; 12:54–13:9; 18:8; and 21:32).[87] Wilson finds the solution to this apparent puzzle by positing a "dual situation" that demanded of Luke a "dual response." A church experiencing the parousia delay could lapse into one of two dangerous extremes: fervent renewal of apocalypticism, or denial of the future hope.[88] It appears, then, that Luke directed his delay strand at resurgent apocalyptic hope but targeted the imminence motif at languishing future hope. Wilson places great weight on the pastoral, as opposed to theoretical, sphere in which this two-front battle is waged.[89] Several recent studies of Lukan eschatology have been influenced by Wilson's two-front, pastoral description of Luke's situation and strategy: H. Farrell and J. Ernst (see below), and even A. J. Mattill follow Wilson in his reconstruction of Luke's setting. Yet it remains an open question if this depiction of the correlation between eschatology and situation best accounts for the evidence.

---

[84] See "Lukan Eschatology," *NTS* 15 (1969–70) 330–47. Cf. also the treatments of this topic in *The Gentiles and the Gentile Mission in Luke-Acts* (Cambridge: University, 1973) 59–87; and "The Ascension: A Critique and an Interpretation," *ZNW* 59 (1968) 269–81.

[85] "Lukan," p. 347. Maddox (*Purpose*, pp. 129–30) agrees that the extent of future eschatology in Acts is "only slight," and G. Schneider concedes that "das Parusie-Thema tritt in der Apostelgeschichte gegenüber dem dritten Evangelium auffallend zurück" (*Die Apostelgeschichte* [2 vol.: HTKNT 5; Freiburg: Herder, 1980] 1.336). Both scholars, however, resist the twin conclusions of Wilson — namely, that Acts reflects a different eschatological posture and a much later date of composition (Maddox, *Purpose*, 130–32; Schneider, *Apostelgeschichte*, 1.336). Cf. Franklin, *Christ*, 27, 192 n. 37.

[86] "Lukan," 336–40.

[87] Ibid., 340–43.

[88] Ibid., 345–46.

[89] Ibid., 340, 346–47.

B. R. *Gaventa*, in a brief discussion of Lukan eschatology, opts for a modified version of Wilson's two-document approach.[90] She holds that eschatology figures prominently in the gospel and in the opening chapters of Acts,[91] only to disappear thereafter. Gaventa's resolution of this difficulty rests on a particular appraisal of the function of Acts 1–2 in the whole narrative. These chapters, charged with promise, lay the foundation for all that follows; the fulfillment of the dual promise of Spirit and worldwide mission (Acts 1:8) in the subsequent narrative guarantees the fulfillment of the eschatological promise as well. Luke neither abandons future hope nor relegates it to the remote future.[92]

Gaventa's perception of Luke's setting echoes the approach of Wilson, without, however, raising Wilson's intuition to the level of careful analysis. Between the lines of Acts 1:11 she reads the possibility of a community in which eschatological hope had waned. Acts 1:6–7, on the other hand (cf. Luke 17:20–31; 19:11; 21:7), may address over-eager speculation about the timing of the parousia.[93] Luke, on this reading, affirms the parousia as a future event in the face of both doubt and apocalyptic speculation: the guarantee is provided by promises already fulfilled.[94]

A dual eschatology of an altogether different character is advocated in the writings of E. E. *Ellis*.[95] Like Wilson, he recognizes in Luke-Acts the twin motifs of delay and imminence. Ellis, however, incorporates these eschatological materials into the interpretive framework of a two-stage eschatology. The person of Jesus binds together the two stages, and therefore Lukan eschatology as a whole. Jesus "represents in his resurrection an individual fulfillment of the age to come" (in the present); however, the universal consummation will come only with Jesus' parousia.[96] Ellis departs from the pattern typified by all the studies previously considered in two important respects. First, he emphasizes passages

---

[90] "Revisited."

[91] Gaventa's treatment lacks precision at this point. In one context, she alludes to the "virtual eclipse of the eschaton" after Acts 1–2 (ibid., 35; cf. also p. 34). Elsewhere (p. 34), she concedes that a reader "unfamiliar with Acts," after studying 3:19–21, "might suppose that this is a work dominated by eschatological hope (whether imminent or delayed)."

[92] Ibid., 38.

[93] Ibid., 39. Wilson proposed this dual setting for Acts 1:6–7 and Acts 1:11 in "Ascension."

[94] Ibid., 42. Gaventa does not offer a careful method for identifying the Lukan setting. After observing that the recurring mention of judgment and future resurrection in Acts occurs before non-believing audiences, she asserts: "Apart from 1:6–11, Luke gives no indication that the eschaton or anything pertaining to it was a matter of debate or discussion within the community itself" (p. 35). Such an analysis ignores the evidence of the third gospel and cannot, therefore, yield a convincing description of Luke's setting.

[95] See especially *Eschatology in Luke* (Philadelphia: Fortress, 1972), a revised version of "Die Funktion der Eschatologie im Lukasevangelium," *ZTK* 66 (1969) 387–402; and "Present and Future Eschatology in Luke," *NTS* 12 (1965–66) 27–41.

[96] *Eschatology*, 19–20.

in Luke-Acts suggesting a reorientation of eschatology toward the personal eschaton (at death) of each individual (e.g., Luke 23:43),[97] although he insists such passages are controlled by others stressing the corporate identification of the believer with the risen/exalted Christ.[98] Second, Ellis assigns a weighty role to christology as the center of Lukan eschatology (a theme picked up by J. Ernst, whose contribution will be examined next).

Ellis explicitly poses the question of the setting of Luke's eschatology; his special concern is the polemical function of this theme. Luke corrects an over-eager parousia expectation that was threatening to subvert the church's mission.[99] This polemic reflects Luke's situation, one which, in Ellis' judgment, accords well with tendencies of that historical period (i.e., widespread apocalyptic fever).[100]

In a study largely consisting of reactions to the approaches of Conzelmann, H. Flender and G. Schneider (see below), and Ellis, J. *Ernst* arrives at a view of Lukan eschatology similar to that of Ellis.[101] For Ernst, eschatology in Luke is fundamentally an aspect of Christology: eschatological salvation has drawn near in the person of Jesus.[102] God's kingdom, therefore, is essentially realized in the present, although the culmination is yet to come. Jesus himself represents the kingdom in both present and future dimensions.[103] Ernst follows Ellis not only in assigning a pivotal role to the person of Jesus, but also in the resultant two-stage eschatology. Ernst detects in Luke-Acts intimations of an individualizing eschatology; systematic reflection is, however, absent. This individual eschatology,[104] which does not displace the general eschatology, stems from Luke's Christology: Jesus is the "Vollender des individuellen Lebens" as well as the salvation-bearer in a general sense.[105] In his discussion of Luke 21, Ernst concludes that Luke makes no precise assertions regarding the interval preceding the End.[106]

---

[97] "Present," pp. 35–40. See the discussion in Excursus 1 below.

[98] *Eschatology,* 20. By appealing to the solidarity of believers with Christ, Ellis differs from J. Dupont and G. Schneider, who discern in Luke-Acts a shift toward eschatology focused on the individual's death (see below).

[99] Ibid., 19. In another context, Ellis mentions political messianism and a heavenly or "spiritual" understanding of the resurrection as likely heretical foils for Luke's eschatology (p. 15).

[100] Ibid., 18–19.

[101] *Herr.*

[102] Ibid., 111–12.

[103] Ibid., 60.

[104] For proponents of an individual eschatology (i.e., eschatology focused on the destiny of the individual) in Luke, see the discussion of Dupont and Schneider below.

[105] Ibid., 87.

[106] Ibid., 73–74.

Occasional suggestions concerning Luke's setting are scattered unsystematically throughout Ernst's monograph. He has recourse to the two-front hypothesis of Wilson at one point,[107] but in another place substitutes a new doctrinal error for Wilson's picture of waning future hope. Perhaps, Ernst proposes, Luke refuted both an exclusively future oriented preaching ("stubborn apocalyptic enthusiasm") and a realized eschatology that expected nothing further from the future.[108] Ernst is inclined to minimize the impact exerted on Luke's eschatology by parousia delay. In the first place, he points out that Luke already encountered the delay theme in the pre-Lukan tradition (and not everything contained in the tradition transmitted by Luke is actually "Lukan").[109] Second, Ernst sees Luke's revision of the inherited eschatology as motivated less by the experience of delay than by christological reflection.[110]

4. Approaches Emphasizing the Present Fulfillment of Eschatological Hopes

Among the dichromatic positions surveyed, those of Ellis and Ernst draw an explicit distinction between present and future phases of eschatological fulfillment. Similar views —though without the christological concentration —are advanced by H. Farrell and R. Maddox. The particular stress placed by both on the present fulfillment of eschatological hopes and the thoroughness of these inquiries justify special consideration here.

But before turning to a summary of these two studies, it is fitting to consider briefly an earlier article by H. J. *Cadbury* which anticipated the emphasis on present fulfillment in Lukan eschatology.[111] Cadbury sketched a perspective on eschatology in Acts without seeking to develop a full treatment of the theme in the Lukan writings. Following Conzelmann's then fresh thesis, he noted that Luke emphasizes delay. He also observed, however, that the expectation of a future eschaton remains intact, that, indeed, assurance concerning the final events is strengthened, not weakened, by acceptance of the delay.[112] Cadbury addressed the objection that the eschatological factor is especially slight in Acts by arguing that eschatology is presupposed in the narrative, as indicated by the presence of such rubrics as "resurrection" and "kingdom."[113] Nevertheless,

---

[107] Ibid., 46.

[108] Ibid., 48. Two important treatments of Luke's eschatology to be discussed below, those of H.-W. Bartsch and C. H. Talbert, make extensive use of the argument that Luke countered an over-realized eschatology. Ernst refrains from ascribing such a crucial role to this possible component of Luke's setting.

[109] Ibid., 50. This claim raises an important issue of method to which I will return in the last section of chapter 1.

[110] Ibid., 68.

[111] "Acts and Eschatology," in *The Background of the New Testament and Its Eschatology*, ed. W. D. Davies and D. Daube (Cambridge: University, 1964) 300-21.

[112] Ibid., 320-21.

[113] Ibid., 310.

Cadbury discerns that the main weight of Lukan eschatology rests upon present fulfillment: "Luke on the whole has more to say about recent or present fulfillment of past prophecy than about present adumbrations of future expectations."[114]

How does Cadbury correlate this eschatological view with Luke's setting? He seems to think that practical conditions compelled Luke to counter an over-expectant attitude (delay was, in truth, what should be expected). Luke, then, sought to discourage a premature eschatological expectation.[115]

The contribution by H. *Farrell* represents the most extensive, sustained exegetical examination of eschatological materials in Luke-Acts to date,[116] and will accordingly receive detailed consideration here. Several passages in Luke-Acts emphasize the present dimension of eschatology (Luke 1–2; 4:16–30; 9:27; 17:20–21; Acts 2:16). These texts lead Farrell to conclude that "the present realization of the Kingdom of God in Jesus and the church is the dominant motif in Luke's thought." Luke contended for "the real presence of the Kingdom of God in the person of Jesus."[117] Accordingly, the whole period initiated by Jesus and continuing in the church's proclamation is characterized by the realization of the kingdom in a "non-apocalyptic and non-transcendent" form.[118] Luke's stress on present fulfillment does not, however, supplant expectation of a visible, external, apocalyptic consummation of the kingdom.[119] Several texts expressing this future dimension prevent such an interpretation (Luke 12:35–48; 17:22–18:8; 21:5–36; Acts 1:11; 3:21). In Farrell's judgment, these materials render impossible the remote-eschaton interpretation of Conzelmann. Luke is motivated by an awareness that his church may stand at the conclusion of the "times of the Gentiles" (Luke 21:24) and at the edge of the appearance of the cosmic signs that will usher in the End.[120] With the arrival of Paul and the gospel in Rome, the scriptural program (God's plan for history) has been completed and the culminating cosmic signs may occur at any time.[121]

---

[114] Ibid., 315.

[115] Ibid., 316, 320.

[116] "The Eschatological Perspective of Luke-Acts" (Boston: Boston University Ph.D. dissertation, 1972). The length of Farrell's study, some 284 pages, is exceeded only by the massive dissertation of J. Zmijewski (*Die Eschatologiereden des Lukas-Evangeliums* [Bonn: Peter Hanstein, 1972]), 572 pages in length but limited to analysis of Luke 17 and 21.

[117] "Perspective," 86–87.

[118] Ibid., 83.

[119] Ibid., 87. Farrell criticizes Conzelmann's failure to recognize this double nature of the kingdom (pp. 23–25), an aspect of Farrell's thesis that conforms closely to the approach of Ellis (whose two-stage eschatological formulation Farrell cites with approval, p. 185).

[120] E.g., ibid., 101, 163.

[121] Ibid., 279.

The results of Farrell's work are indeed impressive. Here for the first time one meets an attempt to do justice to the full range of data.[122] Nevertheless, Farrell fails to integrate the present-fulfillment and future-consummation themes into one eschatological perspective.[123] He can only invoke Wilson's two-front hypothesis to explain the tension between present and future in Luke-Acts.[124] Not until the conclusion, and then only sketchily, does Farrell turn to a more convincing resolution of the duality in Luke's eschatology. There Farrell contends that Luke narrates in Acts the fulfillment of the scriptural promise of gospel-proclamation to the end of the earth. As a result, Acts must be viewed as "history in service of eschatology on a grand scale."[125] Luke's concern in reporting the world mission is to demonstrate that "now one may *properly* expect the cosmic signs and the Parousia."[126]

A satisfactory dovetailing of the two strands in Lukan eschatology would appear to require an accurate correlation with the Lukan setting. On this issue, Farrell does not succeed, although he does sprinkle comments about Luke's situation liberally throughout his dissertation. He accepts Conzelmann's thesis that parousia delay prompted Luke to the eschatological construction that is at the heart of his project (differing with Conzelmann primarily on the question of the time-perspective).[127] It is consistent with this setting, for example, that Luke closes the discourse of Luke 21:5-36 with a series of exhortations revolving

---

[122] Especially significant is Farrell's insistence on the controlling function of scripture in shaping Luke's eschatological perspective ("Perspective," 234-79). The discussion of this theme, inspired by L. C. Crockett's dissertation, "The Old Testament in the Gospel of Luke with Emphasis on the Interpretation of Isa. 61:1-2" (Brown University, 1966), is one of the most useful sections of the study (although its isolation, as a self-contained chapter, from the earlier attempt to lay an exegetical foundation for Luke's eschatological point of view undermines the coherence of the study as a whole).

[123] Symptomatic is the separation of Luke 17:20-21 and 17:22-18:8, necessitated by Farrell's distinction between present and future texts. Commenting on the Transfiguration in Luke 9:28-36, however, Farrell asserts: "By giving such a proleptic manifestation of the future Kingdom of God, Luke intends to confirm the reality of the present, non-glorious realization of the Kingdom in Jesus and to assure the certainty of the consummation of that Kingdom in its glorious, apocalyptic form. This fits in with the basic thrust of Luke to stress the present reality of the Kingdom of God . . . in order to strengthen the faith of his church in the future manifestation" (p. 46). This attempt to bring together the present and future texts, all too rare in the dissertation (cf. only pp. 193-94), moves in the right direction. It seems to me more helpful, however, to focus on the theme of fulfillment of promise in the present, rather than the presence of the kingdom. A set of (eschatological) promises already fulfilled provides reassurance that as yet unfulfilled promises will have their day (cf. Gaventa, "Revisited").

[124] "Perspective," 193-94. See the summary below of Farrell's depiction of the Lukan situation.

[125] Ibid., 275.

[126] Ibid.

[127] E.g., ibid., 92, 173.

around readiness for the end-time. This passage appears to indicate "the serious threat of complacency in the church of Luke's day."[128] Indeed, Farrell detects in the composition of Luke 21 a carefulness "which evidences a debate in the church regarding the correct understanding of this topic."[129] The proposed setting of Luke gains concreteness when Farrell goes on to assert:

> Our basic assumption is that Luke is writing in the seventies after the destruction of Jerusalem at a time when the second coming is called into question. The basis for the doubt is the ambiguity which exists in the Markan prophetic traditions.[130]

In another context Farrell describes the parousia as the "central issue confronting the church of his day."[131]

To this point in the presentation, the argument is clear and coherent. Yet Farrell, in seeking to integrate the present and future motifs, introduces new elements into the Lukan setting. Here, in essentials, he follows Wilson's two-front reconstruction, though with some reformulation:

> From these two emphases it seems very likely that Luke faced a battle on two fronts. On the one hand, the recent developments had caused some to falsely proclaim that the End was imminent or immediate. To this Luke replied with an encouragement for patience and with instruction regarding the clarity of the coming cosmic signs and dissolution that were to precede the Parousia. On the other hand, others were sceptical and doubted apparently both the reality of the present realization and also the future consummation of the Kingdom of God. . . . To this Luke replied with a stress on the fulfillment and an underscoring of the promise yet remaining. . . . Thus, Luke is not combating apocalyptic *per se*. His primary concern is to gain the recognition of the presence of the Kingdom. And he does this by distinguishing himself from and rejecting false imminentistic apocalyptists and carefully setting forth the proper future apocalyptic expectations, including cosmic signs, in the light of the reality of the presence of the Kingdom of God.[132]

The chief difficulty in this analysis lies in the first battlefront assigned to Luke. To put the issue sharply, Farrell places Luke in opposition to the very view that he claims Luke otherwise represents (that is, hope of an imminent End). Farrell stumbles at this juncture because he has not sufficiently discriminated between the narrative situation and Luke's own social setting.[133] Failure to

[128] Ibid., 163.

[129] Ibid., 171.

[130] Ibid., 174 n. 1.

[131] Ibid., 182. Farrell claims that the primary function of the ascension in Luke-Acts is to anticipate the parousia. Although Acts 1:11 clearly points forward to the parousia, it is an exaggeration to speak of the ascension's primary function in those terms.

[132] Ibid., 193–94.

[133] That is, the narrative rules out imminent hope in those (narrative) settings where it would be premature. (Cf. Hiers, "Problem," 148, 150, 155. Hiers' narrow focus on the infallibility of Jesus as the motivating factor is problematic, however.) If Luke is to make

correlate successfully Luke's setting and his theological view has prevented an otherwise careful probe of Lukan eschatology from achieving a cogent synthesis.

Like Farrell, R. *Maddox* argues that present fulfillment of eschatological hopes represents Luke's primary emphasis, although he differs from Farrell by discerning a reduction of importance for future eschatology in Luke-Acts.[134] Maddox draws a distinction between the kingdom of God and the day of the Son of man. The kingdom in Luke-Acts is essentially a present reality, though it must be consummated in the future![135] This present kingdom one enters through faith. On the other hand, the day of the Son of man is an event lying in the future. Nevertheless, this ultimate, apocalyptic completion of eschatology recedes in importance (if not in time) in Luke-Acts, according to Maddox![136] Luke's interest centers not in a long-extended period of waiting, but rather in the confident, joyful conviction that the essential expectations of the end-time have already been realized![137]

Maddox rejects the view of Luke's setting that is prevalent among scholars working in Conzelmann's shadow. Parousia delay is not the central issue![138] Moreover, in contrast to Braumann, he does not regard persecution as a serious problem confronting Luke's church![139] Instead, Maddox envisages for Luke-Acts a Christian audience of about the sixth decade of the church's history, for whom

---

imminent hope viable in his own setting, he must show that such hope was misplaced in earlier contexts. After all, the eschatological promises did not then come to fruition! I will develop this hypothesis in chapters two and three of the dissertation.

[134] *Purpose,* 100–57. For a similar view, based on an analysis of Luke 22:13–20, see W. Bösen, *Jesusmahl, Eucharistisches Mahl, Endzeitmahl: Ein Beitrag zur Theologie des Lukas* (Stuttgart: Katholisches Bibelwerk, 1980). Bösen contends that, for one who participates in the communion of the eucharistic meal, the "Gottesgemeinschaft" of the end-time is already, here and now, actualized "vorwegnehmend" (pp. 75–76). The meal of the end-time will bring to completion the salvation actualized for the between-time in the eucharistic meal. Bösen also offers a glimpse of Luke's situation: toward the close of the first century, the connection of the believer to Jesus came to be threatened by daily difficulties; the enthusiasm of the imminent-expectation phase had faded away, and disappointment, discouragement, and resignation remained. In such a setting, Luke sought to move believers to new zeal and to active engagement in their daily living (p. 139).

[135] Ibid., 136–37, 143. For a clear presentation of the present character of the kingdom in Luke-Acts, see O. Merk, "Das Reich Gottes in den lukanischen Schriften," in *Jesus und Paulus,* ed. E. E. Ellis and E. Grässer (Göttingen: Vandenhoeck and Ruprecht, 1975) 201–20.

[136] Here Maddox parts company with Farrell, who gives particular emphasis to the eschatological tenor of Acts. Maddox asserts that the eschatological hope has less prominence in Acts (*Purpose,* 130–31).

[137] Ibid., 139. In this sense it is permissible to speak of the period of the church as "charged with eschatology."

[138] Ibid., 115.

[139] Ibid., 91–99.

the consciousness of a wide and almost certainly permanent rift between Christians and Jews now posed an acute theological problem. This division between Judaism and Christianity might be taken to mean that Christians were excluded from the community of salvation. Under pressure from Jewish propaganda, Christian faith was troubled by the haunting question: How could non-Jews hope to find value in a movement rooted in Judaism, yet repudiated by the leaders of the Jewish people? In this context, Luke's aim was that of "clarifying the Christian self-understanding."[140] Luke's two-volume work was designed to reassure the Christian community concerning the validity of the tradition and faith in which it stood.[141] Hence Luke's emphasis on present fulfillment of God's saving purposes, which governs the Lukan eschatology and, in fact, lies at the center of Luke's purpose in writing.[142]

Before I proceed to the next type of approach to Luke's eschatology, it is appropriate to note here the position taken by J. *Fitzmyer* in his commentary on Luke.[143] Fitzmyer recognizes that Luke does not completely abandon expectation of an imminent End, although he has coped with the issue of the delay. Fitzmyer suggests, however, that the two-pronged set of eschatological statements (pivotal in the view of Wilson, e.g.) in Luke-Acts in all likelihood reflects pre-Lukan traditions.[144] According to Fitzmyer, Luke does not de-eschatologize the kerygma; on the contrary, Luke knows well the importance of the eschatological materials he has inherited, and so he preserves them. At the same time, Luke endeavors to shift attention away from exclusive concentration on imminence to a realization that the present period of the church, too, has a place in God's salvation history.[145]

Concerning the situation that shaped the Lukan eschatology, Fitzmyer spurns Conzelmann's thesis that the eschatological viewpoint of Luke represents a response to a crisis prompted by delay. He also rejects the position (described under the next heading below) that Luke directed his eschatological emphases against a gnostic identification of parousia and resurrection/ascension. The decisive factor in Luke's shift of emphasis from the eschaton to the present was his desire to present a still valid guide for conduct today. Luke dulls the eschatological edge of some sayings of Jesus in order to make of them "a hortatory device for everyday Christian living."[146]

[140] Ibid., 181, 184.

[141] Ibid., 186.

[142] Ibid., 183.

[143] *The Gospel According to Luke,* (2 vol.; AB 28–28A; Garden City: Doubleday, 1981, 1985).

[144] Ibid., 1.234: ". . . the two-pronged set of statements that one finds in the Lucan Gospel is not necessarily all of Luke's own making. There is reason to think that this double attitude was part of a pre-Lucan tradition."

[145] Ibid., 1.235.

[146] Ibid.

5. Lukan Eschatology as Correction of an Over-Realized Eschatology

If Farrell and Maddox assign great weight to the dimension of present fulfillment in Lukan eschatology, precisely the opposite occurs in the work of H.-W. Bartsch and C. H. Talbert, both of whom contend that Luke crafts his eschatological message to oppose an over-realized eschatology. H.-W. *Bartsch* has, in several publications, advanced the view that Luke holds to an imminent hope and directs his eschatological formulation against Gnostic-like speculation that mistakes the resurrection and exaltation of Jesus for the events of the parousia.[147] Bartsch acknowledges, with Conzelmann and others, that Luke-Acts betrays a historicizing tendency. Luke "historicizes" all events which are, with reference to his own time, past. However, this historicizing tendency does not entail an abandonment of imminent hope, as Conzelmann thought. Rather, Luke intensifies imminent eschatological expectation.[148] Bartsch perceives this Lukan perspective as a deliberate turning away from the original eschatological conviction of primitive Christianity, namely, that with Jesus' death and resurrection the end-time had already broken in.[149] Needless to say, this position presupposes a picture of primitive Christian eschatology radically different from that assumed by most scholars, and forcefully described by Grässer.[150]

Luke's eschatological point of view was, according to Bartsch, shaped with a view to the correction of a mistaken theological understanding. This attempt to correlate eschatology and setting is similar to Conzelmann's approach (and to that of most other scholars who have addressed the topic) in that it conceives of the setting as one in which theological or ideational correction is required.[151] The theological problem in this reading of the Lukan writings, however, is not parousia delay but erroneous identification of resurrection and parousia. Therefore, although Bartsch anticipates Wilson's later two-front description of Luke's setting, the shape of the battle he sees being waged by Luke is quite different. Bartsch pictures an "Auseinandersetzung" against two fronts: first, the belief "dass das Ende unmittelbar mit Jesu Sterben und Auferstehen gekommen sei (19,11; 21,9,12)"; second, the skeptical view "dass sein Kommen darum noch lange aussteht (12,45!)."[152] In other words, the situation in which Luke writes is

---

[147] Bartsch presents his approach in commentary style in *Wachtet aber zu jeder Zeit: Entwurf einer Auslegung des Lukasevangeliums* (Hamburg-Bergstedt: Herbert Reich, 1963), and in numerous articles: "Parusieerwartung und Osterbotschaft," *EvT* 7 (1947–48) 115–26; "Zum Problem der Parusieverzögerung bei den Synoptikern," *EvT* 19 (1959) 116–31; "Early Christian Eschatology in the Synoptic Gospels," *NTS* 11 (1964–65) 387–97.

[148] *Wachtet,* 123.

[149] Ibid., 121.

[150] In *Problem,* which builds upon the foundation of a Jesus who holds to an unqualified, imminent future hope, and which then traces the successive transformation of eschatological beliefs in light of the phenomenon of parousia delay.

[151] See *Wachtet,* 7. The insistence of Wilson, Cadbury (see below), and Braumann, e.g., on the pastoral, practical dimension of Luke's activity is, of course, an exception.

[152] Ibid., 123.

characterized by both languishing future hope and gnostic speculation. This approach stands or falls not only on its peculiar reconstruction of pre-Lukan eschatology, but also on this highly unusual correlation of Luke's eschatology and setting. In any case, Bartsch does make an important contribution by insisting on the presence of living imminent hope in Luke-Acts, and by pointing out with clarity that Luke's so-called historicizing tendency simply makes past events past.

The most energetic proponent of the thesis that Luke's eschatology (indeed, his literary enterprise as a whole) was designed to oppose a gnostic orientation to Christian faith has been C. H. *Talbert*.[153] Talbert's approach approximates closely that of Bartsch. Luke retained belief in an End close at hand, Talbert maintains. However, the author of Luke-Acts also sketches the stages of history that must precede the parousia. Why this periodization of history? First, Luke depicts past events as past. Second, he seeks to counter an over-realized eschatology that mistakenly discerned in Jesus' ascension (and in Pentecost) the coming of the kingdom of God![154]

It is already apparent that Talbert takes seriously the problem of correlating Luke's eschatology with his situation. Luke 19:11–27, for example, indicates that an eschatological problem is agitating Luke's church. However, Talbert minimizes the role played by parousia delay, preferring to ascribe that motif (e.g., in Luke 12:38, 45) to Luke's *sources*. It is therefore incorrect to draw inferences regarding Luke's own setting from this seeming struggle over delay![155] Talbert is also persuaded that no false apocalypticism is raging in Luke's church![156] Instead, it appears (to Talbert) that someone in that church is misinterpreting the Jesus tradition as locating the eschaton in present experience. Talbert even goes so far as to say that someone is employing Jesus' words (Luke 17:20–21) to undergird the claim to have experienced the eschaton now![157] In order to lend added plausibility to his hypothesis, Talbert calls attention to spiritualized, realized eschatology as a problem widespread in the early church![158] In a word, Talbert detects the clue to Luke's thought not in parousia delay but in "the pressure of heresy in the Lucan community."[159]

---

[153] The most significant and fullest presentation of Talbert's position on Luke's eschatology is "The Redaction Critical Quest for Luke the Theologian," in *Jesus and Man's Hope*, ed. D. G. Buttrick (Pittsburgh, 1970) 171–222. See also *Literary Patterns, Theological Themes, and the Genre of Luke-Acts* (Missoula: Scholars, 1974); *Luke and the Gnostics* (Nashville: Abingdon, 1966); and *What Is a Gospel?* (Philadelphia: Fortress, 1977).

[154] "Redaction," 173, 176, 183–85.

[155] Ibid., 189–91.

[156] Ibid., 185–86.

[157] Ibid., 179–81, 191.

[158] Ibid., 192, with appeal to 1 Corinthians; 2 Tim 2:17b–18; Philippians 3; 2 Thessalonians 2; Tertullian, "On the Resurrection of the Flesh," 19; Hippolytus' account of the Naassenes; etc.

[159] Ibid., 213.

This approach correctly recognizes the persistence of imminent expectation in Luke-Acts; moreover — and this is of special importance for my undertaking — Talbert grapples earnestly with the connection between Luke's theological view and Luke's setting. Nevertheless, Talbert's portrayal of "anti-Gnostic" Luke has found few followers; his view of the relation of Luke's eschatological view to his setting remains suspect. The decisive question is: what manner of correlation between eschatological perspective and situation best fits the evidence? Especially granted Talbert's handling of the delay motif in Luke-Acts (it reflects an essentially pre-Lukan struggle), what features of the Lukan writings may be used to draw inferences regarding Luke's setting, and on the basis of what criteria? To these questions we will return in the final section of chapter 1.

6. Approaches Emphasizing the Centrality of the Ascension in Lukan Eschatology

The pivotal role of the ascension in Luke's eschatology has informed the positions of H. Flender and E. Franklin. H. Flender arrived at his systematic orientation to the topic in reaction to the study by Conzelmann.[160] Luke's starting point, in the analysis of Flender, is not history but rather the exaltation of Christ. Indeed, it is significant for Luke's eschatology that the ascension, not the resurrection, introduces the world to come: Luke thereby avoids the danger of presuming a direct connection between the resurrection of Jesus and the general resurrection.[161] Discernible in Luke-Acts is a shift of weight from the parousia to the ascension: "Functions previously assigned to Christ at the parousia are transferred to the exaltation." Flender dares to assert: "For Luke exaltation and parousia are identical. Jesus' goal is achieved with his exaltation. The parousia is the manifestation on earth of the Lordship into which Jesus has entered in heaven."[162] Obviously, this interpretation sharply contradicts the views of Bartsch and Talbert. A significant result of this stress on the ascension is a peculiar transposition of horizontal into vertical eschatology in Luke-Acts. The temporal framework for eschatology is subordinated to a (Platonic) spatial juxtaposing of the earthly and the heavenly. Because salvation has already been consummated in heaven, Luke is "no longer tied down to an imminent end."[163]

In the light of this heavily theological approach to Luke's eschatological perspective, it is hardly surprising that Flender rejects Conzelmann's salvation-history model as simplistic and one-dimensional. To do justice to Flender's reading of Luke, it is important to observe that he does not argue that Luke has simply postponed the parousia and replaced it with the exaltation. "Christ, now enthroned in heaven, keeps alive the expectation of his coming on earth." The

[160] English translation: *St. Luke: Theologian of Redemptive History,* tr. R. Fuller and I. Fuller (Philadelphia: Fortress, 1967).

[161] Ibid., 57, 19. This last point resembles the approach of both Bartsch and Talbert.

[162] These two quotations are excerpted from ibid., pp. 91 and 94 n. 3, respectively.

[163] Ibid., 60–61 n. 6.

introduction of Jesus' ascension does not imply a reduction of the eschatology, but it does mean a transformation has occurred.[164]

What of Luke's setting? Flender concedes that ongoing history has as its corollary the delay of the parousia. However, as Luke 22:69 illustrates, the "real problem exercising the community was not the continuation of time, but the certainty of Christ's final victory."[165] Flender's relatively abstract, theoretical picture of Luke's project does not lead him to elaborate on this hint. In another context, Flender provides an equally general description of the situation that prompted Luke to his literary endeavor. The era in which he lived dictated for Luke a threefold task as an historian: (1) to preserve the unique character of the Christ event in continuing history; (2) to resolve the problem of the historical continuity between Israel and the Church; and (3) to describe the presence of salvation in the Christian community over time. Without minimizing the importance of these theological concerns in Luke-Acts, it is fair to say that Flender does not present a concrete glimpse of the Lukan situation.

In two studies less governed by systematic-theological interests, E. *Franklin* arrives at a similar emphasis on the function of the ascension in the narrative of Luke-Acts.[166] Like Flender, Franklin contends that the stress shifts from parousia to ascension. The ascension, not the parousia, is the event that fulfills the hopes of Israel.[167] Franklin also agrees with Flender that this shift does not involve a reduction, but rather an interpretation, of pre-Lukan eschatological expectation. Although the ascension constitutes the climax of Luke's narrative, the parousia remains intact; indeed, it is not necessarily expected to be long delayed.[168] Still, the parousia undergoes a distinct relativizing in Luke-Acts; no

---

[164] Ibid., 99. Flender's emphasis on vertical eschatology carries with it unfortunate terminological consequences. It appears that the word "eschatology" is removed from any considerations of time; in Flender's hands, "eschatological" becomes synonymous with "heavenly" or "divine." See, e.g., p. 114: Luke treats the destruction of Jerusalem as eschatological because "it is a symbolic embodiment of God's dealings with the world" (cf. p. 167).

[165] Ibid., 102.

[166] "The Ascension and the Eschatology of Luke-Acts," *SJT* 23 (1970) 191–200; *Christ the Lord: A Study in the Purpose and Theology of Luke-Acts* (Philadelphia: Westminster, 1975), especially pp. 9–47. G. Lohfink (*Die Himmelfahrt Jesu* [Munich: Kösel, 1971]) and E. Kränkl (*Jesus der Knecht Gottes* [Regensburg: Pustet, 1972]) likewise place the ascension of Jesus at the center of Luke's narrative (and eschatology). See, e.g., Lohfink, *Himmelfahrt,* 201, 259–61; Kränkl, *Knecht,* 185–86, 204. Like Franklin, Lohfink holds that Luke does not push the End into the remote future, even though he has given the period between Jesus' resurrection and parousia its own weight in salvation history (*Himmelfahrt,* 260–61). On the other hand, Kränkl argues that Luke has solved the problem of delay by focusing his eschatological conception in Jesus the resurrected and exalted Lord, rather than Jesus the returning one. The question of the timing of Jesus' parousia has consequently become irrelevant (*Knecht,* 204).

[167] *Christ,* 27, 41.

[168] "Ascension," 192, 200.

longer the ground of hope, it becomes one event among others witnessing to the kingdom of God![169] Concerning the timing of the parousia, Franklin maintains that Luke expects the End in the near future, if not immediately. A delay has certainly occurred, and Luke and his contemporaries stand at a considerable distance from the life of Jesus. In order to sustain the faith of his contemporaries — a faith shaken by the non-occurrence of the parousia — Luke must therefore remove from the parousia the significance that it possessed in Mark. Hence the constitutive importance of the ascension![170]

Franklin's perception of the Lukan setting has already begun to surface. Luke's situation is characterized by "doubts, persecutions, and disappointments."[171] Standing at some distance from the time of Jesus, Luke's readers "are still oppressed and hopes are beginning to fail. In the face of this, Luke maintains that the parousia, though delayed, is nevertheless a certainty and one that will come about soon."[172] The failure of the parousia to appear is, then, a central concern of Luke. In fact, Luke 18:8b points to a widespread crisis of confidence in Luke's own day![173] To be sure, Franklin's reconstruction of this setting is not developed systematically or methodically; nevertheless, it does offer a coherent, consistent diagnosis, one which will need to be taken into account in my own analysis.

7. Approaches Emphasizing Individual Eschatology in Luke-Acts

Our discussion of Ernst's *Herr der Geschichte* adumbrated the problem of "individual eschatology" — concentration on the personal eschaton of the individual at death — in Luke-Acts![174] J. Dupont and G. Schneider have focused attention on this feature of the Lukan writings. J. *Dupont* discerns in Luke an intense interest in the destiny of the individual after death![175] At the same time,

[169] *Christ*, 16, 19.

[170] Ibid., 19–20.

[171] Ibid., 47.

[172] Ibid., 19.

[173] Ibid., 10, 19.

[174] For a concise, balanced discussion of this question, see Maddox, *Purpose,* 103–05. Maddox concludes "that there is indeed a small element of 'individual eschatology' in Luke-Acts" (p. 104). He suggests that Luke has accepted, to a slight degree, an alternative way of thinking that he places alongside the traditional, apocalyptic eschatology. Maddox also cautions against the notion that this phenomenon is unique to Luke; he points to Phil 1:23; 1 Thess 4:15–17; and 1 Cor 15:51–52 (p. 105).

[175] See especially "L'après-mort dans l'oeuvre de Luc," *RTL* 3 (1972) 3–21; and "Individuelle Eschatologie," in *Orientierung an Jesus*, ed. P. Hoffmann (Freiburg: Herder, 1973) 37–47. Dupont has also published exegetical treatments of eschatological materials in Luke-Acts other than those bearing upon the issue of individual eschatology: e.g., "Les discours de Pierre dans les Actes et le chapitre XXIV de l'evangile de Luc," in *L'Evangile de Luc: Problèmes littéraires et théologiques*, ed. F. Neirynck, 329–74; "La Parabole du Maître qui Rentre dans la Nuit (Mc 13,34–36)," in *Mélanges Bibliques*, ed. A. Descamps

though, Dupont perceives no elimination by Luke of the collective (future) eschatology. Nor does Luke abandon hope in the future return of Christ.[176] These two aspects of Lukan eschatology—individual and collective—run parallel, never being brought into mutual relationship.[177] Nevertheless, in Dupont's judgment, Luke regards as decisive the fate of the individual at death. This individual eschatology, then, entails a certain relativizing of the collective, future eschatology: the present must be taken with full seriousness, for it is no longer provisional in character, but has a finality of its own.[178]

Dupont refrains from reflection on the problem of the setting for this Lukan perspective, apart from one general comment. The individual aspect of Lukan eschatology, expressed in such passages as Luke 12:16-20; 16:19-31; and 23:43, is one manifestation of the "individualistischen Mentalität der griechischen Welt der ausgehenden Antike."[179]

G. *Schneider* has also called attention to an individualizing tendency in Luke's eschatological perspective.[180] The element of delay, and of a period of time stretching out until the parousia, is obvious in Luke-Acts. Schneider suggests (on the basis of Acts 1:6-8) that the worldwide mission necessitated a delay in the parousia, and that the Spirit's sending made this delay (in service of mission) possible.[181] Despite the attainment of the "end of the earth" (Acts 1:8) by Paul in Acts 28, Schneider denies that Luke reckoned with an imminent End (cf. Acts 26:29). In light of the passage of time, involving the deaths of believers before the consummation of the kingdom, Luke was moved toward an individualizing of the "Parusieproblematik."[182] Accordingly, the individual's fate prior to the parousia figures prominently in Acts 7:56, 59 and Luke 23:42-43.[183]

(Gembloux: Duculot, 1970) 89-116; "La Parabole du Figuier qui Bourgeonne," *RB* 75 (1968) 526-48.

[176] "Individuelle," 37, 45.

[177] Ibid., 46.

[178] Ibid., 47.

[179] Ibid. Interest in the status of the individual before the parousia is also a corollary, in theory at least, of the parousia delay.

[180] See, e.g., *Parusiegleichnisse im Lukas-Evangelium* (Stuttgart: Katholisches Bibelwerk, 1975); and *Apostelgeschichte*. A convenient distillation of Schneider's view is provided in an excursus on "Parousia and Parousia-Expectation" in *Apostelgeschichte,* 1.336-39. Cf. the theological reflections presented in "Anbruch des Heils und Hoffnung auf Vollendung bei Jesus, Paulus und Lukas," in *Lukas, Theologe der Heilsgeschichte: Aufsätze zum lukanischen Doppelwerk* (Bonn: Peter Hanstein, 1985) 35-60, especially 51-56.

[181] *Apostelgeschichte,* 1.338; *Parusiegleichnisse,* 88-89. Only the activity of the Spirit permitted fulfillment of the program prophesied in scripture for the period before the End (Luke 24:44-47); see the discussion in *Apostelgeschichte,* 1.338.

[182] *Apostelgeschichte,* 1.338; *Parusiegleichnisse,* 78-84, 89.

[183] *Apostelgeschichte,* 1.338. On Acts 7:56,59 (the martyrdom of Stephen and his vision of the standing Son of man) and individualizing eschatology, see also C. K. Barrett,

Schneider differs from Dupont in arguing that individual and collective eschatology do *not* remain parallel, unintegrated concepts; on the contrary, the line probably leads from the collective eschatology to the individual statements.[184] According to Schneider, the retreat of the parousia theme in Acts is due to Luke's freedom in handling his sources, not to a later date of composition (as Wilson infers).[185] As the importance of the parousia retreats, all the more definitive becomes the destiny of the *individual* after death.[186] Schneider arrives at the conclusion that Luke's eschatological perspective paints a unified picture: all statements of imminence are suppressed or reinterpreted. Luke's parousia hope focuses on readiness (on the part of the individual) for the Lord's sudden coming (at whatever time, imminent or delayed); the imminence of the parousia is not central.[187] In Schneider's view, the church's experience of parousia delay is the decisive factor in Luke's eschatological reformulation.[188]

8. Concluding Observations

The preceding discussion has shown something of the diversity of opinion on Lukan eschatology. In fact, recent debate has led to an impasse. Even if Conzelmann's thesis of "uneschatological Luke" no longer enjoys the supremacy it once could claim, no rival theory has supplanted it. The range of disagreement is immense. Concerning the timing of the End, Luke is seen to be both an advocate (Mattill, Hiers, Francis) and an enemy (Conzelmann, Haenchen, Grässer, Zmijewski) of imminent hope.[189] The balance between present and future in the structure of Luke's eschatology tips now toward the present (Farrell, Fitzmyer, Maddox), now toward the future (Mattill, Hiers). Many scholars regard Luke and Acts as consistent with respect to the role of eschatology (Francis, Smith, Farrell), but others drive a wedge between the two volumes (Wilson, Gaventa; cf. Schneider). The weight of Luke's eschatological emphasis falls in some cases on the parousia (Mattill), in others on the ascension (Flender, Franklin, Kränkl), and in others still on the history that stretches out between these two moments (Conzelmann, Zmijewski). Finally, the setting that prompted Luke's formulation of future hope varies from discouragement and doubt induced by parousia delay (Franklin, Kränkl), to an outbreak of apocalyptic enthusiasm (Haenchen, Ellis), to a combination of these two factors in a war

---

"Stephen and the Son of Man," in *Apophoreta: Festschrift für Ernst Haenchen,* ed. W. Eltester (Berlin: Töpelmann, 1964) 32–38.

[184] *Parusiegleichnisse,* 81.

[185] Ibid., 85.

[186] Ibid., 94.

[187] Ibid., 91.

[188] Ibid., 95.

[189] Farrell manages to combine both views. Kränkl claims that the question of timing is irrelevant for Luke.

waged on two fronts (Wilson, Mattill, Farrell, and Gaventa), to gnostic absorption of the parousia into Jesus' resurrection/ascension (Talbert, Bartsch).

Confusion stems not only from varying exegetical conclusions but also from haphazard, unsystematic inferences about the setting which underlies the text of Luke-Acts. The number of proposals for Luke's eschatological view and his situation, all claiming to find warrant in the text, but often enough turning out to be mutually exclusive, justifies a renewed attempt to draw—with as much methodological precision as is possible—correlations between the Lukan eschatological perspective and a posited Lukan setting. By following such a path, I aim in this study to point beyond the present impasse.

The complexity of this research survey is also symptomatic of another source of confusion in recent research. Luke's eschatological perspective is not one-dimensional, although it is often treated as though it were. Ordinarily, attention is focused on the question of chronology or timing: When will the arrival of the kingdom of God (parousia of the Son of man) occur? This has been by far the most hotly contested aspect of debate. However, the presence, out on the periphery of the discussion, of studies which are concerned more with the content of the eschatological fulfillment than with its timing—notably the probes of individual eschatology in Luke, but also several works examining the inter-relationships among Israel, church, and kingdom[190]—serves as a reminder that Luke's eschatological perspective represents a matrix composed of several variables.

Among the elements merging to form this perspective, four are of special importance. First is the *timing* of the eschatological program and its completion. Second is the *content* of the eschatological program, specifically of its completion at the eschaton. What did Luke expect to happen, and to whom? Here crucial sub-issues include the individual vs. cosmic scope of salvation; the destiny of Israel, of unbelieving Jews, of Gentile believers, and of the nations; and the nature and beneficiaries of judgment and restoration. Third is the *significance* of the eschaton, and of eschatology in general, in Luke's total perspective. What is the precise weight of the eschatological program and its completion in Luke-Acts? Fourth is the *situation* that shaped Luke's eschatological viewpoint. In other words, what is the (social) function of eschatology in Luke's total perspective? My point is simply that one reason for such a bewildering variety of approaches to Lukan eschatology is that the subject has several dimensions.

Because of the limits of space, this dissertation will not attempt a comprehensive treatment of all variables comprising Luke's eschatological perspective.

---

[190] To mention only a few of the recent studies: the paradigm-shifting articles by J. Jervell, gathered in *Luke and the People of God* (Minneapolis: Augsburg, 1972); G. Lohfink, *Die Sammlung Israels: Eine Untersuchung zur lukanischen Ekklesiologie* (Munich: Kösel, 1975); D. Tiede, *Prophecy and History in Luke-Acts* (Philadelphia: Fortress, 1980).

I will focus on the first and fourth elements outlined above, namely, the timing of the eschatological scenario and its completion, and the correlation between eschatology and situation in Luke-Acts. However, the second and third aspects of the Lukan eschatological matrix will never be remote from our immediate concerns. Before turning to an analysis of the pertinent texts (chapters two and three),[191] I will address significant issues of method raised by this survey of research and outline the method to be employed in the constructive section of the dissertation.

B. METHODOLOGICAL ISSUES

Redaction critical study of the synoptic gospels has undergone transformation since Conzelmann first applied such methods to Luke-Acts. To an increasing degree, Lukan scholars have tempered their redaction critical orientation with appreciation of the full dimensions of the author's finished literary product as a whole.[192] Moreover, under the impact of social-scientific methods of analysis,

---

[191] The selection of passages has been determined by the course of previous research and by my own methodological position. The eschatological discourses of Luke 17 and 21, the account of Jesus' ascension in Acts 1:3–11, the Joel quotation in Acts 2:17–21, and the last half of Peter's speech in Acts 3 (vv 19–26) have formed the center of debate and so receive detailed consideration in the present study. Although Luke 12:35–48 has remained on the periphery of the discussion, I include a section on this passage because it is pertinent to eschatology—indeed, I will argue that it establishes a baseline for future expectation in Luke-Acts. Similarly, Luke 19:11–27, though not prominent in treatments of Luke's eschatology, receives attention here because it places Jesus' Jerusalem ministry in relation to the eschaton. In addition, I bring Luke 1–2 and Acts 28:17–31 into the discussion because these passages (seldom introduced into the previous debate) form Luke's narrative beginning and conclusion, and in so doing place his entire literary project in connection with the hope and future of Israel.

[192] For a sampling of position statements on this question, see Ellis, *Eschatology*, 2–3; R. A. Edwards, "The Redaction of Luke," *JR* 49 (1969) 392–405; L. T. Johnson, *The Literary Function of Possessions in Luke-Acts* (Missoula: Scholars, 1977) 12–28; Maddox, *Purpose*, 19–20; Fitzmyer, *Luke*, 1.144; D. Juel, *Luke-Acts: The Promise of History* (Atlanta: John Knox, 1983) 5, 8; J. B. Tyson, "Source Criticism of the Gospel of Luke," in *Perspectives on Luke-Acts*, ed. C. H. Talbert (Danville: Association of Baptist Professors of Religion, 1978) 24–39, 38–39; D. R. Adams, "The Suffering of Paul and the Dynamics of Luke-Acts" (New Haven: Yale University Ph.D. dissertation, 1979) 7–8, 54–55; P. F. Feiler, "Jesus the Prophet: The Lucan Portrayal of Jesus as the Prophet Like Moses" (Princeton: Princeton Theological Seminary Ph.D. dissertation, 1986) 17–27. Illustrative of the trend in Lukan redaction critical work is the approach of Ellis, who rejects the assumption that "pre-Lukan" = "non-Lukan": "All of the material in Luke is in some sense 'Lukan' from the fact that Luke includes it. If the traditional material has acquired a Lukan shape, the editorial material also may have a traditional character. In choosing sources, as much as in his *ad hoc* elaboration, Luke is expressing his concerns and preferences" (*Eschatology*, 3). In his critique of the work of M. Dibelius, Adams ("Dynamics," 7–8) observes that Dibelius' work was limited by the assumption "that in a

research on the gospels has shown new sensitivity to the social matrices that shaped these literary texts. In parts one and three of this discussion of methodology, I will locate my study in relation to these concerns. The middle section will explain my approach to the meaning of "eschatology" in Luke-Acts.

1. What Is "Lukan"?

Underlying current debate regarding the application of redaction critical methods to Luke[193] is the fundamental question: what patterns of thought, what literary dynamics, what theological and historical perspectives may be characterized as "Lukan"? The pioneers in the study of Lukan redaction (Conzelmann, Haenchen) focused attention on Luke's modifications of his sources, especially Mark, in constructing a picture of Lukan theology. Those areas in which Luke demonstrably parted company with the traditions that he wove into his narrative offered the key to Luke's own theological orientation and purposes.

There can be no doubt that such a procedure sharpens one's analysis of the text. The question remains, however, whether such an approach by itself does not yield skewed results. Luke did not, after all, expect his audience to grasp the meaning of his narrative with a synopsis in hand. Luke rather entrusted the whole of his composition to his readers, and we must be confident that Luke viewed his writing as a fair presentation of his perspective. To be sure, whenever an author incorporates traditions, there is the possibility that the two layers will not coincide in every respect. Yet we need to consider the probability that pre-Lukan traditions (redacted or not) are as much a vehicle of the Lukan perspective as are alterations made to them. The inference that traditions have been included by Luke *against* his own views should not be arrived at too hastily. In the specific instance of eschatological traditions, the explanation given by Conzelmann and Grässer for passages expressive of imminent hope—namely, that Luke has transmitted them without allowing them to shape his own view—is a hypothesis of last resort.

Clear evidence of Lukan redaction of his sources must, of course, be granted full value in any analysis of Lukan composition. Nevertheless, recognition of these data must be balanced by sensitivity to synthetic features of Luke's writing: the literary "architecture," to use Talbert's category,[194] narrative transitions,

---

composite writing, the author's message is to be found in his editorial work and free composition, not in the traditions he employed. Over against this assumption, we would argue that an author's message is to be found in his final product — tradition, redaction and free composition considered as one. A text conveys its meaning as a totality, and while it may be convenient to start with redactional features, that convenient beginning should not be allowed to stand for the whole of the interpretive enterprise" (cf. pp. 54–55).

[193] See the preceding footnote.

[194] Of Talbert's numerous literary analyses of Luke-Acts, the fullest presentation of his literary method is *Literary Patterns, Theological Themes, and the Genre of Luke-Acts* (Missoula: Scholars, 1974).

beginnings and endings, thematic repetition, and other literary clues to the meaning of Luke's story in its finished form. The literary analyses of Luke-Acts recently presented by L. T. Johnson suggest the heuristic power of such serious attention to the entire narrative.[195]

The above discussion has assumed the necessity of reading the two volumes of Luke's work as one literary composition. That assumption appears to be the prevalent one in current study of Luke and Acts, and need not be justified here.[196] Nevertheless, Dibelius' position on the differing scope and specificity of sources for the two volumes remains valid.[197] Luke probably had fewer and less detailed sources at hand for the composition of Acts than was the case in the gospel;[198] Luke had a correspondingly greater measure of freedom in compiling the stories and speeches of Acts. Indeed, in the case of eschatology, G. Schneider concludes that the muting of imminent eschatology in Acts stems precisely from this relative freedom of the author, who is not (as he was in the gospel) bound by the presence of abundant eschatological materials.[199] This is certainly a hypothesis worth considering, although the present study will opt for a different explanation, in part because I take with greater seriousness than does Schneider the responsibility of the author for the *totality* of his composite writing.

The position that will guide this examination of Luke-Acts is that the gospel and Acts must be approached differently, insofar as tradition-redaction analysis is concerned. In the gospel, Luke's treatment of his sources (where extant, or recoverable ["Q"] with some precision) will be scrutinized closely and accorded due weight.[200] In Acts (as also in Luke 1-2), the absence of any reliably reconstructed sources requires that tradition-redaction analysis take a back seat to the literary analysis of the finished product.[201] With respect to both volumes,

---

[195] See above all *The Literary Function of Possessions in Luke-Acts* (Missoula: Scholars, 1977).

[196] See, e.g., Maddox, *Purpose*, 3-6; D. L. Tiede, *Prophecy and History in Luke-Acts* (Philadelphia: Fortress, 1980) 11-16; Juel, *Promise*, 1-2; Johnson, *Possessions*, 12-14. On this point the view of H. J. Cadbury has prevailed (see *The Making of Luke-Acts* [New York: Macmillan, 1927] 8-9).

[197] Several of Dibelius' essays on Acts are conveniently gathered in *Studies in the Acts of the Apostles*, tr. M. Ling and P. Schubert, ed. H. Greeven (London: SCM, 1956). See especially the first essay on "Style Criticism of the Book of Acts."

[198] A point contested by Jervell ("The Problem of Traditions in Acts," in *Luke and the People of God* [Minneapolis: Augsburg, 1972] 19-39).

[199] *Parusiegleichnisse*, 85.

[200] While I recognize the present debate over synoptic source theory, stimulated in large part by the work of W. R. Farmer, I am persuaded that a form of the conventional "two-source theory", with allowance for the continuing formative effect of oral traditions alongside written sources, best explains the (admittedly complex) data. Accordingly, I will assume that Luke has employed Mark, a tradition in common with Matthew, and numerous oral traditions, in composing his gospel.

[201] See Tyson, "Source," 24-39, for a view of source-redaction analysis of the gospel that has affinities with that advocated here for Acts.

however, redactional analysis using Luke's sources as a baseline *and* literary analysis of the whole narrative will be used as mutually supplementary procedures. The literary function of a passage in the context of Luke-Acts as a whole will be a governing concern at every phase of the study—both for the assessment of Luke's theological perspective and for the formulation of a hypothesis concerning Luke's situation.

In seeking to discern a "Lukan" eschatological perspective, therefore, I will be charting a middle course between two extremes. I will not adopt the procedure of a literary analysis of the final form of the whole narrative which neglects tradition-redaction probes (where such are appropriate). Nor, at the other pole, will I focus all attention on redactional transformations of Luke's sources, to the neglect of the entire work in its present form. The two approaches will operate together. Similarly, where the probability exists that Luke has taken up antecedent traditions, these will be taken seriously as evidence for Luke's view, yet not uncritically, as if the two layers of tradition necessarily coincide in all points.

2. What Is "Eschatological"?

Perhaps the greatest single source of confusion in recent study of Lukan eschatology is the lack of terminological precision. One scholar's "eschatology" is another's "history." Luke, there can be no dispute, composed a narrative that presupposes a considerable expanse of early Christian history. To Conzelmann and Grässer, among others, this fact compels the judgment that Luke has transformed eschatology into history. Taking into account the period that followed the time of Jesus, Luke allowed the eschaton to retreat to the distant horizon. However, to Borgen and Francis, among others, this phenomenon requires the conclusion that Luke has eschatologized history! In the light of the end-time bestowal of the Spirit (Acts 2:17), the entire period of the church's mission is eschatological in quality. Yet more is involved than word games (historicizing of eschatology or eschatologizing of history?). The two camps of scholars arrive at divergent answers on questions of pivotal importance in the present study: What is the relation of the eschaton to history, and what is the character of each? When, from Luke's own vantage point, will the eschaton occur? Scholars who perceive Luke as a historicizer of eschatology tend to deny any imminent hope to Luke; those who see Luke as an eschatologizer of history tend to affirm it. Consequently, this dissertation will attend to close exegesis of the kind likely to turn up a clear (descriptive) answer to the question, "When the eschaton?", from Luke's perspective. The crucial issue is: What manner of relationship (temporal and otherwise) does Luke envisage between historical events and the eschaton that he awaits?

Broad definitions of "eschatology" will hinder, rather than facilitate, this exegetical task.[202] In employing the expression "eschatological perspective,"

---

[202] J. B. Chance, in his recent Duke University Ph.D. dissertation, "Jerusalem and the Temple in Lucan Eschatology" (1984), adopts a broad definition of eschatology. The result

therefore, I refer to the point of view adopted in Luke-Acts in relation to the eschaton—the final consummation of God's plan and the end of history, insofar as Luke portrays it. In opting for such a narrow definition, I hope to be able to elucidate the ways in which the Lukan perspective on the end-time functions within Luke's story (and, by inference, within Luke's community), and the ways in which it relates to the present and past of Luke's community(ies).

3. What Constitutes Evidence of Luke's Setting?

The research survey documented the claim that lack of clarity concerning Luke's setting has contributed to our confusion about Luke's eschatological perspective. What features of the text of Luke-Acts may legitimately be appealed to as evidence of the setting in which the document emerged?[203]

---

is imprecision. For example, when Chance speaks of eschatological fulfillment in the apostolic "rule" over Israel (the Jerusalem narrative in Acts), he must qualify that description with such terms as "proleptic" and "partial" (pp. 284–96). After all, as Chance concedes (p. 294), Pentecost is not for Luke "*the* eschatological event without remainder. The community still awaits the restoration of all things." What requires explanation is the connection between strictly eschatological fulfillment (still awaited) and present fulfillment of scriptural promise for the period preceding the End. How does the eschaton impinge upon the present experience of the church? Use of the term "eschatology" for both aspects of Luke's presentation blurs the issue.

[203] I will not attempt a full-scale reconstruction of Luke's social setting (a task for which too little evidence is presently available). Rather, this study examines one aspect of Luke's setting, namely those features that have shaped the end-time perspective presented in Luke-Acts. For recent discussion of Luke's social setting, see E. A. La Verdiere and W. G. Thompson ("New Testament Communities in Transition: A Study of Matthew and Luke," *TS* 37 [1976] 567–97); Adams ("Dynamics," 296–305); L. T. Johnson ("On Finding the Lukan Community: A Cautious Cautionary Essay," in 1979 SBL *Seminar Papers*, vol. 1, ed. P. J. Achtemeier [Missoula: Scholars, 1979] 87–100); B. J. Hubbard ("Luke, Josephus, and Rome: A Comparative Approach to the Lukan *Sitz im Leben*," in 1979 SBL *Seminar Papers*, 1.59–68); R. J. Karris ("The Lukan Sitz-im-Leben: Methodology and Prospects," in 1976 SBL *Seminar Papers*, ed. G. W. MacRae [Missoula: Scholars, 1976] 219–33; "Poor and Rich: The Lukan Sitz im Leben," in *Perspectives on Luke-Acts*, ed. C. H. Talbert [Danville: Association of Baptist Professors of Religion, 1978] 112–25; "Windows and Mirrors: Literary Criticism and Luke's Sitz im Leben," in 1979 SBL *Seminar Papers*, 1.47–58; "Missionary Communities: A New Paradigm for the Study of Luke-Acts," *CBQ* 41 [1979] 80–97); F. Mussner ("Die Gemeinde des Lukasprologs, in *Studien zum Neuen Testament und seiner Umwelt,* 6–7 [1981–82] 113–30); D. M. Sweetland ("The Lord's Supper and the Lukan Community," *BTB* 13 [1983] 23–27); D. B. Kraybill and D. M. Sweetland ("Possessions in Luke-Acts: A Sociological Perspective," *Perspectives in Religious Studies* 10 [1983] 215–39); S. Arai ("Individual- und Gemeindeethik bei Lukas," *Ann Japan Bib Inst* 9 [1983] 88–127); Feiler ("Prophet," 293–304). Luke's treatment of possessions and of the rich and the poor has figured prominently in recent analysis of Luke's setting. On the role of possessions in Luke-Acts, see further Johnson (*Possessions*) and D. P. Seccombe (*Possessions and the Poor in Luke-Acts* [Linz: Studien zum Neuen Testament und seiner Umwelt, B, Band 6,

Given the present enthusiasm for (and relative novelty of) the application of social-scientific models to the study of New Testament writings, the need for caution is great. L. T. Johnson has emphasized the pitfalls accompanying the quest for the Lukan community.[204] In Johnson's view, the primary obstacle derives from Luke's literary pretensions: "there is every reason to believe that the composition of Luke's work was motivated above all by the demands of his overall literary and theological aims."[205] Accordingly, individual elements within the literary structure have their primary function within a literary, not a social, context.[206] Even apart from barriers to setting that are distinctive to Luke-Acts within the New Testament, Johnson notes the limits of the "mirror method" in working with any text:

> The study of Paul's letters reminds us that even in documents of a genuinely occasional nature, not every element in the writing is determined by the place, the people, or the occasion. Some things are there because of the demands of genre, the impetus of tradition, the logic of argumentation, the inertia of scriptural citations, and the idiosyncratic perceptions of the author. Responsible exegesis takes these factors into account *before* using passages as a mirror to community problems.[207]

Only when diverse elements of Luke-Acts are viewed in relation to the literary whole is it then appropriate to ask about Luke's readers and setting.[208]

Because of the level of uncertainty involved, this task requires an increased dose of methodological rigor. For example, pre-Lukan traditions—while a

---

1982]). Both Karris ("Missionary," 89) and Seccombe (*Possessions,* 17) criticize Johnson (*Possessions*) for reducing the theme of possessions in Luke-Acts to the status of literary symbol. Johnson's position (developed in "Cautious") is that inferences about Luke's social setting must follow identification of the literary function of the materials of Luke's narrative.

[204] "Cautious."

[205] Ibid., 92.

[206] Ibid. It should be noted, however, that while Johnson identifies Luke's primary motivation as literary and theological, his discussion proceeds as if he really meant literary aims alone. Such theological designs as may have shaped Luke's literary project are themselves related to a concrete social setting. (Moreover, literary genre also has social location.) For all the hazards accompanying the quest (rightly noted by Johnson), we must finally return to the question of Luke's setting.

[207] Ibid., 89. For discussion of the limits (and benefits) of sociologically attuned reading of New Testament texts, see, e.g., G. Theissen, *The Social Setting of Pauline Christianity* (Philadelphia: Fortress, 1982), especially pp. 175–200; J. G. Gager, *Kingdom and Community: The Social World of Early Christianity* (Englewood Cliffs: Prentice-Hall, 1975); R. Scroggs, "The Sociological Interpretation of the New Testament: The Present State of Research," *NTS* 26 (1980) 164–79; W. A. Meeks, *The First Urban Christians: The Social World of the Apostle Paul* (New Haven: Yale University, 1983).

[208] Ibid., 94.

vehicle of Luke's literary and theological aims — may reflect pre-Lukan settings more accurately than Luke's own situation. Accordingly, in drawing inferences regarding Luke's situation, I will weigh carefully clear signs of Lukan redaction that also have a bearing upon the situation that shaped the document. Yet composition critical analysis of the narrative as a whole will continue to assume a coordinate role in this facet of the study.[209] At the same time, the literary functions of particular passages will be kept in view when the move is made from the literary text to description of both theological perspectives and social situation.

In the course of the research survey, it became apparent that the presence of both delay and imminence motifs in Luke-Acts had evoked a variety of explanations. An increasingly popular assumption (S. G. Wilson, Gaventa, Farrell, Mattill, Ernst) has been that Luke was waging a two-front battle. With the delay motif he sought to defuse overheated apocalyptic fervor, and with the element of imminence he countered fading eschatological hope. This particular reading fails to distinguish between the narrative setting — the setting within the story — and Luke's own situation. Luke wrote in a setting in which parousia delay and a period of worldwide mission were data of history. In such a context, in order for Luke to maintain parousia hope[210] as a credible position, it would be necessary for him, in constructing his narrative, to show imminent expectation to have been inappropriate during the ministry of Jesus, the early years of the church's mission, and at the destruction of Jerusalem (hence the element of delay). The prominence of delay in Luke-Acts does not, therefore, rule out imminent hope in Luke's own time. Serious miscalculation may accompany the failure to discriminate between Luke's narrative setting and his own situation.[211] Since confusion of literary and social setting has been commonplace in study of Lukan eschatology, my own analysis of the relationship between Luke's eschatological point of view and his situation will deliberately emphasize this distinction.

---

[209] Luke's perception of his situation is witnessed not only in his modifications of his sources but also in his shaping of the entire narrative. Still, materials that appear to reflect pre-Lukan settings more accurately than Luke's own situation will be treated with special caution.

[210] Luke does not use the term παρουσία(cf. Fitzmyer, *Luke,* 2.1171); nevertheless, Luke expects Jesus' return (Luke 12:40; 17:24, 30; 18:8; 21:27; Acts 1:11; 3:20–21), and Acts even conforms the ascension account to traditional parousia imagery. It is therefore appropriate to apply the expression "parousia hope" to Luke.

[211] Cf. W. Schenk, "Naherwartung und Parusieverzögerung: Die urchristliche Eschatologie als Problem der Forschung," *Theologische Versuche* 4 (1972) 47–69, 50: ". . . Lukas rechnet nicht mit einem fernen Ende, weil er nur im Blick auf vergangene Ereignisse enteschatologisiert, nicht aber im Vorausblick auf künftige. Nur eine Nichtdifferenzierung an diesem Punkte kann ihm generelle Enteschatologisierung und Fernerwartung zuschreiben." Schenk's discussion of Lukan eschatology builds on the foundation laid by H.-W. Bartsch.

2
Eschatology and Situation in the Gospel of Luke

A. LUKE 1-2 AND THE "HOPE OF ISRAEL"

One of the striking literary features of Luke-Acts is the recurrence of the theme, the "hope of Israel," at the conclusion of each volume of the two-volume work. At the end of the gospel, two disciples speak of their disappointment to a risen "incognito" Lord: "We had hoped that he was the one to redeem Israel" [ἡμεῖς δὲ ἠλπίζομεν ὅτι αὐτός ἐστιν ὁ μέλλων λυτροῦσθαι τὸν Ἰσραήλ] (Luke 24:21). And at the end of Acts Paul discloses to Roman Jews that he had become a prisoner at the initiative of Jerusalem Jews, yet ironically because of the "hope of Israel" [ἕνεκεν γὰρ τῆς ἐλπίδος τοῦ Ἰσραήλ] (Acts 28:20). His apologia picks up a recurring motif of the defense speeches of Acts 21-26: ἐλπίς occurs on Paul's lips in 23:6; 24:15; and 26:6-7![1]

Both the ending of Luke and that of Acts intimate that nothing less than the hope of Israel—specifically, the hope of Israel's redemption—is at stake in the course of Luke's story of Christian beginnings. This suggestion finds confirmation in Luke 1-2; Luke-Acts opens with two chapters announcing the dawn of an era in which the hope of Israel now attains decisive fulfillment. This section of the dissertation aims to elucidate the function of Luke 1-2 within the narrative of Luke-Acts,[2] using as the focus of attention the

---

[1] The substance of this "hope" is not necessarily uniform. For example, in the apologetic contexts of Acts 21-26, Luke's Paul appears to narrow the focus of Israel's hope to the event of resurrection from the dead, now fulfilled in the figure of Jesus (cf. Acts 13:32-33). Luke 24:21, on the other hand, links the disciples' hope to the expected redemption of Israel, a connection which picks up the theme of pious Israel awaiting redemption, in Luke 1-2. Although the resurrection and ascension of Jesus are pivotal events in Luke's presentation of the hope of Israel—promised to "the fathers" and now fulfilled in relation to Jesus—the content of Israel's hope is not to be reduced to resurrection.

[2] Conzelmann was driven, on methodological grounds, to exclude Luke 1-2 from his analysis of Lukan theology (*St. Luke*, 22 n. 2; 172). Yet virtually no one else has followed his lead. Even H. H. Oliver ("The Lucan Birth Stories and the Purpose of Luke-Acts," *NTS* 10 [1963-64] 202-26) and W. B. Tatum ("The Epoch of Israel: Luke I-II and the Theological Plan of Luke-Acts," *NTS* 13 [1966-67] 184-95)—who are convinced by Conzelmann's epochal understanding of Lukan theology—criticize him on this point. The

theme — crucial to an understanding of Luke's eschatological perspective — of the hope of Israel.

1. The Function of the Hymns and Annunciations within Luke 1-2

R. E. Brown has noted that the hymns of Luke 1-2 and the speeches of Acts serve analogous functions:

> The speeches of Acts and the hymns of the infancy narrative are both compositions reflecting older material, but compositions which convey to the reader the tonality of the character to whom they are attributed and which comment upon the significance of the context in which they are uttered.[3]

Anticipating the method of Acts, Luke relies heavily in Luke 1-2 upon inspired speeches which interpret the course of events. In the endeavor to illumine the role of these chapters in Luke's narrative, therefore, I will focus upon the speeches, i.e., the hymns and annunciations, contained in Luke 1-2.[4]

---

most forceful defense of the positive function of Luke 1-2 in the Lukan corpus comes from P. S. Minear ("Luke's Use of the Birth Stories," in *Studies in Luke-Acts,* ed. L. E. Keck and J. L. Martyn [Nashville: Abingdon, 1966] 111-30). Minear discovers in Luke a "theology of the time of fulfillment"; the "hope of Israel" is at stake in the narrative of Luke-Acts from beginning to end (pp. 116, 120, 129). The birth stories are, therefore, pivotal in Luke's theological presentation. S. W. Ryoo reaches a similar conclusion ("The Lukan Birth Narratives and the Theological Unity and Purpose of Luke-Acts" [Boston: Boston University Th.D. dissertation, 1969]). R. C. Tannehill ("Israel in Luke-Acts: A Tragic Story," *JBL* 104 [1985] 69-85) and L. Gaston ("The Lucan Birth Narratives in Tradition and Redaction," in 1976 SBL *Seminar Papers* [Missoula: Scholars, 1976] 209-17) claim that Luke 1-2 raises expectations (revolving around fulfillment of the hope of Israel) that the subsequent narrative shatters. Recent study of the role of Luke 1-2 in Luke-Acts confirms my selection of the "hope of Israel" as the focal theme in my discussion of these chapters. What remains unclear is the question of precisely how the concept, "hope of Israel," functions in Luke's story — and in his setting.

[3] *The Birth of the Messiah* (Garden City: Doubleday, 1979) 243; cf. p. 347. Cf. Juel, *Promise,* 20-21: The hymns and "prophetic outbursts" of Luke 1-2 "are appropriate to the situation, yet they offer an interpretation of events that both foreshadows what is to come and relates them to promises and motifs familiar from Israel's past. The hymns provide an interpretive framework within which the entire story can be understood." D. R. Adams, however, rightly cautions against preoccupation with the speeches of Luke-Acts, to the neglect of narrative material, in analysis of the literary and theological dynamics of the text, in his Yale Ph.D. dissertation, "The Suffering of Paul and the Dynamics of Luke-Acts" (New Haven, 1979).

[4] For the most recent discussion of the genre of this material, see S. Farris, *The Hymns of Luke's Infancy Narratives: Their Origin, Meaning and Significance* (JSNTSup 9; Sheffield: JSOT, 1985) 67-85. Farris identifies as hymns the Magnificat (1:46-55), the Benedictus (1:68-79) and the Nunc Dimittis (2:29-32), and he limits his analysis to these

By means of corresponding angelic annunciations and inspired prophetic speeches, Luke 1-2 unfolds in parallel fashion the preparation, appearance, and significance of John and Jesus.[5] These chapters are permeated with the atmosphere of Luke's Greek Bible.[6] Even apart from the clear allusions to Old Testament texts, the style is scriptural (Septuagintal),[7] and the content of the stories equally so. Luke's readers are to see epitomized here the best faith, piety, obedience, and (2:25, 38) expectation of God's people Israel. When God intervenes in the continuing history of Israel by sending Gabriel to the devout priest Zechariah, the stage onto which that angel steps is one on which the dramatic story of God's people Israel has been enacted through the ages.

a. Gabriel's Annunciation to Zechariah (Luke 1:13-17)

The story begins[8] with a heavenly message interrupting the priestly service of the childless priest Zechariah. Not only does Zechariah have impeccable

---

three passages. Despite diverse form, all the hymns and annunciations of Luke 1-2 serve to interpret the events being narrated; accordingly, this section will treat five "hymn/speeches" of special importance for my subject (1:13-17; 1:30-33[35-38]; 1:46-55; 1:68-79; 2:29-32, 34-35).

[5] On the structure of these chapters, see J. M. Creed, *The Gospel According to St. Luke* (London: Macmillan, 1930) 6; Brown, *Birth,* 248-53; Fitzmyer, *Luke,* 1.313-15; and R. Laurentin, *Structure et Théologie de Luc I-II* (Paris: Gabalda, 1957) 32-34. Laurentin contends that the parallelism between John and Jesus serves to contrast the two figures. Fitzmyer's assessment is more accurate: "there is a step-parallelism at work, i.e. a parallelism with one-upmanship" (1.315). The important point is that, while Jesus' superiority to John is clearly established in the birth narratives, the two are at the same time closely associated, and precisely with a view to their respective roles in bringing to fulfillment God's promise—the hope of Israel. John readies the λαός (Luke 1:17) and orients them to the salvation which is effected through gracious forgiveness of sins (1:77-78). Jesus accedes to the throne of David (1:32-33) and accomplishes the salvation prepared by John (1:68-71).

[6] On Luke's use of the Old Testament, see especially M. Rese, *Alttestamentliche Motive in der Christologie des Lukas* (Gütersloher: Studien zum Neuen Testament 1, 1969); T. Holtz, *Untersuchungen über die alttestamentlichen Zitate bei Lukas* (Berlin: Akademie, 1968); L. C. Crockett, *The Old Testament in the Gospel of Luke* (Brown University Ph.D. dissertation, 1966). For useful treatments of Luke's use of the Old Testament in Luke 1-2, see the commentaries of Fitzmyer, Brown (*Birth*), Creed, and Plummer.

[7] See, e.g., H. J. Cadbury, *The Making of Luke-Acts* (New York: Macmillan, 1927) 213-38; H. F. D. Sparks, "The Semitisms of St. Luke's Gospel," *JTS* 44 (1943) 129-38; Fitzmyer, *Luke,* 1.107-27, 312; F. L. Horton, "Reflections on the Semitisms of Luke-Acts," in *Perspectives on Luke-Acts,* ed. C. H. Talbert (Danville: Association of Baptist Professors of Religion, 1978) 1-23; and M. D. Goulder and M. L. Sanderson, "St. Luke's Genesis," *JTS* 8 (1957) 12-30. The last-mentioned work is overly imaginative in its portrayal of Luke 1-2 as Luke's midrashic composition; however, Goulder and Sanderson have rightly captured the biblical (Septuagintal) flavor of these chapters.

[8] On the function of Luke 1:1-4 in the Lukan corpus, see most recently S. Brown, "The

priestly credentials (1:5); both he and Elizabeth are paradigms of Jewish piety and obedience (1:6). Like Abraham and Sarah, however, this couple has reached advanced age without experiencing the blessing of a child (cf. 1:7 and Gen 18:11). With Zechariah fortuitously (ἔλαχε, 1:9) present in the sanctuary, the scene is prepared for a dramatic new beginning.

God initiates that new beginning through the intermediary Gabriel.[9] At this point in the narrative, the revelation is private; not only is Zechariah evidently alone in the sanctuary (anxiously awaited by "all the multitude of the people" outside, 1:10), but also the penalty received for his initial skepticism (1:18) — he is silenced until the prophesied birth has occurred (1:20) — serves to underscore the private nature of the divine communication. Not until the "Benedictus" subsequent to the birth of John (1:68–79) will Zechariah's inspired interpretation of this good news become public.

Gabriel informs the aging priest that his prayers have been answered,[10] and that a son is on the way (1:13–14). The primary function of the announcement, though, is to spell out the role that this promised child will play in the story to follow. In a manner evoking memories of Samuel, the angel declares that John will abstain from strong drink (1:15; cf. 1 Sam 1:11), and will be filled instead by the Holy Spirit.[11] The weight of the angelic message falls, however, on the final two verses, which specify John's future function in relation to his people Israel. While he is not identified with Elijah,[12] John is assuredly given the role associated

---

Role of the Prologues in Determining the Purpose of Luke-Acts," in *Perspectives on Luke-Acts,* ed. C. H. Talbert (Danville: Association of Baptist Professors of Religion, 1978) 99–111. The discussion here is limited to 1:5–2:52.

[9] Laurentin (*Structure,* 45–46) and Chance ("*Jerusalem,*" 239–40) lay particular stress on the eschatological connotation of Gabriel's appearance in Luke 1. Chance appeals to Dan 8:17 and 9:24ff (where Gabriel discloses details of the apocalyptic timetable to Daniel), and to 1 En 40:9 and 54:6 (where Gabriel is one of four chief angels active in executing judgment for the "Lord of Spirits"). Similarly, Brown, *Birth,* 270–71. Gabriel certainly brings from Daniel to Luke's narrative his role as conveyer and interpreter of visions; however, the absence of other indicators of end-time developments in the immediate Lukan context calls into question the assumption that the "eschatological atmosphere" of Daniel 8 and 9 (Brown, *Birth,* 271) colors Luke's story as well.

[10] Verse 13 implies that Zechariah's prayer included the request for a child. Note that the promise of the birth of a son follows directly (καί) on the assurance that the priest's prayers have been heard: ". . . because your prayer has been heard, and your wife Elizabeth will bear you a son." This supposition is confirmed by vv 7, 18.

[11] Already Luke 1:41 anticipates the fulfillment of the prophecy that John will be endowed with the Spirit "from the womb of his mother" (1:15). At Mary's approach, John, still within the womb, leaps, and his mother, filled with the Spirit, blesses "the mother of [her] Lord."

[12] It was precisely the association of John with Elijah in 1:17, 76 that (along with other features of these chapters) compelled Conzelmann to discard Luke 1–2 from his portrayal of Lukan theology (see *St. Luke,* 22–27). Elsewhere, Luke seems to be careful to avoid any

with Elijah in Jewish tradition (Mal 3:1; 4:5-6 LXX; Sir 48:10).[13] Essentially, John's task will be to *prepare* the people by bringing them to *repentance* (note the twofold use of ἐπιστρέφω, 1:16, 17). In the position of a precursor,[14] John will make ready a prepared people, that is, a people who have heard the summons to repent.[15]

In the ongoing story of God's people Israel, a new era has dawned. Zechariah's predecessor-models, Abraham (father of a nation) and Hannah (mother of a king-maker), each stood on the brink of the fulfillment of a great covenant-promise. The same is true of Zechariah; the instrument of God's final work of restoration among his people has appeared. The note of expectancy is intense: for what will this "prepared people" be ready?

b. Gabriel's Annunciation to Mary (1:30-33 [35-38])

Once again in a private divine disclosure, this time to the young woman Mary,[16] the reader is apprised of an astonishing new development. Mary will give

---

identification of John as Elijah. For a clear discussion of the issue, see J.-D. Dubois, "La figure d'Elie dans la perspective lucanienne," *RHPR* 53 (1973) 155-76. Dubois argues forcefully that Luke gives the part of Elijah to Jesus, not John. For a less successful attempt to deal with this tension within the Elijah materials of Luke, see Oliver, "Birth," 216-19. Oliver suggests that Luke elsewhere suppresses the identification of John with Elijah because he has already made that identification in Luke 1-2 and wishes to throw the full weight of that association on the pre-ministry period (!). Feiler ("Prophet," 251-87, especially pp. 261-65) offers a carefully nuanced discussion of the interplay in Luke-Acts among the figures Jesus, John, and Elijah. Feiler shows that Luke has constructed an Elijah typology in his portrayal of Jesus (part of Luke's presentation of Jesus as the eschatological prophet), but that Jesus contrasts with Elijah in important respects (a point overlooked by Dubois). At the same time, Feiler points to Luke 1:17 and 7:27 as evidence that Luke does consider John to be the Elijah-like forerunner of Jesus (pp. 263-64). Because Luke's John is not Elijah redivivus (1:17: "in the spirit and power of Elijah"), potential confusion with the Elijah-Jesus typology is averted.

[13] So also Chance, "Jerusalem," 240-41; Feiler, "Prophet," 263-64. Chance lists the assigning of Elijah-like features to John as one of several features of Luke 1-2 that give the Lukan infancy narrative an "essentially eschatological character" (pp. 239-46).

[14] Most likely with respect to God, not Jesus (αὐτοῦ in v 17 must have as its antecedent κύριον τὸν Θεόν of v 16). The referent of κυρίῳ in v 17 is less clear: the title κύριος is given to Jesus in 2:11 (cf. 1:43), and the imagery of John making ready the people for Jesus' activity is certainly apt. In any case, the work of John is characterized as one of preparation.

[15] Interestingly, John's activity is characterized here as a making ready for the Lord (via repentance), and Jesus (the Lord) will later be seen to prepare his disciples for the eschatological "day" (e.g., 12:40).

[16] In contrast to the depiction of Elizabeth and Zechariah, Mary's credentials pass by unmentioned. Her genuine piety is portrayed dramatically instead, with the trusting response of 1:38.

birth to a son who will fulfill—in an eternal reign!—the long-disappointed covenant-promise to David. In words reminiscent of the promise of a child to Abraham and Sarah (Gen 16:11; 17:19 LXX; also cf. 1:37 and Gen 18:14 LXX), Gabriel announces the advent of a son to be named Jesus (1:31). As the annunciation to Zechariah introduced the function of John with respect to God's λαός, the annunciation to Mary introduces the function of Jesus. The speech first defines the significance of this child to be born: he will be "great" (μέγας),[17] and will receive the appellation "son of the most High" (1:32; cf. "son of God" in 1:35). Verses 32b–33 state the functional significance of this title: Jesus will be son of God in that he will take up David's throne. The language indicates that the promise to David in 2 Samuel 7 now finds in Jesus its final realization (cf. 2 Sam 7:12-13, 16 LXX). A kingdom over Israel ("house of Jacob," 1:33), and one without end (cf. 2 Sam 7:13, 16), is hereby inaugurated.

In combination, the explicit reference to the promise to David and the allusion—by stylistic imitation—to the promise to Abraham suggest that the appearance of Jesus brings to fruition all the hopes of Israel. This interpretation receives confirmation in Mary's hymn-speech (1:46–55), where the covenant-promise to Abraham is explicitly mentioned (1:55), and in Zechariah's hymn-speech (1:68–79), where language tied to both covenant-promises surfaces ("house of David," his παῖς, 1:69; "his holy covenant" with the "fathers," 1:72; the oath to Abraham "our father," 1:73). Against Gaston's claim that this is but a naive and enthusiastic expression of Jewish hopes,[18] one which—due to the subsequent harsh events—Luke could not unambiguously affirm, the identity of the speaker must be taken with full seriousness. We have to do here with prophetic announcements of which God, through his angel Gabriel, is the author![19] The ensuing narrative will indeed make clear that the hope of Israel requires redefinition (in light of the rejection of Jesus and the inclusion of the Gentiles), but even this redefinition has God as author and scripture as warrant (programmatically, e.g., in Luke 4:16–30 and 24:44–47). Luke offers no hint that he prefaces his account of Jesus' career with a nostalgic, "tongue-in-cheek" glance at Israel's hope for a better day. The insistent reappearance of this theme throughout Luke's story suggests, on the contrary, that Luke views Israel's hope and God's promise with full seriousness. There can be no Christian eschaton that does not satisfactorily—and definitively— address these Jewish expectations.

---

[17] For the import of the absolute use of "great" here (in contrast to the expression "great before the Lord" employed of John in 1:15), see Fitzmyer, *Luke,* 1.325; Laurentin, *Structure,* 35.

[18] Gaston, "Tradition," 212–14.

[19] See also Tannehill ("Israel in Luke-Acts: A Tragic Story," *JBL* 104 [1985] 69–85, 72), who characterizes those who make such assertions in Luke-Acts as "reliable spokespersons."

c. The Magnificat (1:46-55)

The connectional role played by Mary's visit to Elizabeth in 1:39-56 is unmistakable. This pericope brings the two unborn agents of God's salvation into direct encounter, and clarifies the relation of John to Jesus as that of subordinate to Lord (especially 1:42-45).[20] The meeting also provides the occasion for another speech elaborating the meaning of these developments. Mary's[21] hymn of praise is a veritable mosaic of scriptural passages, the song of Hannah in 1 Sam 2:1-10 being the basic model; so Luke aligns this human voice with the divine message.

In the Magnificat, Mary sings God's praise on behalf of all the lowly who benefit from God's activity of reversal.[22] Verses 46-53 are, in fact, governed by the two themes of God's praise and reversal.[23] Jesus will, in the course of the narrative, also align himself with God's turning of the tables on the "high and mighty" (to note just two particularly important examples: the citation from Isaiah 61 and 58 in Luke 4:18-19; and the balanced beatitudes and woes, 6:20-26). The climax of the hymn-speech, however, picks up once again the theme of God's faithfulness to his promise to Israel (1:54-55). In the present context, these verses evidently assert that — given the clear signs of God's present decisive intervention in the saga of Israel — God has not forgotten his people (μνησθῆναι ἐλέους, 1:54b), but (in language influenced by Isa 41:8-9) has come to

---

[20] See, e.g., the discussion in Brown, *Birth,* 339; Fitzmyer, *Luke,* 1.357.

[21] For treatments of the once hotly contested text-critical problem, see, e.g., Brown, *Birth,* 334-36; Fitzmyer, *Luke,* 1.365-66. Although certain observations favor the ascription of the hymn to Elizabeth (Hannah serves *Elizabeth* better as a model, especially if the ταπείνωσις of v 48 is taken as a reference to childlessness; one would expect, were Mary the speaker, "and *she* said to *Elizabeth*" in 1:56), the weight of the manuscript evidence and the flow of the narrative both require that, at least in Luke's story, Mary be the inspired speaker. Verses 42-45 demand some reaction from the mother of Elizabeth's Lord.

[22] For an imaginative and especially well-argued (though finally unsuccessful) identification of Mary as the "daughter of Zion" and as the "ark of the Lord," see Laurentin, *Structure,* 64-81, 90-91. Note the cautious assessment of Brown in *Birth,* 319-28. More promising is Laurentin's characterization of Mary as "Israel personified" in that she is possessor of the promise (pp. 93-94).

[23] On the motif of role reversal in Luke-Acts, see, e.g., Adams ("Dynamics," e.g., p. 293) and C. H. Cosgrove ("The Divine ΔΕΙ in Luke-Acts," *NovT* 26 [1984] 168-90). Cosgrove characterizes Luke-Acts as a "doxology to the God of surprise reversal" (p. 190). Cf. also Chance ("Jerusalem," 244), who aligns this Lukan motif with the eschatological reversal expressed in such texts as Isa 57:15-21; 61:1-11; 1 En 92-104. Of particular interest for our project is the manner in which Adams correlates the persistent pattern of role reversal in Luke with the Lukan setting. Adams holds that the monotonous regularity of Luke's dialectic of adversity and divine aid ("each seeming defeat turns into triumph, and each triumph leads in turn to a new series of challenges that reinvoke the dialectic of adversity and divine aid") is all to the good for the author, "who seeks for his own community the strongest ties possible with the past" (p. 293).

their aid (1:54a). This timely assistance represents nothing other than the fulfill-ment of God's word of promise to Abraham and to Abraham's descendants (1:55). The content of the Magnificat indicates that Abraham's promise is realized concretely in the merciful help now to be shown to Israel, specifically in the blessing of the lowly and turning away of the powerful. Jesus' public ministry will in Luke's hands accomplish just this mission. The important point here, though, is the claim of this scripture-inspired speech that God has acted (note the string of aorists throughout the hymn) to fulfill his promise to Abraham.

d. The Benedictus (1:68-79)

After the birth and naming of John—all confirming Gabriel's prophetic announcement—Zechariah is finally able, under the inspiration of the Holy Spirit, to interpret the surprising chain of events which has overtaken him. It is significant that Zechariah's speech is portrayed as both a blessing of God (εὐλογητός, v 68, picking up the narrative setting of v 64: "he spoke blessing God") and prophecy (v 67). In fact, with the insertion of vv 65–66 and the dual description of the hymn as a blessing/prophesying, Luke accomplishes two tasks with the hymn-speech. First, it comments upon the overall import of the births of John and Jesus (1:68–75). Second, it develops further the function of John in relation to Jesus (1:76–79).[24]

The first section of the Benedictus (vv 68–75) fills out the notice of v 64 ("he spoke, blessing God"). The basis for this praise of the God of Israel is that, as promised long ago by the prophets (v 70, employing language that will recur in Acts 3:21b), God has visited (ἐπεσκέψατο, "looked favorably upon,"[25] v 68) his

---

[24] The structure, origin, and relation to present context of the Benedictus have been widely discussed. The essay by P. Vielhauer, "Das Benedictus des Zacharias" (*ZTK* 49 [1952] 255–72), has been particularly influential. Vielhauer sought to establish the unity of 1:76–79 and its origination in a baptist milieu, but he also integrated the hymn, as used by Luke, into Luke's theology of a universal *Heilsgeschichte* (the latter point on pp. 271–72). More recent treatments of the questions raised by the passage may be found in J. Gnilka, "Der Hymnus des Zacharias," *BZ* 6 (1962) 215–38; Brown, *Birth,* 377–92; Fitzmyer, *Luke,* 1.374–90; and Farris, *Infancy,* 26–30, 127–42. Gnilka argues that the Benedictus originated in Jewish Christian circles standing in close proximity to the Testaments of the Twelve Patriarchs ("Hymnus," 237–38). Luke incorporated this Jewish Christian hymn, adding only 1:70. Farris contends that Luke has inserted 1:76–77 into a hymn encompassing vv 68–75, 78–79 in order to connect it to the surrounding narrative (*Infancy,* 26–28, 131–32).

[25] The term ἐπισκέπτομαι, in the sense of "visit," is an especially significant one in Luke-Acts. Seven of eleven New Testament occurrences of the verb appear in the Lukan corpus: Luke 1:68, 78; 7:16; Acts 6:3; 7:23; 15:14, 36. Also relevant is the use of the noun ἐπισκοπή (Luke 19:44) with the meaning "visitation." The Lukan usage of ἐπισκέπτομαι indicates that God has indeed visited his people in the healing, prophetic ministry of Jesus. Whether that visitation results in redemption (the assumption of 1:68) or judgment (the prophecy of

people, effecting redemption through the agency of a Davidic salvation-bringer (vv 68b-69). In the light of Gabriel's message to Mary (1:32 — "David his father"), it is likely that the salvation-effecting activity of Jesus is in view. Verses 71-75 describe the σωτηρία to be given by God through the activity of Jesus (and John). True to the merciful covenant with the "fathers," fulfilling the oath sworn to Abraham (vv 72-73), God rescues his people from their enemies (vv 71, 74a), the purpose being the unhindered,[26] holy, and righteous service of God (vv 74-75). Against Gaston, who stresses the theme of rescue from enemies in the hymn,[27] it is important to note that this theme serves as the precondition of genuine, free service of God. *That,* the hymn appears to suggest, is the goal of Israel's expectation. It is in terms of that goal that fulfillment of the promise in Luke and especially Acts must be seen.

The second section of the hymn, with its shift to the second person singular ("And you, child . . ."), expressly answers the question posed by the narrative through the insertion of vv 65-66: what, the neighbors query, will this child of Zechariah and Elizabeth amount to? John will receive the appellation "prophet of the most high" (v 76) and will (recalling the motif of 1:17) precede the Lord in order to make ready his path. While the identification of John as a prophet is new, the twin themes of precursor and preparer echo the angel's announcement to Zechariah. The most important advance in the Benedictus, however, comes with v 77: the task of preparation to be assigned John is, specifically, that of giving "to [the Lord's] people knowledge of salvation." Salvation will occur in (or through, ἐν) the forgiveness of sins (v 77), which is itself grounded in God's mercy (v 78a).[28] Needless to say, the twin motifs of salvation and forgiveness will

---

19:44) depends upon the response of God's people to the visitation. This will be an important clue toward the solution of the problem: what happens (in Luke-Acts) to the hope, the promise, of Israel?

[26] Note how the serving of God "free from fear" (1:74) corresponds to the "boldness" (παρρησία) which typifies the apostolic preaching in Acts.

[27] "The Lucan Birth Narratives in Tradition and Redaction," in 1976 SBL *Seminar Papers,* ed. G. W. MacRae (Missoula: Scholars, 1976) 209-17, 214. I am here concerned to make sense of the present form and context of the hymn, whatever earlier traditions may be incorporated within it.

[28] While Jesus is the central bearer of this salvation-through-repentance/forgiveness, Luke depicts John in similar terms in Luke 3:3: "And [John] went into all the region around the Jordan, preaching a baptism of repentance for the forgiveness of sins." This partial coalescing of the functions of John and Jesus suggests the possibility that 1:78b-79 pertains to the ministry of John, not Jesus. Contrary to Fitzmyer's translation (*Luke,* 1.375, 387-88), v 78b does not mark a new beginning syntactically; rather it continues the accumulation of loosely connected clauses elaborating John's role as precursor (v 75). Only the noun ἀνατολή in v 78b — if it is a strictly messianic term here — points definitively to Jesus (in the hymn's Lukan context). Certainly the ὁδός-imagery of v 79 fits John's later message (3:4, 5). In any case, the hymn taken as a whole praises God for the decisive saving activity which will soon begin in the ministry of John and culminate in the work of Jesus (extended through his apostles).

run like a thread through the ensuing narrative. Through Jesus, and the apostolic mission which he inaugurates, salvation will come to Israel, and to the nations as well.[29]

Although vv 78b-79 contain no unambiguous reference to John or to Jesus,[30] the merging in v 78 of the imagery of the divine visitation (ἐπισκέψεται),[31] elsewhere linked to Jesus, with the probably messianic term ἀνατολή,[32] points to Jesus as the likely figure in view.[33] If so, vv 76-79 not only answer the question (v 66) concerning John's identity and significance but also relate John's function to that of Jesus. John prepares the people for the salvation, light, and peace that Jesus, the Davidic ruler, will bring.[34]

In any case, the outcome of the appearance of these two sons of Israel will be the fulfillment of the prophetic promises of light in death's darkness (v 79a) and of peace (v 79b). In general terms, the hymn of Zechariah both advances and makes specific the theme of 1:54-55. That is to say, it spells out in detail just how God will, true to his word to the "fathers," succor Israel. The Benedictus leaves no doubt that the new era that has arrived in conjunction with the births of John and Jesus brings to fruition all the highest hopes of God's people. Nearly all the key words are present: salvation; redemption; forgiveness; peace. (Add to these the theme of David's descendant ruling over the nation [1:32-33].) The Jewish hope will not be disappointed! At the same time, if my reading of the hymn in its present form is correct, then a process of redefinition of that hope is already underway. For the salvation that the Davidic King will bring seems to focus on release from sins and freedom for service as much as on rescue from enemies.[35]

[29] Even as 1:74-75 qualify the conceptuality of salvation as "rescue from enemies" by associating it with genuine service of God, so also v 77 (especially 77b) qualifies this σωτηρία as, ultimately, a religious concern.

[30] Vielhauer has, indeed, argued that *originally* the ἀνατολή of v 78 pointed to John ("Benedictus," 266).

[31] Since σπλάγχνα is the antecedent of οἷς in v 78, this visitation "from on high" (= "from heaven"; cf. Luke 24:49) will be a gracious one: "because of the merciful heart by (in) which a dawn from on high will visit us."

[32] For discussion of the source and meaning of this term, see Chance, "Jerusalem," 243; Brown, *Birth,* 373-74; Fitzmyer, *Luke,* 1.387. The noun ἀνατολή sometimes denotes the rising of stars or sun (e.g., Matt 2:2, 9; T. Levi 18:3; cf. especially Mal 3:20). In three passages in the LXX, however, the same word translates the Hebrew *semah* ("sprout," "shoot"), designating an heir of David (Jer 23:5; Zech 3:8; 6:12; cf. 4QBless 3; 4QFlor 1:11). Luke 1:79 ("to shine on those who sit in darkness . . .") suggests that the "dawn from on high" is a rising light; nevertheless, the context makes a messianic nuance likely as well (v 69: note the combination of the terms "visit," "his people," "salvation" in vv 68-69 and 77-78; the explicit mention of David in v 69 would then be matched by the implicit reference ἀνατολή in v 78b).

[33] But see footnote 28 above.

[34] Cf. Fitzmyer, *Luke,* 1.386.

[35] Cf. Fitzmyer (*Luke,* 1.386), who argues that the overtones of political deliverance early in the hymn are here spiritualized.

To speak of a spiritualization of the hope of Israel would be an overstatement, for the imagery of Davidic kingship and of deliverance from enemies is present in bold relief. Nonetheless, the *possibility* at least has surfaced that Luke perceives the fulfillment of Israel's hopes as something other than the physical restoration of land and kingdom to Israel. This is, in fact, a question of crucial importance for understanding Luke's eschatological perspective. Does Luke expect, as one reading of these chapters would suggest, a final, future, physical restoration of Israel?[36] Or does Luke's narrative show, rather, the manner in which the hope of Israel has actually been realized, its restoration effected (or begun) through the worldwide mission? Depending on the interpretation, Luke will have a quite different picture of the eschaton. By the conclusion of this study, when the ending of Acts comes up for scrutiny, the problem of the relationship between the hope of Israel and eschatology (in the strict sense of the term) must receive a clear answer. For the present, it suffices to reiterate that the hymns and annunciations so far considered indicate that the narrative about to unfold must be seen in light of the age-old promises and hopes of Israel.

e. The Nunc Dimittis (2:29-32, 34-35)

Yet another voice joins the chorus praising God for the fulfillment of Israel's hope, when the aged Simeon meets the infant Jesus in the temple.[37] The story emphasizes the divine authentication of Simeon's message, inasmuch as the Spirit's guidance of the pious old man is noted three times (2:25-27). Like John's parents, Simeon is a devout, law-abiding Jew (v 25); moreover, like those persons enlightened by Anna in 2:38, he is an *expectant* man of faith. They are said to expect the redemption of Jerusalem; he awaits the consolation of Israel (2:25). Presumably the two expressions have a single λύτρωσις in view.[38]

What better spokesperson for the fulfillment of Israel's hope than just such an expectant Jew? A mixture of narrative and direct speech (vv 26, 29-30) confirms the messianic identity of Jesus (already established in Gabriel's annunciation to Mary). The infant Jesus is identified with God's salvation (v 30),[39] and

---

[36] A sharp statement of this thesis is offered by A. W. Wainright, "Luke and the Restoration of the Kingdom to Israel," *ExpTim* 89 (1977) 76-79. See also the extensive discussion, slightly more nuanced, in Chance ("Jerusalem," especially 299-301).

[37] Certainly the angel's message and heavenly doxology in 2:10-14 merit inclusion among the interpretive speeches of Luke 1-2. As Zechariah's hymn (1:68-79) constitutes a public disclosure of the meaning of John's birth (with an eye forward to Jesus' birth), so this chorus of heavenly voices represents a public disclosure of the import of Jesus' birth. Because this disclosure consists in an impressive *christological* concentration (Savior-Christ-Lord) but does not significantly advance the thought relative to the eschatological hope of Israel, I bypass analysis of this pericope in this context.

[38] So also Chance, "Jerusalem," 245-46.

[39] Could this be the reason that the neuter σωτήριον is employed in v 30 (i.e., τὸ σωτήριον [2:30] = τὸ παιδίον [2:27])? It is often assumed that the choice of the neuter noun is influenced by Isa 40:5 LXX (as in Luke 3:6).

Simeon prophesies the universality of the blessing to be bestowed by him (vv 31–32). Although Luke consistently uses λαός to refer to Israel,[40] the plural form with πάντων in v 31 is likely a comprehensive term embracing both the people (singular) Israel (v 32b) and the Gentiles (v 32a). If this judgment is correct, then Simeon's oracle provides the first clear indication that the hope of Israel, embodied in the infant born to Mary, must extend beyond the borders of Israel to the Gentiles. This broadening of the sphere of God's saving activity represents no radical departure, however, for Simeon's prophecy is cast in the words of Isa 42:6; 49:6, 9. Jesus will bring glory for Israel *and* revelatory light for Gentiles.

After a brief mention of the amazement of Jesus' parents, Simeon discerns the first ominous clouds on the horizon: Jesus, the conveyer of salvation, will provoke a divided response.[41] He has been positioned by God in such a manner as to bring to light one's innermost tendencies (v 35), causing the fall and rising of "many" (= "all").[42] Indeed, he will be a sign that will be "spoken against" (εἰς σημεῖον ἀντιλεγόμενον; cf. Acts 28:22). Not only does Simeon's speech anticipate the Gentile destination of Israel's hope; it also adumbrates the rejection of Jesus at Nazareth, then at Jerusalem. It is crucial to observe that Luke's Simeon does not dilute the promise and hope of Israel when he introduces these qualifying motifs. He himself epitomizes Israel's expectancy and here acknowledges the decisive fulfillment of its hope. At the same time, he prophesies that the path will not be entirely free of obstacles (Jesus will experience rejection), nor will that path be confined to the borders of Israel (the Gentiles, too, will be made participants in the long-awaited salvation). To the extent that Simeon's sober words constitute a redefinition of Israel's hope (both themes already present in Luke's scripture, however), the path from Israel's hope to its definitive fulfillment in Jesus is marked by both continuity and discontinuity.[43]

---

[40] See, e.g., N. A. Dahl, " 'A People for His Name' (Acts XV.14)," *NTS* 4 (1957) 319–27; Chance, "Jerusalem," 256.

[41] Still the most provocative discussion of this theme is that of J. Jervell, "The Divided People of God," in *Luke and the People of God* (Minneapolis: Augsburg, 1972) 41–74.

[42] The view, occasionally advanced (e.g., Schweizer, *Luke,* 57), that the fall and rising refer to sequential events in the lives of the same individuals, is out of harmony with the tenor of Luke-Acts as a whole (so also Brown, *Birth,* 460–61; Fitzmyer, *Luke,* 1.422–23). To be sure, those Jews who must bear responsibility for the rejection of Jesus are accorded one final opportunity to repent (Peter's speeches in Acts 2–3 and the Jerusalem mission). However, the overall picture of Luke's story is one of division.

[43] If Conzelmann (*St. Luke*) exaggerates the discontinuity at the expense of continuity (with his epochal saving history), Jervell (*People*) overstates the continuity to the neglect of discontinuity. Chance ("Jerusalem") surveys the texts in both biblical and post-biblical Jewish tradition which betray two distinctive approaches to the eschatological role of the Gentiles. In the first, the nations assault Jerusalem and are overthrown by God (Ezekiel 38–39 is the classic text). In the second, the nations stream to Jerusalem to be instructed in Torah and to worship the God of Israel. Evidently Luke's understanding of the hope of Israel is something of a selective blend of these two approaches: the expression "times

2. The Function of Luke 1-2 in Luke-Acts

a. Luke 1-2 Links the Story of (John and) Jesus to the History of God's People

The language, style, and content of the narratives and speeches of Luke 1-2 converge to connect Luke-Acts as a whole with the story of Israel. The impression generated by these chapters is that one has been immersed in the continuing experience of God's people.[44] Yet, Luke 1-2 also announces that the *closing chapter* in the history of God's people has begun.[45] The hope of Israel is on the verge of realization. For the people of Israel (subsequently, for Gentiles, as well), that hope has led a nation to the crossroads. The point of division, *and* the point of access to participation in the long-awaited salvation of God, is none other than the person of Jesus whose advent is announced in these chapters. In advance of him, readying the people by means of the summons to repentance, is John.

---

of the Gentiles" (Luke 21:24) denotes a period of genuine Gentile domination of Jerusalem, yet no divine overthrow of those Gentile conquerors is portrayed (though the end of this period of domination is presupposed). At the same time, Luke envisages the inclusion of the Gentiles within faithful Israel, yet he narrates a mission proceeding outward from Jerusalem rather than a procession to Jerusalem — an observation calling into question Chance's view that the second tradition (Gentiles streaming to Jerusalem) influenced Luke.

[44] For a suggestive and programmatic characterization of Luke-Acts as the continuation of biblical history, see N. Dahl, "The Story of Abraham in Luke-Acts," in *Jesus in the Memory of the Early Church* (Minneapolis: Augsburg, 1976) 66-86; and "The Purpose of Luke-Acts," in the same volume, pp. 87-98. Cf. Adams, "Dynamics," 296-305. In a discussion of the genre of Luke 1-2, Laurentin (*Structure*) concludes that this narrative is "religious history written in the biblical manner" (p. 98).

[45] Chance ("Jerusalem," 235-48), is especially adamant that Luke 1-2 has an eschatological tenor. He maintains that the primary message of these chapters is that God's promises of eschatological salvation have now come to fruition (p. 238). "While Luke wishes to delineate a continuity between the Old Testament and the events depicted in chapters one and two, the reader becomes aware that something decisively new is about to take place. What is more, this decisively new thing is eschatological" (p. 239). My own analysis of the function of Luke 1-2 within the narrative of Luke-Acts obviously follows a similar path; however, I have deliberately avoided Chance's liberal use of "eschatological" terminology (cf. my discussion of method, chapter one above). The relation of fulfilled hopes and the eschaton is something to be worked out on the basis of Luke's entire narrative, not simply assumed on the basis of common Jewish eschatological patterns (Chance's method), nor as the result of an analysis of Luke 4:16-30 (likewise Chance's procedure). When one opts for a narrow definition of "eschatology" (as I have done), one cannot simply *equate* definitive fulfillment of Israel's hopes and end-time completion of God's plan. The *duration* of the history which connects the beginning of the fulfillment (Luke 1-2) and its completion (Luke 21:25-28) is not a matter of indifference, certainly not when (as in our study) the timing of the end-time completion is a significant variable to be clarified.

The place of Israel in Luke-Acts continues to be a subject of heated controversy.[46] My own judgment on this set of issues must be deferred until consideration of the literary function of the ending of Acts, where the status of Israel forms the climax of the entire composition. For the present, it is enough to point out once again that Luke sets out to continue — indeed, to complete — Israel's history. The language and content of Luke 1-2 conform to the style and stories of the Greek Bible. The phenomenon of Spirit-inspired prophecy is rekindled. The covenant-promises to Abraham and David are explicitly recalled, and are said to have found realization in the new era that dawns with the births of John and Jesus. Luke 1-2, therefore, links the balance of Luke's account to Israel's history by characterizing those coming events as the decisive fulfillment of the hope of Israel.

b. Luke 1-2 Portrays Jesus as the Fulfillment of the Hope of Israel

Specifically, the stories and speeches of these chapters locate the fulfillment of Israel's hope in the person of Jesus.[47] According to Luke 1-2, the blessings that will accrue to Israel with Jesus' advent are manifold. First, Gabriel announces the fulfillment of Nathan's prophecy of a perpetual kingdom for David's son (1:32-33). Of *Jesus'* kingdom there will be no end. Second, the Magnificat implies (and the character of Jesus' public ministry confirms) that Jesus will continue God's activity of role-reversal, turning the tables on rich and poor, strong and weak, lofty and lowly (1:51-53). Third, this extension into Israel's present experience of God's role reversing activity entails succor for Israel, as prophesied by Isaiah (Isa 41:8-9) and as promised to Abraham and his descendants (Luke 1:54-55). Fourth, fulfillment through Jesus of God's covenant-promise to Abraham will finally enable God's people to serve him faithfully, free of fear stemming from the oppression of their enemies (1:72-75). Fifth, Jesus' appearance is prophesied (and the narrative of his ministry will confirm; e.g., 7:16) as the very visitation of God, effecting the redemption of Israel (1:68; cf. 1:78). Sixth, this redemption (salvation) will bring forgiveness of sins (1:77), and light and peace for those shrouded in the darkness — even the darkness of death's shadow (1:78-79). John will prepare this mission of Jesus by readying a repentant people (1:16-17; cf. 1:76). Finally, in fulfillment of God's

---

[46] Among the most important treatments of this theme are: Jervell, *People,* Lohfink, *Sammlung,* F. Bovon, "Israel, die Kirche und die Völker im lukanischen Doppelwerk," *TL* 108 (1983) 403-14; A. George, "Israel dans l'oeuvre de Luc," *RB* 75 (1968) 481-525; J. Gnilka, *Die Verstockung Israels. Isaias 6,9-10 in der Theologie der Synoptiker* (Munich: Kösel, 1961); Dahl, "Abraham"; Tiede, *Prophecy;* Chance, "Jerusalem," Tannehill, "Israel."

[47] It goes without saying that a comprehensive description of the literary and theological functions of Luke 1-2 would elaborate its christological statements. I need only note that the cutting edge is the depiction of Jesus as the one who fulfills God's agenda of promise for Israel. On the christological implications of Luke 1-2, see, e.g., Brown, *Birth,* 309-16; Fitzmyer, *Luke,* 1.335-40, 446-47.

ancient plan announced in scripture (citing specifically Isa 42:6; 49:6, 9), the salvation now to be effected through Jesus will transcend the boundaries of Israel, bringing not only glory to Israel but also the light of disclosure to the Gentiles (Luke 2:32). At the same time, the reader discerns the first ominous sign that not all will warmly embrace the definitive salvation which God offers to Israel (and the nations) in the person of Jesus. Some will oppose him, and their opposition will result in their undoing (2:34-35).

c. Luke 1-2 Announces the Dawn of the Final Fulfillment of the Hope of Israel

The discussion of Luke 1-2 has shown that by placing these stories at the outset of his two-volume work Luke relates Jesus and his church to the history of Israel — fulfillment answering to still outstanding promise. The stories revolving around Simeon and Anna, in particular, are filled with an aura of anticipation. Expectancy is in the air! As for a history of promises left unfulfilled, hopes disappointed, God is about to deliver! The foundational covenant with Abraham, similarly the covenant-promise to David, the λύτρωσις of Israel and of its holy city, the blessing of peace — all these ingredients of Israel's hope are a step away from realization! Moreover, the setting of so many of these episodes in the temple at Jerusalem can only serve to corroborate the sense of expectation, given the prominent role played by both temple and Jerusalem in conventional Jewish eschatological hopes.[48]

There can be no doubt that in the ensuing narrative Luke will be addressing these expectations that he has generated on the part of his readers. At the same time, Luke has already provided clues that the fulfillment reinterprets and redefines — at least in some measure — the hope of Israel. For all their enthusiastic celebration of fulfillment, these chapters anticipate a division within Israel over the one who accomplishes that fulfillment. For all their insistence on the satisfaction of *Israel's* hope, these chapters (true, to be sure, to the original promise to Abraham) press out beyond Israel to the nations. For all their expectation of the deliverance of a nation, these chapters seem to throw their weight on religious issues touching the faithful within it.

Luke 1-2 are indeed an integral part of the movement of the whole narrative of Luke-Acts. They set in motion a chain of events that answers to the highest hopes of Israel. As such, they engender a correspondingly high set of expectations on the part of Luke's readers. The beginning of Luke's story dramatizes the dawn of the fulfillment of Israel's hope, even as it casts a shadow over this joyous disclosure. The agents of God's salvation will meet repudiation from "many" within Israel. The hope, moreover, is something yet to be precisely defined, for it appears to embrace national (an unending kingdom of David's son) and religious (forgiveness of sins) concerns in tension (or unreflective ambiguity).

---

[48] See Chance, "Jerusalem," 217, 236-38. In my judgment, however, Chance reads too much eschatology into the fact of the temple and Jerusalem settings of Luke 1-2, in part due to the fuzziness of his definition of eschatology.

Further (with a view forward to the story of Acts and then back again), it is hinted that inclusion of Gentile believers is intrinsic to the hope of Israel. The following exegetical study will attend to several of the most weighty eschatological statements made by Luke's narrative. Thereafter, we must return to this set of questions posed by Luke's beginning, to discern how he finally disposes of them in his ending (Paul at Rome in Acts 28). In the end-time picture which Luke paints, what place does he reserve for the hope of Israel?

First, however, one agenda item remains to be considered in this discussion of Luke 1–2. What light does the foregoing analysis shed upon the matter of Luke's setting? Both Tannehill and Gaston infer from Luke's post-70 C.E. context that the hope of Israel, painted in such glowing colors in Luke 1–2, cannot be taken at face value. Either Luke is writing a tragic story concerning the outcome of Israel's hope (Tannehill), or it is impossible that he could have composed such a story, with the actual course of history mocking its hopes at every turn (Gaston).[49] These two opinions, however, do not exhaust the range of possibilities for Luke's post-70 setting. In neither case is the assumed (undifferentiated) setting established from Luke 1–2 itself; on the contrary, it is presupposed on other grounds and then used as an interpretive key for these texts.

My own procedure will be different. Only through a cumulative evaluation of evidence for Luke's setting, derived from Luke's whole narrative, will a hypothesis regarding Luke's situation be formulated. Luke 1–2 provides the first important clues, but nothing further will be hazarded at present. The beginning of Luke's story makes clear that Luke-Acts stems from a Christian community or communities in which the Jewish scripture (in Greek translation) is treasured and its stories and language well known. While Luke may be atypical of his community or communities in the depth and range of his biblical knowledge, it is reasonable to suppose that his audience included persons who would be familiar enough with the heritage of Israel to appreciate the way in which the narrative brings that heritage to life. At the very least, some form of contact with contemporary Judaism is likely on the basis of these chapters, even if that contact entailed direct competition with the synagogue.[50] The data supplied by Luke 1–2 are certainly explicable on the traditional assumption that Luke-Acts is the product of Gentile Christianity. A Gentile Christian community at this remove from its origins is likely to require rediscovery of its beginnings. So Adams has characterized Luke-Acts as a "roots" phenomenon; Luke writes this narrative in order to counter the force of "social amnesia."[51] The Gentile composition and missionary orientation of Luke's community are so dominant that "he must demonstrate to the wavering within and to the skeptics without that this

---

[49] Tannehill, "Tragic," 72; Gaston, "Tradition," 213–14.

[50] Adams ("Dynamics") adopts this hypothesis from Dahl and uses it as the springboard for provocative ruminations on the problem of the Lukan setting (see especially pp. 296–305).

[51] Ibid., 296.

new development has its own hidden elements of continuity, and thus its own prominent place in God's plan."[52] But what does the situation of Luke's Christian community—which has appropriated for itself the heritage of Judaism—have to do with eschatology? That question will remain with us throughout the dissertation.

B. LUKE'S APPEAL FOR VIGILANCE: LUKE 12:35–48

Luke first introduces extended discourse material revolving around eschatological themes in Luke 12:35–48.[53] This passage is an appeal for vigilance; it summons the disciples, hence Luke's community, to alertness in expectation of Jesus' return. Whatever their referent in pre-Lukan stages of the tradition, Luke employs the parables of this pericope as "parousia"-parables,[54] and the motif of uncertainty regarding the timing of this event pervades the section. But "ignorance of the hour" serves a paraenetic theme which controls the whole discourse-and-dialogue sequence of 12:1–13:9. The redactional insertion of Peter's question in 12:41, moreover, heightens the responsibility of the disciples (Luke's community) relative to the crowds (those outside the Christian community). These three issues define our agenda for discussion of 12:35–48: (1) ignorance of the hour; (2) the appeal for vigilance; (3) the special responsibility of Luke's community.

1. "The Son of Man is Coming at an Hour You Do Not Suspect" (Luke 12:40, 46)

This segment (12:35–48) contains three parables or parable-like sayings. Each presupposes the uncertain timing of an awaited event. In 12:36–38,[55]

---

[52] Ibid., 301.

[53] The entire cycle of speeches and dialogue contained in 12:1–13:9 addresses various paraenetic motifs related to eschatology: faithful witness under the duress of persecution, reinforced with imagery of judgment (12:4–12; cf. 21:12–19); riches as a life-and-death issue for the individual (12:16–21); cares of this life as a distraction from one's proper orientation, the kingdom of God (12:22–34; cf. 17:26–30; 21:34–36); Jesus' mission portrayed using fire, death-baptism, and division as judgment imagery (12:49–53); discerning the signs of the times (12:54–56), which demand reconciliation (repentance) before judgment overtakes (12:57–59); two current events and a parable employed as a warning of the doom that hastens upon those who refuse to repent (13:1–9). The parable of the barren fig tree (13:6–9) is of particular importance for Luke's eschatology. It characterizes the present as a temporary period of leniency which will soon give way, if the fruits (of repentance) do not appear, to final destruction. J. Dupont in particular has fastened upon 12:4–6, 16–21 as indicative of an "individualizing" tendency in Lukan eschatology. On this question, see Excursus 1 below.

[54] Note the explicit mention of the coming of the Son of man in 12:40. Of course, the term parousia does not occur (Luke never uses this word; cf. Fitzmyer, *Luke*, 2.1325).

[55] This is special Lukan material, although it has points of contact with Matthew's parable of the ten virgins awaiting a wedding party (25:1–13).

servants waiting for their master to return from a feast keep alert, in order that they may open at once (εὐθέως; v 36) when he knocks, even if he should return in the second or third watch of the night (v 38). In the second "parable" (12:39[56]), the image of a thief breaking into one's home hinges on the homeowner's ignorance of the moment of the crime ("If the master of the house had known at what hour the thief was coming, he would not have allowed his house to be broken into"). The parable contrasting faithful and unfaithful[57] conduct of a steward/servant (12:42–46[48])[58] invokes ignorance of the hour as a prelude to the unfaithful servant's punishment: "The master of that servant will come on a day he does not expect and at an hour he does not know. . . ." (v 46). In addition to much of the imagery and wording of the parables themselves, Luke takes over from Q (cf. Matt 24:44) a saying linking the last two parables (the householder victimized by burglary and the faithful/unfaithful servant, present in the same order in Matthew as in Luke): "You also, be ready, because the Son of man is coming at an hour you do not suppose" (Luke 12:40). If the parables of Luke 12:35–48, together with their connecting material, are parousia-parables in Luke, they have essentially one point to make about the coming of the Son of man: it will occur at an undetermined moment.

Of course, Luke in this instance follows the tradition that he has inherited. The motif of ignorance of the hour pervades this pericope not because of Lukan redaction, narrowly conceived, but because of the character of the pre-Lukan tradition. Two observations suggest, however, that Luke agrees with the perspective on the parousia expressed in that tradition.[59] First, Luke's hand *is* clearly seen in the formulation of 12:41–42a.[60] Second, by assembling these parousia-parables, all crystallized around the same perspective on the parousia, Luke has composed what approaches a first eschatological discourse.[61] In other words, the weight and concentration of this section of the journey narrative indicate that Luke has a stake in its message. Acts 1:6–8 supplies additional evidence that Luke

[56] Q material (cf. Matt 24:43).

[57] See 12:46: ἀπίστων. Matthew (24:48) characterizes the second servant as "evil."

[58] Q material: cf. Matt 24:45–51.

[59] Cf. Conzelmann, *St. Luke*, 108.

[60] So also Fitzmyer, *Luke*, 2.985. Bultmann, *Synoptic Tradition*, 335. Marshall (*Luke*, 533), on the other hand, considers it likely that Luke here reworks transitional material already present in his source. Two arguments oppose Marshall's view. First, it is likely that Luke constructs Peter's question in the light of Mark's conclusion to the eschatological discourse (Mark 13:37), otherwise unused by Luke. Second, Luke often inserts such questions to introduce new discourse material (Luke 1:34; 3:10, 12, 15; 10:26; 12:57; 17:37; Acts 2:6–7, 37; 8:30, 34; 9:5; 10:4; 16:30; 19:3; on eschatological themes, cf. Luke 13:23; 17:20; 19:11 [indirect questions]; Acts 1:6). See also R. Schnackenburg, "Der eschatologische Abschnitt Lk 17,20–37," in *Mélanges Bibliques* (Gembloux: Duculot, 1970) 213–34, 217.

[61] In contrast to Matthew, who combines into one climactic eschatological discourse (Matt 24–25) traditions placed by Luke in chapters 12, 17, and 21.

affirms the view of the parousia expressed in Luke 12:35–48. Jesus' reply to the disciples' question concerning the timing of the restoration of Israel's kingdom (Acts 1:6) describes such matters of chronology as the prerogative of God, outside the sphere of concern of believers (v 7). Ignorance of the timing of the eschaton is, therefore, a fundamental axiom of the Lukan eschatological perspective. The date and hour of the coming of the Son of man remain unknown and unknowable. Luke 12:35–48 serves the important function of establishing this baseline for all subsequent statements about the end-time in Luke's narrative. No matter what else Luke-Acts may assert about the eschaton, one aspect must go undefined, and that is the precise moment of the eschatological consummation. Ignorance of the hour rests, as Acts 1:7 states and the parables of 12:35–48 imply, on the freedom and prerogative of God. The master of the house may return whenever he chooses.

Uncertainty about the timing of the End is not, however, primarily a doctrinal question for Luke and his community, if Luke 12:35–48 is any indication. Ignorance of the hour forms the presupposition for each of these parables; nevertheless, the governing motif is a paraenetic one. The burden of this pericope is its summons to a particular manner of living.

2. Ignorance of the Hour Demands a Life of Vigilance and Fidelity

Luke accomplishes the transition[62] to a new theme in 12:35–48 with a call to readiness cast in scriptural language: "Let your loins be girded and your lamps burning" (v 35).[63] This appeal to be prepared for immediate activity sets the tone for the series of parables that follows. Jesus pronounces a blessing upon servants awaiting their master's return who keep watch continually (12:37, γρηγοροῦντας).[64] The fact that Luke depicts all the servants, rather than just one doorkeeper, as standing ready to open the door to their master, suggests that the parable has been shaped with a view to its application to the Christian community.[65] Verse 40 explicitly grounds the mandate to be ready (ἕτοιμοι) in the uncertain time of arrival of the Son of man.

The parable of the faithful and unfaithful steward/servant expands the summons to vigilance by connecting it to faithful activity during the period of the master's absence. Jesus pronounces a blessing upon the servant who is

---

[62] Verse 34 actually flows without grammatical transition (asyndeton) into v 35. The shift is one of content.

[63] The first half of the exhortation picks up the wording of Exod 12:11. The periphrastic participles (περιεζωσμέναι and καιόμενοι) suggest a mode of life characterized by this posture of readiness, not a single instance of such conduct.

[64] Cf. Mark's threefold use of γρηγορέω in 13:33–37. The imperative γρηγορεῖτε forms the climax to Mark's version of the discourse.

[65] Cf. Dupont, "La Parabole du Maître qui Rentre dans la Nuit (Mc 13,34–36)," in *Mélanges Bibliques* (Gembloux: Duculot, 1970) 89–116, 103–04.

faithfully executing his assigned tasks when the master returns (v 43). Luke takes up this theme from the tradition (cf. Matt 24:46); however, he accents it by adding vv 47–48, which address the negative consequences of failure to do the master's will. This pericope urges not a simple posture of readiness (which might be misconstrued as passivity), but a vigilant way of life oriented toward the duties assigned by God (= the "master").

Because Luke and his community live without knowledge of the day of reckoning (the coming of the Son of man) — and this is an agnosticism based on principle — the appeal for constant alertness and faithful activity acquires motivating force. There is the prospect of blessing for those who show themselves to be vigilant, faithful servants (vv 37, 38, 43). Loss and punishment, however, await the lax and those who fail to fulfill their duties (vv 39, 45–48). Luke's readers remain uncertain when they will be called to account; they can be sure of a positive outcome, however, if they *continually* stand ready for eschatological judgment. Concern with ethos and a living eschatological hope go hand in hand.[66] If the eschatological denouement is to be expected at any time — though that time cannot be predicted — then we have to do with living eschatological hope, not with the expectation of a remote eschaton. At the same time, it is not a matter of indifference what one does while waiting.

Luke identifies the disciples as the recipients of this call to vigilance and fidelity. From the standpoint of Lukan composition, Luke's readers (community) form the audience addressed. Nevertheless, the transitional question posed by Peter (12:41), in conjunction with Luke's selection of the word "steward" (οἰκονόμος; v 42) and the distinction drawn by vv 47–48 between differing levels of knowledge of the master's will, has prompted the view that Luke targeted a narrower audience — community leaders — for at least a portion of the paraenesis. This reading of v 41 has a direct bearing on the question of Luke's setting and will, therefore, receive detailed consideration in the next section.

3. "Lord, Are You Telling this Parable to Us or to Everyone?" (Luke 12:41)

Many exegetes maintain that Luke 12:41, 47–48 narrows the focus of responsibility to a leadership group within the Christian community.[67] The discourse

---

[66] Fitzmyer characterizes Luke's eschatological perspective with the attractive slogan: Luke shifts emphasis "from the *eschaton* to the *sēmeron*" (*Luke*, 1.234, 2.1355). Certainly, Luke develops the paraenetic side of his eschatological theme (e.g., 12:35–48; 17:26–30; 21:34–36). One must not too hastily assume, however, any reduction in importance of the eschatological expectation *per se.* Apocalyptic hope and ethical concern are far from strangers to each other!

[67] So, e.g., Grässer, *Problem,* 94; Ernst, *Herr,* 41 n. 45; Fitzmyer, *Luke,* 2.989 (tentatively). Cf. Schneider (*Parusiegleichnisse,* 28–29, 37): Luke shifted the emphasis from paraenesis for disciples to warning of community leaders. Chance ("Jerusalem," 315), on the other hand, assumes — without supporting argument — that Luke 12:41 refers the parable to the entire community.

would, on this reading, warn leaders within Luke's own community against failure to fulfill their special ministry—a failure linked to delay in the eschaton. Nevertheless, this interpretation misconstrues the literary function of v 41. Reexamination of the discourse's targeted audience is necessary.

In a transitional verse (41) stemming from Lukan redaction,[68] Peter asks Jesus concerning the intended audience of the preceding parable:[69] "Lord, are you telling this parable to us or to everyone?" Since the last mention of Jesus' audience in 12:22 names the disciples, Peter's query appears to differentiate between the disciples as a delimited group and the people as a whole (the "crowd"; cf. 12:1, 13, 54). This conclusion is reinforced by the striking formulation of 12:1: "Meanwhile, when the myriads of the crowd had gathered so as to trample one another, [Jesus] began to say to his disciples. . . ." Chapter 12, indeed, is composed of discourse material addressed to alternating audiences: vv 1-12, disciples; vv 13-21, crowd; vv 22-53, disciples; vv 54-59 (13:9), crowd. Peter's question (v 41), therefore, presses for a distinction between the disciples (the Christian community) and the crowd (those outside the community).

Certain features of the text have nevertheless been seen as clues that Luke addresses this paraenetic instruction to the leaders of his community. Luke replaces the "faithful servant" (δοῦλος) of Q with a "faithful steward" (οἰκονόμος) who, as the following verses show, has authority over the other servants of the household.[70] Verses 47-48, moreover, distinguish between two levels of responsibility, with knowledge of the master's will as the discriminating factor: those

---

[68] See footnote 60 above. Talbert ("Quest," 188) contends that even if v 41 is not entirely redactional, it is a "Lucan adaptation of tradition for redactional purposes." The net result, for exegesis, is the same in either case.

[69] It is likely that "this parable" refers back to the parable-material, with application, of vv 36-40, not just to the immediately preceding parable image of v 39. In any case, the use of the singular ("this parable") rules out reference to teaching given before v 35. Therefore, Peter asks about the audience who are to hear the summons to readiness in view of the uncertainty surrounding the date of the parousia.

[70] Cf. Matt 24:45 and Luke 12:42. Although the vocabulary differs, Matthew's version depicts the status and responsibility of the "steward" in similar terms: ὃν κατέστησεν ὁ κύριος ἐπὶ τῆς οἰκετείας αὐτοῦ τοῦ δοῦναι αὐτοῖς τὴν τροφὴν ἐν καιρῷ. The observation that Luke reverts to the term δοῦλος after v 42 confirms the impression that "servant," not "steward," originally appeared in Luke's source, but also indicates that the terms are synonymous for Luke. He has chosen a word that aptly characterizes the function of the servant in the traditional parable. In the only other passage in which Luke employs οἰκονόμος (vv 1, 3, 8 in the parable of the unjust steward, Luke 16:1-9 [also addressed to the disciples]), emphasis is placed not on the superior position of the steward (relative to other servants) but on his use of money. *All* disciples—not just their "leaders"—are urged to profit from the example of the steward (vv 8-9). So in 12:42-46, interest centers in the steward's obedience in fulfilling his assigned tasks (vv 43-44), and in the negative consequences of reckless abandonment of those duties under the spell of delay (vv 45-46). A distinction between steward (= church leader) and servant (= member of the community) does not govern the parable, as the interchangeability of the terms δοῦλος and οἰκονόμος shows.

who are "in the know" have greater accountability for obedience to their master's wishes (vv 47–48a), and those who have received much will be expected to produce accordingly (v 48b). These details do not, however, point to community leadership as the intended audience. Rather, the passage heightens the responsibility of the disciples (Luke's community), who—unlike those outside this circle—know the divine will. The privilege of membership within the Christian community carries with it an extra measure of responsibility. The key question is: will the servant (disciple) carry out the wishes of his master—even in the master's absence?[71]

The specific task of the steward of 12:42–46 is provision of grain to the household, and faithful performance of this task will elevate the steward to a position of oversight of the master's entire estate. According to v 45, the danger lies in the servant's recognition of his master's delay in returning. If misled by delay into abuse of the authority entrusted to him, the servant will be overtaken by a day of reckoning which he had left out of consideration due to its seeming remoteness.

The imagery of the parable points to delay in the parousia as a potential obstacle to faithful service in the community.[72] Nevertheless, the problem is not

---

[71] To the crowds, Jesus issues the challenge to recognize the καιρός that now meets them in his ministry (12:54–56). To the disciples, Jesus addresses an appeal for readiness and fidelity during a period, of uncertain duration, stretching out before the End (12:35–48; cf. the analogous relation of message to audience in 17:20–21 [Jesus confronts the Pharisees with the present activity of the kingdom] and 17:22–18:8 [eschatological instruction for the disciples]). This observation further supports the contention that 12:35–48 holds in view the entire community, as distinct from those standing outside. The force of the passage, in light of 12:41, is to accent the special responsibility of members of Luke's community.

[72] Luke 12:38 likewise reflects the phenomenon of delay ("even if he should come during the second or third watch"): see, e.g., Conzelmann, *St. Luke,* 108. Talbert ("Quest," 190), on the other hand (here he follows J. Jeremias, *The Parables of Jesus* [rev. ed.; New York: Scribners, 1963] 57–58), views both allusions to delay (vv 38, 45) as part of the dramatic machinery of the stories. Moreover, because both allusions to delay are present in the pre-Lukan tradition, Talbert claims that any struggle over delay underlying these texts must be assigned to a pre-Lukan setting, not to Luke's setting. This caveat is indeed to be taken seriously. It should be noted, however, that Luke has appended the notice of the night watches (v 38) to a special Lukan tradition that seems complete without it (v 37 forms an effective climax to the story, with the surprising reversal of roles on the part of master and servants). The related material in Mark 13:35 may have prompted Luke to include the night watches. Lukan redaction in 12:35–38 as a whole is not to be underestimated. The double macarism (vv 37, 38; cf. v 43) and especially the correspondence between περιεζωσμέναι in the introductory v 35 and περιζώσεται in the parable itself (v 37)—matching the reversal in role of master and servant—suggest a heavy hand by Luke in vv 35–38 (cf. Schneider [*Parusiegleichnisse,* 30–31], who sees v 35 as secondary but assigns v 38 to Q). If so, then the force of Talbert's warning is partially blunted. If other passages in Luke-Acts support the view that delay was a factor in Luke's situation, not just in the era preceding him, then my reading of Luke's setting in light of 12:35–48 withstands Talbert's criticism. Delay in

delay *per se* but delay as the *occasion* for irresponsibility. The parable depicts irresponsible behavior accompanying uneschatological faith as abuse of authority and dissolute living. It would be hasty to infer that the people of Luke's community were guilty of physical assault against other community members, or that they were drunkards. Such a wooden transfer to the Lukan setting fails to reckon with the traditional nature of the metaphors.[73] What *is* clear is that judgment will overtake even highly placed household servants who: (1) fail to meet their responsibility for care of subordinates; (2) adopt a complacent and cavalier approach to both life and ministry. Despite the fact of delay, Luke's community must expect the certain coming—at any moment!—of the Son of man. This event will call each to account for the fidelity of his or her "stewardship."

The emphasis of this passage on the manner of life pursued during the interim opened up by delay recurs in Luke. Already in 12:22–34 the present discourse opposed routine concerns of everyday life (food, drink, clothing) to the true business of life, seeking God's kingdom.[74] The eschatological discourses of Luke 17 and 21 both contain paraenetic sections in which Jesus describes the destructive consequences of absorption in routine affairs of daily living (17:26–30; 21:34–36). Luke 17:27–28 and 21:34 in particular approach the language of the indictment in 12:45 (ἤσθιον and ἔπινον in 17:27–28; "dissipation and drunkenness," ἐν κραιπάλῃ καὶ μέθῃ, in 21:34).

It would be presumptuous to press the evidence too far. Luke 12:35–48 gives only a fleeting glimpse of Luke's situation. It does appear, however, that parousia delay is a significant element of that situation—not as an isolated ideational problem but rather as a practical issue of ethos. With delay comes a lure toward complacent living correlated with uneschatological faith. The Christians of Luke's community have apparently succumbed (or at least begun to succumb) to that temptation. If such were not the case, he would not have had need to give Luke 12:35–48 its present form and urgent tone. Life "over the long haul" poses an acute challenge to eschatologically oriented faith. This challenge seems to have found a home in Luke's community. Delay provided the occasion for a relaxed, indeed complacent, approach to the tasks of discipleship, and this in turn dictated Luke's response. In view of a parousia that may materialize at any time—though it remains unpredictable—Luke summons readers of his gospel

---

the eschaton represented a challenge to faithful ministry in Luke's community. It is hardly likely that concern over delay in the era before Luke would vanish in his generation.

[73] For indictment of indulgence in "eating, drinking, and drunkenness," see, e.g., Prov 4:17; 23:1–8; Isa 22:12–14; Sir 18:30–19:3; 34:12–21, 25–31; 1 Enoch 98:11; 102:9; T. Reub 2:7; T. Judah 14, 16; T. Benj 6:3 (cf. Luke 7:33–34; 12:19; 17:26–30; 21:34; Rom 13:13; 14:17; 1 Cor 15:32; Gal 5:21; 1 Thess 5:7). Physical abuse of lowly servants would also represent a commonplace image in Luke's age; cf. Ahiqar 3:1–2; 4:15.

[74] Cf. Luke's version of the "choking cares of *living*" in the parable of the sower (Mark 4:18–19; Luke 8:14).

to unrelaxed vigilance and faithfulness to their Christian responsibilities.

Luke 12:35–48 begins to expose the threads connecting eschatology and situation in Luke-Acts. This passage establishes a base from which eschatological hope may not—with respect to its content—waver. The precise date and hour of the arrival of the Son of man, the culminating eschatological image in Luke-Acts, are and must remain unknown. Because that event is not remote but may occur at any moment, believers must remain ever alert, ever true to their assigned tasks. Nevertheless, the pericope mirrors a situation in which, under the spell of parousia delay, Christians within the Lukan sphere are inclining toward a complacent posture in which living eschatological expectation no longer plays any role.

The first full-fledged eschatological discourse in Luke, Luke 17:20–18:8, continues this welding of eschatological and paraenetic motifs, yet moves beyond Luke 12:35–48 in its concrete description of the events of the "last day." Before examining this next discourse, however, I devote an excursus to critical analysis of the view advanced by Dupont and Schneider, partly on the basis of materials contained in Luke 12, that emphasis on the eschaton of the individual plays a pivotal role in Lukan eschatology.

EXCURSUS 1: "INDIVIDUAL ESCHATOLOGY" IN LUKE-ACTS?

The exemplary story of Luke 12:16-21 has—together with other passages in Luke-Acts[75]—given rise to the view that the personal eschaton of each individual at the moment of death occupies a place of special prominence in the Lukan eschatological perspective.[76] This special interest in the fate of the individual after death runs parallel to the traditional collective eschatology; however, Luke offers no reflection on the relationship between the two perspectives.[77] The individualizing tendency in Luke's thought about the last things stems from his

[75] Particularly Luke 12:4-5; 16:19-31; 23:43; Acts 7:55-60; 14:22.

[76] The key contribution is that of Dupont, in two articles: "L'Après-mort dans l'oeuvre de Luc," *RTL* 3 (1972) 3-21; "Die individuelle Eschatologie im Lukasevangelium und in der Apostelgeschichte," in *Orientierung an Jesus,* ed. P. Hoffmann (Freiburg: Herder, 1973) 37-47. Nevertheless, others have perceived Luke as accenting the role of the individual (and the individual's death) in eschatology. See, e.g., G. Schneider, *Parusiegleichnisse,* 78–84; H. Conzelmann, *Apostelgeschichte,* 10; A. Pérez, "Deráš Lucano de Mc 13 a la luz de su 'Teología del Reino': Lc 21,5–36," *EstBib* 39 (1981) 285-313, 303; C. K. Barrett, "Stephen and the Son of Man," in *Apophoreta: Festschrift für Ernst Haenchen,* ed. W. Eltester (Berlin: Töpelmann, 1964) 32-38. For criticisms of this approach to Lukan eschatology, see Ernst, *Herr,* 78-87; Maddox, *Purpose,* 103–05; Mattill, *Last,* 26-40. Unlike Mattill, Ernst and Maddox do acknowledge that "individualizing of eschatology" plays a minor role in Luke-Acts.

[77] "Après-mort," 4, 21; "Individuelle," 37, 46-47. In Dupont's judgment, it is misleading to speak of an "intermediate state" bridging the gap between individual deaths during the period before the End and the End itself.

"Hellenistic formation," from the "individualistic mentality of the Greek world" during this period.[78]

Schneider follows Dupont's exegesis of the pertinent passages,[79] but contends, against Dupont, that the lines of individual and collective eschatology do converge in Luke-Acts. Indeed, Luke 21:19 and 23:43 make clear that the development is *from* collective *to* individual eschatology, for in each of these verses Luke has replaced a traditional statement about the parousia with one about the death of the individual.[80] In addition, while agreeing with Dupont that Luke's interest in individual salvation leads him to give pride of place to the decisive turn that one makes at death,[81] Schneider proceeds to correlate this relativizing of parousia hope with the problem of parousia delay. The passage of time made it necessary for Luke to come to terms with the expanding interval between the deaths of believers and the parousia.[82]

This excursus will examine the thesis of "individual eschatology" by considering, in turn, the key passages: Luke 12:16-21; 16:19-31; 23:39-43; and Acts 7:55-60.[83] The larger questions of the role of the individual in Luke's end-time

[78] "Individuelle," 47; "Après-mort," 21.

[79] See the discussion below.

[80] Schneider, *Parusiegleichnisse*, 81. Dupont does suggest once that "individual eschatology" in Luke-Acts entails a certain relativizing of the collective, future eschatology. That is, Luke's approach involves taking the present more seriously—not as provisional, but as final ("Individuelle," 47). This last formulation points toward the direction in which my own study will proceed. However, it is an insight that is separable from the "individual eschatology" thesis. The decisive character in Luke-Acts of one's present life (of repentance, faith, and faithfulness) is undeniable; the assertion that the decisive moment occurs at one's death is something else altogether.

[81] *Parusiegleichnisse*, 81; Dupont, "Individuelle," 45; "Après-mort," 19.

[82] *Parusiegleichnisse*, 81.

[83] I will not provide separate treatments of Luke 21:19; 12:4-5; and Acts 14:22, often adduced in support of the "individual eschatology" position. Schneider (*Parusiegleichnisse*, 81; cf. Dupont, "Après-mort," 18) claims that in Luke 21:19 a statement about the parousia ("one who endures to the end," Mark 13:13) is replaced with one focused on the individual's death ("by your endurance you will gain your souls"). The immediate context (vv 12, 16-18) does point to the persecution and death of some believers, yet Schneider inaccurately speaks of a replacement of parousia expectation. Verse 19, after all, stands in a discourse which makes explicit mention of the "coming" of the Son of man (v 27)! Luke has shifted emphasis from the End to life-giving endurance during the period preceding the End. But he still expects the End, and with it the "parousia." As for Luke 12:4-5, Dupont's insistence that the twofold "after" both is a matter of Lukan emphasis *and* necessarily means "*immediately* after" ("Après-mort," 12; cf. "Individuelle," 41) seems to me tenuous. The passage reads: "But I say to you, my friends, do not be afraid of those who kill the body and after this do not have anything further to do. Yet, I will show you whom to fear: fear the one who has authority after killing to cast into Gehenna. Yes, I tell you, fear this one!" This saying does not (as Dupont claims) indicate that this further divine judgment occurs immediately after death, as opposed to the final judgment. Rather, the point is the contrast between human capacity to harm, limited to this life, and limitless

perspective, and of the decisive moment in it, cannot receive definitive treatment here. To these questions we will return in subsequent sections and in the concluding chapter of the dissertation.

1. Luke 12:16-21

He told a parable to them, saying: "The land of a certain rich man prospered. He thought to himself, 'What will I do? For I do not have anywhere to gather in my crops.' And he said, 'This [is what] I will do: I will tear down my barns and build larger ones, and there I will gather in all the grain and my goods. And I will say to myself (ψυχῇ), Self (ψυχή), you have many possessions stored up for many years. Rest, eat, drink, celebrate!' But God said to him, 'Fool! This [very] night they will demand your life (ψυχήν) from you. As for the things that you have readied, whose will they be?' So is one who accumulates treasure for himself and is not rich toward God."

According to Dupont, Luke's redaction of this exemplary story (that is, the addition of v 21[84]) shifts the locus of folly from a failure to consider death to failure to reckon with what comes after death.[85] Because this rich man has not used his wealth to assist the poor (cf. 12:33-34; 16:19-31) but rather has devoted his attention to the business of increasing his own holdings, he will meet divine judgment after his death ("this night").

Without undertaking a full exegesis of this passage,[86] I counter Dupont's analysis with the following observations. First, it is far from obvious that the addition of v 21 shifts attention from the fact of death itself to judgment

---

divine authority to judge. Concerning Acts 14:22 (". . . encouraging [them] to persevere in the faith and [saying] that it is necessary for us to enter the kingdom of God via many tribulations"), it is important to observe that, while the end-time tribulations of apocalyptic texts are here transmuted (the stresses of persecution are in view), the passage does not reduce these ordeals to the experience of the individual, nor does it state that entrance into the kingdom occurs immediately after death. See further Mattill, *Last,* 34-35 (on Luke 12:4-5), 52 (on Acts 14:22).

[84] Widely held to be from Luke. See, e.g., Fitzmyer, *Luke,* 2.971; Creed, *Luke,* 173. For a different view, see Marshall, *Luke,* 524. The absence of this verse in the version contained in the Gospel of Thomas, logion 63, supports the position that v 21 was not part of the pre-Lukan tradition.

[85] "Individuelle," 38; so also Schneider, *Parusiegleichnisse,* 79. In fact, Dupont suggests (39) that the link between v 21 and vv 33-34 (where the motif of a treasure oriented toward God is interpreted in terms of almsgiving) shows the dominance of the perspective of the individual's death throughout the whole of vv 13-34.

[86] I simply note that vv 16-21 serve as a commentary on v 15 (so also Fitzmyer, *Luke,* 2.971 [v 15c]), and also prepare for the section vv 22-34, which culminates in an appeal for generous behavior for which the rich fool constitutes a negative model. The key word ψυχή (which appears three times in vv 16-21) is picked up in vv 22, 23, and the activities of eating and drinking (v 19) likewise resurface in vv 22, 29. The juxtaposition of the two pericopae yields a contrast between inappropriate and appropriate orientation toward worldly possessions.

immediately after death. The argument that this verse must be interpreted by way of 12:33–34 ("treasure in heaven")[87] is dubious. Verse 21 (like v 20) expresses God's disapproval of the conduct portrayed—this much is to be granted. However, what evidence in the text points to the moment immediately after death as the occasion when God exercises judgment? Verse 20 presents untimely death itself as the judgment: the expression "they (will) demand your soul (life)" is a euphemism for death, not judgment.[88] Second, moreover, the presence of the motifs of "eating and drinking" and absorption in business affairs in other, manifestly eschatological contexts in the gospel (e.g., 12:45; 17:26–30), actually directs the imagery of this parable against Dupont's conclusion. Luke's eschatological perspective does involve divine judgment for the kind of posture depicted here, but that judgment is elsewhere explicitly tied to the parousia. An irresponsible style of life in the present jeopardizes one's status at the eschaton, and to that extent the present becomes of decisive importance for eschatology. Nevertheless, it is not the moment of death but the ultimate verdict of God at the parousia that is conclusive.

The traditional nature of this story requires no demonstration.[89] Jewish wisdom devoted extensive reflection to the problem of wealth in relation to righteousness/wickedness, and to human finitude.[90] Luke was no innovator, therefore, in posing the question of the individual in relation to eschatology. It may be that the individual has an important part to play in Luke's end-time perspective; however, that aligns him with many predecessors and contemporaries[91] and need not justify the special ascription to Luke

[87] Dupont, "Individuelle," 38–39.

[88] See Wis 15:8: a potter who has fashioned a "god" out of clay will soon return to the earth when the soul [= life] loaned to him is recalled (. . . τὸ τῆς ψυχῆς ἀπαιτηθεὶς χρέος). So also Epictetus, Discourses 4.1,172 (following the LCL translation): "For the sake of what is called freedom some hang themselves, others leap over precipices, sometimes whole cities perish; for true freedom, which cannot be plotted against and is secure, will you not yield up to God, at his demand, what he has given (. . . ἀπαιτοῦντι τῷ Θεῷ ἃ δέδωκεν οὐκ ἐκστήσῃ;)?" Cf. Sir 11:19: ". . . when he says, 'I have found rest, and now I will eat of my goods,' and he does not know what season will come; and he will leave these things to others, *and he will die.*"

[89] Cf. Ps 38:7 LXX; Eccles 6:1–6; 1 Enoch 97:8–10. On the affinities between Luke's material on possessions and 1 Enoch 92–105, see S. Aalen, "St. Luke's Gospel and the Last Chapters of 1 Enoch," *NTS* 13 (1966–67) 1–13; G. W. E. Nickelsburg, "Riches, the Rich, and God's Judgment in 1 Enoch 92–105 and the Gospel according to Luke," *NTS* 25 (1978–79) 324–44.

[90] Classic texts in Ecclesiastes. The appellation addressed to the rich man ("Fool!") already points toward the Jewish wisdom literature.

[91] Note the emphasis placed on judgment of the individual in PsSol 5:4; 9:5. Cf. the ruminations on theodicy and the destinies of the "few" righteous and "many" sinners in 4 Ezra; and the depiction in 1 Enoch of the Garden of Eden (paradise) as place of residence for the elect and righteous ones (60:7–8, 23; 61:12; 70:1–4; 77:4; 106:7–8). Rabbinic discussions presuppose the necessity of the individual's being called to account for Torah

of a tendency to "individualize eschatology." Further evidence will accumulate as we proceed.

2. Luke 16:19-31

Luke 16:1-13, the story of the unjust steward, and 16:19-31, the story of the rich man and Lazarus, form another pair of passages juxtaposing positive and negative models for use of possessions.[92] The villain of vv 19-31, by neglecting the destitute beggar Lazarus, failed to employ his wealth properly. When the parable portrays the outcome of these two lives — the callous rich man is consigned to torment in Hades (vv 23-24), while the poor beggar enjoys rest and bliss "in the bosom of Abraham"[93] — it does so without any mention of final judgment. From these details, Dupont infers that the "but now" of v 25 refers to the time immediately after death, when the circumstances of Lazarus and the rich man are reversed — independent of any eschatological event.[94] The parable must be read from the vantage point of individual eschatology.[95] Yet, the notion of an intermediate state may not be read into the story, Dupont insists.[96]

A full treatment of this passage would take us far afield.[97] Three points in

---

observance. So, e.g, even Sanhedrin 10:1: "All Israel — there is for them a share in the world to come." It is not only the Israelite nation but also individuals comprising Israel who will have a share in the world to come. See the discussion in E. P. Sanders, *Paul and Palestinian Judaism* (Philadelphia: Fortress, 1977) 181-82. Additional material on the relation of individuals to the collective eschatology within Judaism may be found in E. Schürer, *The History of the Jewish People in the Age of Jesus Christ*, rev. and ed. G. Vermes, F. Millar, and M. Black (2 vol.; Edinburgh: T. & T. Clark, 1979) 2.544-47.

[92] The intervening verses (16:14-18) link the two passages and prepare for the climax of the parable in vv 19-31. Verses 14-15 identify the Pharisees as the audience for the following parable. As for vv 16-18, the relationship between the law and prophets, on the one side, and the kingdom of God, on the other, is additive. The law and prophets remain operative during the era of kingdom proclamation (vv 17-18 elucidate the difficult v 16 in these terms). Moreover, the law and prophets should suffice to elicit from Abraham's children the appropriate manner of living (v 30). Even the resurrection of one from the dead will not deflect the unrepentant from their course (v 31; this statement points forward through Luke 24 into the Acts narrative: Jesus' resurrection will not persuade those who, bent on their own destruction, refuse to repent in response to the apostolic preaching).

[93] This image appears in T. Abr 20:14.

[94] "Après-mort," 17; "Individuelle," 44.

[95] Dupont proposes to understand the beatitudes and woes of Luke 6:20-26 in light of this parable. Those who hunger now will be sated in the "then" that follows a person's death. The contrast is between the conditions of one's earthly life and those of the after-life ("Individuelle," 44; "Après-mort," 17).

[96] "Individuelle," 47; "Après-mort," 4.

[97] In particular, a plethora of Jewish texts shed light on the questions of the location and chronology of this residence in company with, or isolation from, the patriarch Abraham. The closest parallel to the depiction of Lazarus' bliss comes from the "A"

response to Dupont's exegesis will suffice, however. The first concerns the traditional nature of the parable, a piece of special Lukan tradition that has been lightly redacted.[98] Behind this parable may be detected a variant of a folktale of Egyptian origin.[99] Although the traditional character of 16:19-31 has led some to minimize its place in Luke's eschatological perspective,[100] the author has

---

Recension of the T. Abr 20:14: the "mansions of [God's] holy ones, Isaac and Jacob, are in [Abraham's] bosom [in Paradise], where there is no toil, no grief, no moaning, but peace and exultation and endless life" (see the translation by E. P. Sanders in *The Old Testament Pseudepigrapha*, 1, ed. J. H. Charlesworth [Garden City: Doubleday, 1983] 895. Sanders dates the document within the period 75-125 C.E.). It is of interest that the T. Abr combines the notion of a preliminary judgment following the death of an individual (Abel is cast in the role of judge) with a final judgment by God (see especially 13:1-8; a third judgment, by the whole of Israel, is thrown in for good measure, thereby meeting the description of three witnesses in Deut 19:15 LXX). See the comment by Sanders, *Pseudepigrapha*, 1, 890 n. 13a.

According to 4 Ezra, too, the final judgment is preceded by an interim period during which the righteous enjoy rest (7:95, in chambers guarded by angels) but sinners wander about in torment (7:80). These conditions of rest and torment which immediately follow death are only the prelude to the end-time judgment (7:32, 84, 95). Until the eschaton, the souls of the righteous dead wait in their guarded chambers in Hades (4:33-43). Although the material from 4 Ezra does not agree in every detail with the parable of Luke 16:19-31 (e.g., the tormented sinner is depicted as wandering in 4 Ezra; however, one of the torments is precisely the vision of the righteous in their guarded habitations! [7:85]), the common themes suggest that Lazarus and the rich man are experiencing — within their separate abodes in Hades — the interim reversal of condition which anticipates God's final judgment. For consideration of 1 Enoch, see below.

[98] Cf. Fitzmyer, *Luke*, 2.1125: "The amount of non-Lucan formulation in the story is . . . noteworthy." Fitzmyer lists the "few traces of Lucan redaction" that are discernible. I am inclined to assign Luke a more prominent role than does Fitzmyer in the composition of vv 27-31. Although the first part of the parable (vv 19-26) finds parallels in extrabiblical sources, the second part (vv 27-31) stands alone. Whether this conclusion to the parable comes from Luke or his tradition (Fitzmyer prefers to regard the parable as a unity and to ascribe it to Jesus [*Luke*, 2.1127]), it certainly accords with central motifs in the larger narrative (see note 92 above). Verses 19-26 emphasize the reversal of fortunes — focused on possessions — that the after-life brings. Verses 27-31 assert that the unrepentant rich will not alter their way of life even if one returns, resurrected, from the dead. Cf. Bultmann, *Synoptic Tradition*, 178; Fitzmyer, *Luke*, 2.1126.

[99] The tale was copied in Demotic on the obverse of a Greek document from 47 C.E. It illustrates retribution in the next life for conditions of this life, using the reversal of the fortunes of a rich man and a poor man. See H. Gressmann, "Vom reiche Mann und armen Lazarus: Eine literargeschichtliche Studie," *Abhandlungen der königlichen preussischen Akademie der Wissenschaften* (Berlin: Königliche Akademie der Wissenschaften, 1918); cf. Fitzmyer, *Luke*, 2.1126-27; Schweizer, *Luke*, 260. Cf. also the reversal motif in 1 Enoch 103-5.

[100] Maddox (*Purpose*, 103) remarks: ". . . this pre-existing tale offered the possibility of dramatizing pictorially the seriousness of each individual's responsibility for his conduct

made it part of his narrative, and we must take it seriously.

Second, however, it is misleading to speak of a new orientation of eschatology toward the individual and his or her death. In addition to the Jewish texts already cited,[101] the apostle Paul preceded Luke in reflecting (though rarely, in extant writings!) on the post-death, pre-parousia state of the believer (2 Cor 5:4-10; Phil 1:23), his governing apocalyptic eschatology notwithstanding.[102] The collective, cosmic, and future expectation of Jewish and Christian apocalyptic texts had, long before and alongside Luke, found room for rumination on the status of the individual between death and final judgment.

Third, the affinities between Luke 16:19-31 and 1 Enoch (particularly chap. 22) place a question mark beside Dupont's contention that the parable cannot have envisaged an intermediate state.[103] Although the composite nature of 1 Enoch has as its corollary a variety of eschatological conceptions throughout the document, certain patterns do emerge. In 1 Enoch 91-108, a section revolving around the two paths of the righteous and the sinners, the end-time judgment dominates the scenery (91:15-16; oscillation of consolation for the righteous and woes to sinners, chaps. 94-105; 103:8; 104:3-5 ["the day of the great judgment"]). Prior to this "day of the great judgment," all—righteous and sinner alike—descend into Hades to await the final judgment (e.g, 102:4-11). Already a distinction is drawn, however, between the condition of the righteous after death and that of the sinner. The souls of the evil will experience tribulation in Sheol (103:7) before they proceed to the final judgment. The souls (or spirits) of the righteous, on the other hand, will know joy and good fortune (103:3-4).[104]

during his lifetime. It is no more necessary to believe that Luke took this eschatological description literally than it is to believe that every modern Christian who tells or retells a story about Saint Peter as gate-keeper 'of the pearly gates' has seriously conflated Rev. 21:10ff. with Matt. 16:19 to produce the eschatology which he really holds." Yet, despite the folk character of the tale and the absence of such a picture of the after-life elsewhere in Luke-Acts, the story is not to be dismissed. To be sure, where Abraham figures in the Lukan depiction of the kingdom, the setting is (outside this passage) the eschatological banquet (see Luke 13:23-30). But that function of Abraham does not preclude a post-mortem, pre-eschaton role for him as conveyer of (intermediate) blessing. Luke 16:19-31 indicates that Luke envisages an existence in blessing or torment after the individual's death and before the end-time.

[101] See note 97 above.

[102] Cf. Ernst, *Herr,* 85.

[103] Aalen ("Enoch," 1-13) calls attention to the striking affinities in language and phraseology between 1 Enoch 91-105 (in Greek) and Luke's special material. Certainly, the two texts share a common disdain for riches and a corresponding expectation of God's reversal of fortunes (e.g., 1 Enoch 94:6-11; 96:4-8; 97:8-10).

[104] For discussion of 1 Enoch 103:7-8, see Aalen ("Enoch," 9) and Mattill (*Last,* 30). Aalen rightly discerns in 103:7-8 two stages in the lot of the wicked: preliminary punishment in Hades (v 7), followed by the "great judgment" (v 8).

The visions of book one of 1 Enoch shift the center of gravity away from the eschatological judgment to the interim condition of the two classes of humanity (that is, the righteous and sinners). Chapter 22, in particular, develops the theme of the contrasting fortunes of the two groups in the interim before the eschaton.[105] The divine policy for the post-death, pre-eschaton interim is one of separation (22:9-14). In fact, three separate dwelling-places are carved out in Hades, the first for the righteous, the second for sinners who went unpunished during their lifetimes, and the third for sinners who have already been punished. The righteous ones enjoy rest during their residence in Hades, while sinners suffer torments. Despite the seemingly ultimate character of these rewards, explicit mention of the "great day of judgment" (v 11) is made. 1 Enoch 22 is especially important for the exegesis of Luke 16:19-31 because in both passages a separation of righteous and sinner subsequent to death is depicted, together with reversal of circumstance. The location of the compartment of the righteous in Hades may also guide the reading of Luke 16:19-31 and 23:43 in relation to eschatology. Lazarus may enjoy the bliss of Abraham's bosom in "Paradise" (23:43; cf. T. Abr 20:14), located within Hades. In any case, the imagery of 1 Enoch 22[106] — along with other affinities between Luke and 1 Enoch — suggests, against Dupont, the counter-thesis that the parable in Luke 16:19-31 envisages an in-between state, even though no explicit mention of end-time judgment appears.[107] The interim role reversal which overtakes the rich man and Lazarus does not replace an eschatological climax.

Precisely how Luke understood this parable is inaccessible to us; however, vv 27-31 are a clue to its function within his narrative. With specific reference to one's orientation toward material possessions, this parable reinforces the demand for repentance with a graphic picture of role reversal after death. This is the force of the passage, not the chronology of the judgment involved. There is no denying the pivotal role played here by the conduct of the individual as determining factor in his or her destiny, *and* no denying that Luke pictures a post-mortem existence for the individual prior to the end-time. To suggest,

[105] That this material is not a peculiarity of 1 Enoch may be seen from the similar imagery in 4 Ezra 7:75-101 and T. Abr 11.

[106] To round out the sketch of eschatological perspectives in 1 Enoch, I simply point out that the Similitudes of chaps. 37-71 enhance the separation between the righteous (elect) ones and sinners. In this section the term "Paradise" (or "garden of Eden," or "garden of life") is regularly applied to the interim abode of the righteous, elect ones (60:7-8, 23; 61:12; 70:1-4). This temporary separation is sealed at the judgment at which the Son of man (Enoch) presides. Along with T. Abr 20:14, 1 Enoch's identification of Paradise as the interim residence of the righteous (not located in heaven) will prove significant in the analysis of Luke 23:39-43.

[107] Luke did not need to import the motif of end-time judgment into the story because his primary point—the reversal of fortunes in divine judgment—was sufficiently established without it.

however, that "individual eschatology" replaces collective, future expectation in this passage is to move far beyond the evidence.

3. Luke 23:39-43

> Now one of the criminals who had been hung [on the cross] reviled [Jesus], saying: "Aren't you the Christ? Save yourself and us." But the other one responded by rebuking him [the first criminal]: "Do you not even fear God? For you are [condemned] with the same punishment, and we justly, for we have done things deserving of what we are receiving in return. But this man has done nothing amiss." And he said, "Jesus, remember me when you go into [come in?] your kingly rule." And [Jesus] said to him, "Truly, I tell you, today you will be with me in Paradise."

In typical fashion,[108] Luke's account of Jesus' crucifixion narrates a divided response to Jesus on the part of the two criminals executed alongside him.[109] The artistry of the episode lies in the manner in which Jesus answers affirmatively — in the case of the second criminal — the sarcastic request of the first criminal: "Aren't you the Christ? Save yourself, and us" (v 39b). When the second criminal repents,[110] he receives from Jesus assurance of association with Jesus after death ("today!").[111]

But what is the sense of that assurance, "Today you will be with me in Paradise"? Dupont argues that Jesus in v 43 corrects the criminal's eschatological viewpoint: "The salvation which the criminal requests for the end of time falls to him even today, in the moment of his death."[112] Jesus substitutes

---

[108] Programmatically at Luke 2:34-35.

[109] Of course, Luke diverges in this respect from Matthew (27:44). Whatever the extent of Lukan composition in 23:39-42, the saying of Jesus in v 43 bears the marks of pre-Lukan tradition, notably the Lukan *hapax legomenon* παράδεισος (which, however, appears only twice in the rest of the New Testament [2 Cor 12:4; Rev 2:7]) and the introduction of the saying with "Amen," a rare phenomenon in Luke-Acts (cf. only Luke 4:24; 12:37; 18:17, 29; 21:32; see Fitzmyer, *Luke*, 1.536-37, 2.1510).

[110] The behavior, if not the terminology, suggests this conclusion.

[111] Cf. Dupont ("Individuelle," 45), who comments that the meaning of v 43 is to be found in the preceding conversation: Jesus can only show his Messiahship through exercise of his saving power.

[112] "Individuelle," 45; cf. "Après-mort," 19. Fitzmyer (*Luke*, 2.1510) holds that the σήμερον of 23:43 should not be construed calendrically, but rather in the sense of the "now" of messianic salvation inaugurated by Jesus (cf. Ellis, "Present," 36-37). This line of interpretation eases the tension between this verse and the prevalent Lukan conception that Jesus' ψυχή remained in Hades and his body in the tomb until his resurrection "on the third day" (cf. Mattill, *Last*, 32). If "Paradise" here refers to the interim residence of the souls of the righteous dead before the parousia, then Jesus' saying must mean "today" (calendrically), for Jesus would soon be raised up from the realm of the dead, then exalted to heaven. Thereafter, the criminal would no longer be "with Jesus" until the end-time. If "Paradise" does not have end-time bliss but rather interim refreshment for its content, then Jesus' point in v 43 would be: "You need not wait until the establishment of my kingly rule

for parousia-centered salvation a new perspective: although Luke does not deny Jesus' future glorious coming, the pivotal event is entrance into the realm of the saved at the death of the individual.[113]

Examination of the background and usage of the term παράδεισος will clarify the sense of Jesus' word of consolation.[114] "Paradise" has its origin in the Old Persian *pairidaêza*, meaning "enclosed space." The earliest attestation of παράδεισος in Greek is in the writings of Xenophon, with reference to the parks of Persian royalty and nobility.[115] The LXX employed παράδεισος for the "garden of Eden" in Gen 2:8 and "the garden of God" in Gen 13:10. This equation became the springboard for subsequent Jewish usage of the noun. "Paradise" often assumed an eschatological connotation; the blessings intended by God in the creation of humanity find fulfillment at the consummation of history.[116] Nevertheless, a popular usage of "Paradise" identified it as the dwelling place of the righteous dead between death and the general resurrection of the end-time.[117]

Given the variety of meanings assigned to "Paradise" in the Jewish literature, and the absence of the concept elsewhere in the Lukan corpus, Luke's understanding of v 43 must remain elusive. However, the view that Paradise refers here to an interim residence for the righteous dead, prior to their final vindication at the end-time judgment, has the advantages of fitting well with Luke 16:19–31 and cohering with the conceptuality of 1 Enoch[118] — not to mention resolving the apparent inconsistency with Luke's presentation of Jesus' itinerary after his death. If this position is correct, then verse 43 yields the following meaning: "Today, when we enter the abode of the dead, you will be with me in the place of refreshment apportioned to the righteous." The passage represents

---

to enjoy the blessings of God in fellowship with me. This very day we will be together in the (temporary) abode of the righteous."

[113] "Après-mort," 19; cf. Schneider, *Parusiegleichnisse*, 83–84.

[114] For discussion of the origin, use, and meaning of "Paradise," see J. Jeremias, "παράδεισος," *TDNT* 5, 765–73; Fitzmyer, *Luke*, 2.1510–11; Mattill, *Last*, 33–34; Marshall, *Luke*, 872–73.

[115] Xenophon, *Anab.* 1.2,7; 2.4,14; *Cyrop.* 1.3,14. Cf. the Hebrew *pardēs* ("a treed park"), which appears in Cant 4:13; Eccles 2:5; Neh 2:8.

[116] E.g., Ezek 31:8; T. Levi 18:10; Rev 2:7; cf. SibOr frag 3, 48–49. In T. Levi 18:10 the author speaks of the restoration of paradise in the era of the raising up of the eschatological priest.

[117] E.g., PsSol 14:3; T. Abr 11:10 ("A" recension); 20:14; ApocAbr 21:6; 1 Enoch 60:7–8, 23; 61:12; 70:1–4; cf. 2 Enoch 8:1; 42:3–14 (in 2 Enoch Paradise is prepared for the righteous and appears to be inhabited now, yet the accent falls on Paradise as eternal inheritance). On the diversity of Paradise traditions in 1 and 2 Enoch, see F. I. Andersen's translation of 2 Enoch in *Pseudepigrapha*, ed. Charlesworth, 1, 114–15 n. 8b. The location of Paradise varies considerably in the texts, including sites on earth, Hades, and the third heaven (third heaven in 2 Enoch 8:1). Paul's visionary trip to Paradise (2 Cor 12:4; in view of 2 Enoch, likely identical to "third heaven" in v 2?) is probably to be classed with these texts.

[118] A text that shares other affinities with special traditions in Luke's gospel.

no new departure into the fertile fields of "individual eschatology," nor does it hand over the finality of end-time judgment to the moment of the individual's death. The decisive feature of Luke 23:39–43 is not so much the "today" —which corrects parousia hope—as it is the promise of fellowship with Jesus for the penitent![119]

4. Acts 7:55–60

On all counts, the content of Acts 7:55–60 is striking: the bare fact of the Son of man saying (v 56) in this setting; the image of the Son of man *standing* at God's right hand; the petition of v 59 ("Lord Jesus, receive my spirit"), which echoes Jesus' own dying words (Luke 23:46); and the prayer of forgiveness (v 60). C. K. Barrett has advanced the thesis that Luke narrates in this passage a private, personal parousia of the Son of man for the martyr Stephen![120] Barrett suggests that Luke was conscious of the problem of believers' deaths (cf. 1 Thess 4:13) for eschatological expectation, and that he came to perceive the death of the individual as an eschaton which would be marked by a personal parousia of the Son of man![121] Such is Stephen's experience at the event of his martyrdom. Luke has pushed eschatological expectation in an individualistic direction![122]

Without entering into debate over the various interpretations that have been offered of the standing Son of man in 7:56,[123] I do venture to say that Barrett has placed enormous weight on this small detail in the text, with precious little corroborating evidence from other parts of Luke-Acts. Verse 59 *may* indicate that Jesus, Son of man, has stood up to receive the spirit of Stephen. Even granting this reading of the passage for the moment, it does not, however, follow that Luke depicts Stephen as the model of every Christian, who on dying experiences a private parousia. Everything in the account of Stephen (notably, the Jesus/Stephen parallels) serves to highlight his extraordinary status, not his representative quality.

If my exegetical probes of the other passages in this excursus have been on target, then Barrett's hypothesis of a "personal parousia" finds no support elsewhere in Luke's narrative. In any case, as even Barrett admits,[124] the traditional expectation for an eschaton of cosmic proportions remains intact in Luke-Acts. Whatever interest Luke may have had in the status of individual believers

---

[119] Cf. Ellis, "Present," 35–40; Ernst, *Herr,* 86–87. Ernst observes of Luke 23:42–43 that the author does not wish to develop a doctrine about the after-life, but rather to speak of salvation in its connection to Jesus.

[120] Barrett, "Stephen," 36–37.

[121] Ibid., 35. Barrett has chosen his words carefully; he does not maintain that Luke replaced *the* eschaton—which remains part of his future expectation—with the termination of the individual's life.

[122] Ibid., 38.

[123] Barrett provides a useful survey of options in "Stephen," 32–35.

[124] "Stephen," 35.

between their deaths and the parousia.[125] Luke's central interest in the realm of things eschatological was to foster a positive correlation between the end-time intervention of God—still a matter of hope—and the faith and manner of living of believers in the present. Luke does indeed accent the role of the individual in relation to eschatology. (This is no invention of Luke's.) However, it is not the moment of death, but the present situation of the believer—with the necessity of repentance, faith, vigilance, and faithfulness—that decides one's eschatological outcome.[126] And without the prospect of an impending, universal day of reckoning, this urgency of the present would dissolve. In short, the theory of "individual eschatology" places the accent in the wrong place.

C. INSTRUCTION FOR THE "DAY OF THE SON OF MAN": THE ESCHATOLOGICAL DISCOURSE OF LUKE 17:20-18:8

Luke 12:35-48 assumed the certainty of the Lord's return to call his servants to account for their conduct during his absence. However, the uncertain timing of that certain return—together with its implications for the believers' manner of living—governed the passage. This first Lukan eschatological "discourse"[127] did not elaborate the picture of the eschatological events themselves. Jesus' discourse in Luke 17:20-18:8 fills the gap; in fact, 17:22-37, the heart of the discourse, is without parallel in Luke-Acts in its concentration on the events of the end-time.

Before examining the eschatological perspective of this passage and its clues to Luke's setting,[128] I will consider problems of literary context and structure. This discussion will justify the demarcation of 17:20-18:8 as a unit for study, especially with an eye to the connection between vv 20-21 and the rest of the section. Luke 17:20-21 raises acute interpretive questions, not least among them the meaning of the concept "kingdom of God" in Luke-Acts. After treating such issues at length, I will focus on the portrait of the "day(s) of the Son of man" in 17:22-18:8. The discussion will show that Luke pictures the advent of the Son of man as a sudden, universally manifest, and inescapable event, one which takes people by surprise, thereby effecting a final division among all people. Luke

---

[125] The extent of the data suggests that this was not a pressing item on Luke's agenda. A much more significant product of the parousia delay was the challenge to faith and faithfulness posed by *life* over the "long haul."

[126] Similarly, Geiger, *Endzeitreden,* 192-93: Luke gives every present the weight of the end-time judgment; every present is filled with eschatological judgment and therefore demands eschatological conduct.

[127] Properly speaking, of course, Luke 12:35-48 represents part of a discourse-and-dialogue sequence, selected for analysis in our study of eschatological themes in relation to Luke's setting.

[128] Discussion of Luke 17:20-18:8 will, because of the importance of this material, and because of the necessity to examine in this context the Lukan presentation of the kingdom of God, be disproportionately long.

upholds this vision of the approaching denouement in a situation shaped by delay: for complacent believers absorbed by the routines of everyday living, Luke accents the urgency of preparedness and persevering faith. This is a question of life or death—and the consequences of one's manner of life in the period preceding the sudden appearance of the Son of man are irrevocable.

1. The Literary Context and Structure of Luke 17:20–18:8

Attention to the audiences specified by Luke in this section reveals that 17:22–18:8 forms a unit of eschatological instruction addressed to the disciples. Luke 17:20–21 stands out as a separate piece, both on formal[129] and material[130] grounds; here Pharisees are Jesus' audience. Although 18:9–14 shares with 18:1–8 the theme of prayer, Luke has specified for the parable on humble prayer (vv 9–14) a new audience: Εἶπεν δὲ καὶ πρός τινας τοὺς πεποιθότας ἐφ' ἑαυτοῖς ὅτι εἰσὶν δίκαιοι καὶ ἐξουθενοῦντας τοὺς λοιποὺς τὴν παραβολὴν ταύτην (v 9). The Pharisees are, beyond doubt, the target of this parable.[131] Audience analysis thus lays bare Luke's careful inversion-arrangement of the materials:

17:20–21—Jesus challenges the *Pharisees* to recognize the activity of the kingdom in their midst;

17:22–37—Jesus instructs the *disciples* concerning the appearance of the Son of man;

18:1–8—Jesus addresses to the *disciples* a parable on persevering prayer and the assurance of vindication;

18:9–14—Jesus addresses to the *Pharisees* (implicitly) a parable on role reversal, employing prayer as the illustration and commending humility.[132]

---

[129] The audience here is the Pharisees, and the verses take the form of a skeletal pronouncement story, culminating in the decisive word of v 21b: "For behold! The kingdom of God is ἐντὸς ὑμῶν."

[130] Luke 17:20–21 revolves around the concept "kingdom of God," yet this term is absent from 17:22–18:8, which focuses instead on the day(s) and coming of the Son of man. Moreover, the singularity of language (παρατήρησις and ἐντός are *hapax legomena* in Luke-Acts) and idea (the present kingdom [at least in the dominant interpretation]) in 17:20–21 isolates it from the following verses.

[131] Cf. the language used of the Pharisees in Luke 16:15.

[132] And note the broader pattern of audience alternation throughout the travel narrative (see footnote 151 below). Farrell ("Perspective," 65) advances a similar view, describing 17:20–18:14 as a "characteristic Lukan chiastic construction." Cf. also the structural analysis in Geiger, *Endzeitreden*, 25. Geiger presents the following arrangement of 17:5–18:14:

17:5–6—Introduction of the theme: the disciples ask for faith;
   17:7–10—Humility of the unprofitable servant;
     17:11–19—A thankful Samaritan;
      17:20–37—Last things;

Audience analysis isolates 17:22–18:8 as an instructional discourse concerning eschatological themes. Nevertheless, Luke has left several clues that the juxtaposition of vv 20–21 and the ensuing instruction of disciples is no accident. The most obvious link between the two sections is the verbal correspondence of v 21a and v 23a:

17:21a—Nor will they say, "Lo, here!" or "There!"
17:23a—And they will say to you, "Lo, there! Lo, here!"

Moreover, the theme of the coming of the kingdom in 17:20 (ἔρχεται) and of the Son of man in 18:8b (ἐλθών) creates an inclusio setting apart the entire passage. To be sure, vv 20–21 mention the kingdom of God (three times!), while 17:22–18:8 revolves around the day of the Son of man. However, these two concepts are closely related in Luke, as 21:31 (alongside 21:27–28, 36) shows. There Lukan redaction replaces the vague image of the Son of man at the door[133] with the assertion: "The kingdom of God is near." While kingdom language and Son-of-man language are not synonymous in Luke-Acts, it is likely that the two motifs serve to interpret each other in 17:20–18:8.

The precise character of that reciprocal interpretation has been the subject of debate, however. R. J. Sneed, on the one hand, contends that Luke realized that the eschatological discourse of 17:22–37 raises "unsettling" parousia expectations. Luke therefore attached vv 20–21 to the discourse in order to counter harmful apocalyptic speculation by means of a pronouncement on the presence of God's reign.[134] In other words, vv 20–21 function as an "anti-apocalyptic pericope" which neutralizes the apocalyptic stimuli of vv 22–37.[135] Fitzmyer, on the other hand, suggests that Luke's Jesus uses the Pharisees' question as an opportunity to instruct the disciples not only about the kingdom but also about the coming of the Son of man. Luke probably added this "somber eschatological instruction about the day(s) of the Son of man" because of the problem of delay.[136] According to this view, the two

---

18:1–8—The widow and persevering prayer;

18:9–14—Humility of the tax collector.

[133] The text of Mark 13:29b reads simply γινώσκετε ὅτι ἐγγύς ἐστιν ἐπὶ θύραις. The subject of the verb ἐστιν, however, must be the Son of man (13:26).

[134] Sneed summarizes his view in "The Kingdom's Coming: Luke 17,20–21" (Washington, DC: Catholic University of America S.T.D. dissertation, 1962) 134; see also " 'The Kingdom of God is within You' (Lk 17,21)," *CBQ* 24 (1962) 363–82, 380–81.

[135] "Kingdom," 381. Cf. the similar treatment in R. H. Gause, "The Lukan Transfiguration Account: Luke's Pre-Crucifixion Presentation of the Exalted Lord in the Glory of the Kingdom of God" (Atlanta: Emory University Ph.D. dissertation, 1975) 143. Gause argues that, as vv 20–21 combat a faulty apocalypticism on the part of the Pharisees, so vv 22–37 correct the same error in the Christian community. Cf. also Kaestli, *Eschatologie,* 30.

[136] *Luke,* 2.1167. Conzelmann, *St. Luke* (122–23) views vv 22–37 as interpretation of the preceding teaching. The shift in audience does not indicate a transition to a new theme.

sections do not oppose but rather supplement each other.

Only careful exegesis of the passage as a whole can answer the question of the relationship between vv 20-21 and the balance of the discourse. The point established at this juncture is that our examination of the eschatological discourse must include vv 20-21, even though, on the basis of the distinction in addressees, these verses fall outside the discourse proper. Despite diverse origin,[137] these traditional materials have been woven by Luke into one unit treating eschatological themes.[138]

Our interpretation of the meaning and literary function of 17:20-18:8 must be guided by its placement in the gospel narrative. This passage is the second of three large blocks of eschatological teachings located within the travel narrative.[139] In addition, as recently as 17:11 Luke has reminded the reader of Jesus' destination, Jerusalem. In view of 9:31 and 13:31-35,[140] the association of that city with Jesus' impending rejection and death is clear. Moreover, Jesus' confrontation with the Pharisees has continued unabated, if indeed it has not escalated throughout the "journey."[141] Significantly, 14:1-24, set in the house of a

---

[137] According to Zmijewski, the materials of 17:20-37 may be assigned to Luke's sources as follows: Special Luke, vv 20b, 21b; Q, vv 23-4, 26-7, possibly 28-30, 34-5, and 37b; Mark, vv 31, 33. The remaining materials Zmijewski ascribes to Lukan composition (a convenient summary in *Eschatologiereden*, 520). R. Schnackenburg's analysis is similar, although he is more inclined than Zmijewski to find Q traditions in the passage. Schnackenburg apportions vv 20b-21, 23-4, 26-30, 33, 34-5, 37b to Q ("Der eschatologische Abschnitt Lk 17,20-37," in *Mélanges Bibliques* [Gembloux: Duculot, 1970] 213-34).

[138] For convenience, Luke 17:20-18:8 will occasionally (e.g., in the section heading above) be referred to simply as an eschatological discourse. Properly speaking, as the discussion above has shown, this passage unites a piece of dialogue and a discourse. Advocates of the unity of 17:20-18:8 (at the level of Lukan composition) include: Zmijewski, *Eschatologiereden*, 341; Kaestli, *Eschatologie*, 28; B. Noack, *Das Gottesreich bei Lukas: Eine Studie zur Luk. 17,20-24* (Uppsala: Gleerup, 1948) 40; cf. Schneider, *Parusiegleichnisse*, 75.

[139] In addition to Luke 12, the travel narrative contains 19:11-27, which clarifies the connection between Jesus' journey to Jerusalem, culminating in his rejection and death, and God's kingdom. For recent study of the travel narrative in Luke, see H. Egelkraut, *Jesus' Mission to Jerusalem: A Redaction Critical Study of the Travel Narrative in the Gospel of Luke, Lk 9:51-19:48* (Bern/Frankfurt: Lang, 1976); and D. P. Moessner, "Luke 9:1-50: Luke's Preview of the Journey of the Prophet Like Moses of Deuteronomy," *JBL* 102 (1983) 575-605.

[140] Egelkraut terms this the center of the travel narrative (*Travel*, 177-78).

[141] R. Brawley ("The Pharisees in Luke-Acts: Luke's Address to the Jews and His Irenic Purpose" [Princeton: Princeton Theological Seminary Ph.D. dissertation, 1978]) minimizes the conflict at this point. But Egelkraut (*Travel*) has succeeded in demonstrating that Luke locates most of his polemical material within the travel narrative. Egelkraut concludes that Luke has employed the journey framework to place Jesus in confrontation with Israel. The travel narrative relates Jesus' challenge to Israel, Israel's rejection of Jesus, and her own rejection in turn (summarized on pp. 213-14). This formulation of the

Pharisee[142] culminated in the parable of a great banquet whose invited guests decline to appear and so exclude themselves from the supper (vv 16–24).[143] The parables of chapter 15 justified Jesus' conduct against the criticisms of Pharisees and scribes. Luke 16:14–29 placed Pharisees in the ranks of those who reject the law and the prophets, bringing upon themselves eternal judgment.[144] Luke continues this confrontation between Jesus and the Pharisees in 17:20–21, resuming it again in 18:9–14. Not only their exclusivism and self-assurance but also their kingdom-expectations require correction. As in 11:14–32, but now in condensed form, Jesus in 17:20–21 upbraids kingdom-watching that is predicated upon the observation of signs and so misses the present activity of the kingdom in Jesus' ministry of healing.[145] After this polemical piece[146] which creates the occasion for eschatological teaching, Luke places a series of admonitions designed to equip the disciples (and therefore Luke's community) for the future arrival of the Son of man (17:22–18:8), whose kingdom has already issued its claim in the present (vv 20–21).

The travel narrative serves to cement the division within Israel precipitated

---

function of the journey is too one-sided; it neglects the positive role often given to the Jewish people in the story, as well as the overarching "restoration of Israel" motif that runs throughout Luke-Acts. Egelkraut is as vulnerable to the methodological criticism of selectivity as is Jervell, whom Egelkraut faults for his failure to consider the travel narrative. The rejection and restoration motifs — otherwise stated, the patterns of discontinuity and continuity between Israel and church — must both be given full weight.

[142] Note the use of παρατηρέω in 14:1, anticipating the noun παρατήρησις in 17:20. The participle παρατηρούμενοι in 14:1 has the connotation of a malicious observation: see Farrell, "Perspective," 54; Sneed, "Coming," 58–63.

[143] The striking correspondence between 14:11 ("everyone who exalts himself will be humbled, and one who humbles himself will be exalted") and 18:14 ("everyone of you who exalts himself will be humbled, but one who humbles himself will be exalted") should not escape notice. In each case, the context of eschatological division highlights the judgment-provoking self-assurance which Luke associates with the Pharisees.

[144] Note the conjunction of Jesus' indictment of the Pharisees as lovers of money (16:14) and the assertion of the lasting validity of the law and prophets (16:16–18), corresponding to the following parable's picture of a rich man who has scorned the teaching of the law and prophets (16:19–31).

[145] Luke 11:20: "If by the finger of God I cast out demons, then the kingdom of God has come upon you (ἔφθασεν ἐφ' ὑμᾶς)." Note the healing of ten lepers immediately before the Pharisees' question in 17:20.

[146] Cf. Schnackenburg, "Abschnitt," 215–16; F. Mussner, " 'Wann kommt das Reich Gottes?' Die Antwort Jesu nach Lk 17,20b.21," BZ N.F. 6 (1962) 107–11. For a different view, see A. Strobel, "Zu Lk 17,20f.," BZ N.F. 7 (1963) 111–13; Ernst, Herr, 59. Ernst opposes a polemical reading of v 21 over against the question of v 20a: the ἐντὸς ὑμῶν clearly answers the question of "When?" with "jetzt schon." However, Ernst goes on to assert that entrance into life in Luke-Acts is determined in the present, a fact that unmasks as wrong all questions about "When?" (including that of the Pharisees).

by Jesus' advent![147] Luke 19:11-27 will interpret one side of that division as culpable rejection of Jesus' kingship. Luke 17:22-18:8, in the form of paraenetic instruction for the disciples (community), places that division in the context of the eschaton itself. Although this discourse develops the theme of the parousia with a fullness unparalleled elsewhere in Luke-Acts, it does not stand in isolation from the surrounding narrative. It warns the disciples (believers) to be prepared for the day of the Son of man (as did Luke 12), but, in its portrayal of the events of that day, it also accents the finality of the judgment and redemption that accompany the division effected by Jesus' ministry.

2. Luke 17:20-21 and the Kingdom of God in Luke-Acts

a. Luke 17:20-21

Few passages within the Lukan corpus have proven as elusive as Luke 17:20-21.[148] The occurrence of two Lukan *hapax legomena,* the noun παρατήρησις (v 20) and the preposition ἐντός (v 21)—neither of which is transparent in sense—poses particularly difficult interpretive problems. In addition, the relationship between this pericope's assertions (two negative, one positive) about the kingdom of God and the overall Lukan conception of the kingdom is a complex question. The text of vv 20-21 reads:

Ἐπερωτηθεὶς δὲ ὑπὸ τῶν Φαρισαίων πότε ἔρχεται ἡ Βασιλεία τοῦ Θεοῦ
ἀπεκρίθη αὐτοῖς καὶ εἶπεν·
  οὐκ ἔρχεται ἡ βασιλεία τοῦ Θεοῦ μετὰ παρατηρήσεως,
  οὐδὲ ἐροῦσιν· ἰδοὺ ὧδε ἢ ἐκεῖ,
  ἰδοὺ γὰρ ἡ βασιλεία τοῦ Θεοῦ ἐντὸς ὑμῶν ἐστιν.

Verse 20a is almost certainly from the hand of Luke![149] The insertion of

---

[147] Recall the prophecy of Simeon, Luke 2:34-35; and the inaugural episode at Nazareth, 4:16-30. See Egelkraut's sharp statement of this view in *Travel,* 133-34. Egelkraut argues that Luke addresses differing eschatological perspectives to the two groups that emerge in the course of the narrative. When speaking to opponents, Jesus issues an urgent summons to repentance in view of imminent catastrophe. To the disciples (e.g., in 12:35-48) Jesus emphasizes delay and the dangers of indolence (p. 162; cf. 193-94). Johnson (*Possessions,* 107-12) also notes the alternation of teaching material in the travel narrative. He concludes that "the core of the faithful people is being prepared on the road to Jerusalem," even as "those who are going to reject are rejecting" Jesus (p. 112).

[148] For orientation to the exegetical problems, and to the history of research, consult Noack, *Gottesreich,* 3-38; Sneed, "Coming"; Zmijewski, *Eschatologiereden,* 332-96; Fitzmyer, *Luke,* 2.1157-63.

[149] So Geiger, *Endzeitreden,* 32; Zmijewski, *Eschatologiereden,* 381-82; Fitzmyer, *Luke,* 2.1159; Schnackenburg, "Abschnitt," 217. Sneed, on the other hand, contends that "the brevity and compactness of Lk 17,20a . . . suggests that Lk 17,20f. is one of those instances in which Lk has transmitted what he received without literary alteration" ("Coming," 118). Sneed prefers to see vv 20-21 as a unified pronouncement story of Palestinian origin.

introductory questions is a common feature of Lukan composition.[150] The content of this indirect question is especially significant; on three other occasions Luke sets the stage for eschatological teaching with questions or suppositions about the timing of the kingdom's appearance (19:11; 21:7 [from Mark]; and Acts 1:6). It is also typical Lukan composition to juxtapose within the travel narrative sections featuring Pharisees and disciples.[151] Identification of v 20a as Lukan redaction will supply a key to unlock the meaning (in the Lukan context) of μετὰ παρατηρήσεως, one of the enigmatic expressions in the pericope.

With the exception of a (later) occurrence in Aquila's translation of Exod 12:42, the noun παρατήρησις appears nowhere else in the Greek Bible. Farrell has therefore proposed to interpret the term in the light of Luke's use of the verb παρατηρέω, which does occur in Luke 6:7; 14:1; 20:20; and Acts 9:24.[152] In each instance, the verb connotes a malicious watching directed at Jesus (or Paul). Farrell's proposal gains plausibility when we find the Pharisees as subject of the verb παρατηρέω on two of the four occasions (6:7; 14:1).[153] The combination in Luke 11:14-32 of the motifs of hostile watching and signs from heaven — although the verb παρατηρέω does not appear — further supports this view.[154] According to Farrell, μετὰ παρατηρήσεως in 17:20 means "with malicious observation." The point of the verses is, as in 11:14-32, that Jesus refuses to give signs to people who do not accept him and the signs that he does perform.[155]

This recognition of the nuance of hostility which colors the idea of "observation" in Luke-Acts should not be ignored. At the same time, *Luke's* introduction of Jesus' saying with a question about the "When?" of the kingdom indicates that Luke understands παρατήρησις along the lines of the Hellenistic usage of the noun denoting astronomical observation — that is, scanning the heavens for premonitory signs.[156] The force of this first negative assertion about

---

[150] See, e.g., Luke 13:23, 17:37; 20:13; 24:5; Acts 1:6; cf. Luke 14:15; 19:11. Cf. Geiger, *Endzeitreden,* 32.

[151] Cf. the inversion-arrangement of 17:20-18:14, noted above, and the alternation of audiences in 11:37-54 (Pharisees and lawyers), 12:1-53 (disciples [plus crowd]); 13:31-14:24 (Pharisees), 14:25-35 (crowd [on discipleship]); 15:1-32 (Pharisees and scribes); 16:1-13 (disciples); 16:14-31 (Pharisees), 17:1-10 (disciples). See also Zmijewski, *Eschatologiereden,* 381-82.

[152] See Farrell, "Perspective," 54-56. Only two other occurrences in the New Testament: Mark 3:2 (a parallel to Luke 6:7; however, Luke has added explicit mention of the Pharisees and scribes to Mark's version!); and Gal 4:10.

[153] The hostile observers in Luke 20:20 are the scribes and chief priests.

[154] Also noted by Farrell ("Perspective," 55-56).

[155] Ibid., 56.

[156] See, e.g., Mussner, "Wann;" A. Rüstow, "ENTOC YMWN ECTIN, zur Deutung von Lc 17 20-21," *ZNW* 51 (1960) 197-224; Fitzmyer, *Luke,* 2.1160. Even A. Strobel, who argues energetically for the meaning "religious observance," concedes that the sense "heavenly observation" has the weight in extra-biblical literature ("Die Passa-Erwartung als urchristliches Problem in Lc 17 20f.," *ZNW* 49 [1958] 157-96).

the kingdom would then be: God's kingdom does not come accompanying the search for signs that would announce its arrival. "Star-gazing" is a human activity; the advent of the kingdom is an event independent of human activity — including prediction — and dependent only upon the divine will (cf. Acts 1:7). Therefore, this part of Jesus' answer to the question about the timing of the kingdom rejects the question on principle. Unlike the weather (cf. 12:54–56), the future consummation of the kingdom cannot be accurately forecast. Nevertheless, even as 12:54–56 challenged the crowds to discern the καιρός that had appeared unrecognized among them, so 17:20–21 presses beyond a denial of the possibility of forecasting the kingdom to redirect the Pharisees' gaze to a kingdom in some sense present — though undetected by them (v 21b)![157]

Luke 17:20 rejects all endeavors to forecast the advent of the kingdom of God by sign-watching. This posture is consistent with the thrust of Luke 12:35–48 (with respect to the coming of the Son of man);[158] together with its theological foundation expressed in Acts 1:6–8. That is, the Father has determined the chronology; human beings cannot know it. Luke 17:21a ("Nor will they say, 'Lo, here!' or 'There!' ") brings geographical considerations into the picture. Jesus opposes not only temporal but also geographical pinpointing of the kingdom's arrival. The kingdom of God cannot be localized[159] — except,

---

[157] Grässer (*Problem,* 193–94) points out the contrast between 17:20–21 and 21:29–31. In the latter passage Luke takes up a tradition that affirmed visible signs preceding the End. The Lukan resolution of this tension appears to be that the final cosmic signs preceding the parousia of the Son of man augur an imminent denouement — which is a basis for reassurance for believers — yet do not pinpoint its arrival. The attempt by Strobel, in several articles, to establish the meaning "religious observance" for παρατήρησις in 17:20 has persuaded few interpreters ("Passa-Erwartung;" "A. Merx über Lc 17,20f.," *ZNW* 51 [1960] 133–34; "In dieser Nacht [Luk 17,34]," *ZTK* 58 [1961] 16–29; "Lk 17,20f."). Fitzmyer (*Luke,* 2.1160) labels Strobel's thesis as eisegetical; Schneider (*Parusiegleichnisse,* 39–41) finds it "interesting" but lacking in evidence. Strobel ("Passa-Erwartung," 161–83) places Luke's use of the term παρατήρησις within the context of Jewish calendrical-liturgical practice, specifically the Passover (the "night of observation"). In Strobel's judgment, the use of παρατήρησις in Exod 12:42 (Aquila, cf. Theodotion [*observationis noctem*] and Symmachus [παρατετρημένη]) speaks for its status as a technical term ("Passa-Erwartung," 172). The noun points to Jewish eschatological expectation associated with the night of Passover. According to Strobel, therefore, Luke 17:20–21 corrects early Jewish and Jewish-Christian popular eschatological expectation which fixed the parousia on the evening of Passover ("Passa-Erwartung," 175, 182–83). Since Luke has composed vv 20–21 (in Strobel's view), this polemic against Passover eschatology comes from Luke himself. The primary — and decisive — objection to Strobel's hypothesis is his reliance upon late texts to establish the existence of a firm popular expectation linked to Passover prior to Luke.

[158] See especially 12:40, 46, and recall the discussion above. This is another indication of the close relationship between the kingdom of God and the coming of the Son of man in Luke-Acts.

[159] To the extent that Luke 17:22–37 interprets vv 20–21, Luke explains this denial of any localization of the kingdom by affirming its *ubiquity* (cf. especially 17:24, 26–27, 37).

that is, in its association with the figure of Jesus (v 21b).

Verse 21b appends a positive statement to the first two negations: "For look! the kingdom of God is ἐντὸς ὑμῶν." The meaning of this much-discussed statement[160] revolves around the sense of the preposition ἐντός, which in the New Testament occurs only here and in Matt 23:26.[161] The classical usage of ἐντός is both spatial and relational; it indicates location within or inside certain limits (specified by the dependent genitive).[162] The meaning "inside you (Pharisees)" falters on two impediments. First, nowhere else in Luke-Acts is the kingdom of God described as an inward, spiritual reality. Second, the object of the preposition (= the Pharisees) is incompatible with that reading, for Luke has portrayed the Pharisees in an increasingly negative light in the travel narrative.[163] The context, the contours of Luke's view of the kingdom, and the presence of a plural object of the preposition combine to dictate the translation "among you" or "in your midst." The existence of something within the limits of a collectivity does not necessarily imply its presence inside the individuals who compose the collectivity. While ἐντός with a plural object is uncommon in classical usage, the reading "among" or "in the midst of" is attested.[164]

---

[160] A sampling of studies: Noack, *Gottesreich;* Sneed, "Coming"; Rüstow, "ENTOC;" R. H. Hiers, "Why Will They Not Say, 'Lo, here!' Or 'There!'?," *JAAR* 35 (1967) 379–84; Mussner, "Wann;" C. H. Roberts, "The Kingdom of Heaven (Lk. XVII.21)," *HTR* 41 (1948) 1–8; A. Sledd, "The Interpretation of Luke xvii.21," *ExpTim* 50 (1938) 235–37; J. G. Griffiths, "ἐντὸς ὑμῶν (Luke xvii.21)," *ExpTim* 63 (1951) 30–31; P. M. S. Allen, "Luke xvii.21," *ExpTim* 49 (1937) 476–77; Allen, "Luke xvii.21," *ExpTim* 50 (1938) 233–35; H. Riesenfeld, "Gudrisket — har eller där, mitt ibland människor ellor inom dem? Till Luk 17:20–21," *Svensk Exegetisk Årsbok* 47 (1982) 93–101; Fitzmyer, *Luke,* 2.1160–62.

[161] Properly speaking, ἐντός is an adverb of place, but it is frequently used (as in Luke 17:21) as a preposition. The usage in Matt 23:26 is as a noun: "The inside of the cup."

[162] See the discussion in Sneed, "Coming," 72; Sledd, "Interpretation," 236; Fitzmyer, *Luke,* 2.1160–62; Roberts, "Heaven," 3. Roberts concludes from a survey of the usage of ἐντός in the papyri that "the function of ἐντός is to include or to limit; it implies the existence of something outside with which its object is contrasted" (p. 3). In addition to the dominant local sense, ἐντός occasionally has a temporal sense or points to a limiting sum of money.

[163] Similarly Fitzmyer, *Luke,* 2.1161.

[164] See Xenophon, *Anab.,* 1.10,3; *Hellen.,* 2.3,19; Herodotus, *Hist.,* 7.100,3. For example, the text of Xenophon, *Hellen.,* 2.3,19 runs: ὥσπερ τοῦ ἀριθμοῦ τοῦτον ἔχοντά τινα ἀνάγκην καλοὺς καὶ ἀγαθοὺς εἶναι, καὶ οὔτ' ἔξω τούτων σπουδαίους οὔτ' ἐντὸς τούτων πονηροὺς οἶόν τε εἴη γενέσθαι (translation: "as though this number were of necessity good and true persons, and there could neither be excellent persons outside this group nor wicked persons within it [among them]"). On the other hand, in Plato, *Laws,* 789A, ἐντός with a different plural genitive must mean "inside": οὐδαμῶς γε, ἀλλ' ἔτι καὶ πρότερον τοῖς ἐντὸς τῶν αὐτῶν μητέρων τρεφομένοις (translation: "no, even earlier [we shall prescribe it] for those nourished inside their mothers[' bodies]"). The nature of the dependent genitive and the larger context are important considerations in the attempt to define the function of ἐντός in a given case.

It is often objected against the translation "in your midst" in Luke 17:21 that Luke would have written ἐν μέσῳ had he intended that meaning (e.g., Rüstow, "ENTOC," 213; Allen,

Jesus, then, issues in verse 21b a mandate to the Pharisees to look around them in order to discern the kingdom already at work in their midst![165] In the light of v 20b, the implied continuation of the saying is: "(Look! The kingdom of God is among you) *and you do not observe it.*"[166] The kingdom is not discernible with the mode of observation practiced by the Pharisees (nor by the crowds in 11:14–32).

The force of Luke 17:20–21 is to reject a particular brand of eschatological expectation, which searches for God's kingdom everywhere except where it is actually operative! The effort to pinpoint the date or locale of its manifestation misconstrues the nature of the kingdom. More to the point, because Jesus' hearers (the Pharisees; in chapter 11 the crowd) refuse to recognize the present activity of the kingdom in Jesus' teaching and healing ministry, they will not discern the future coming of the kingdom. How does this interpretation of vv 20–21 cohere with the general perspective on the kingdom of God in Luke-Acts?

b. *The Kingdom of God in Luke-Acts*

The complex picture of the kingdom in Luke-Acts has prompted a wide

---

"Luke xvii.21" [1937] 476). However, given the likelihood that Luke has taken up this word from his source (it is his only use of ἐντός), that argument is not decisive.

[165] The saying thus approximates in function Jesus' claim in 11:20 ("If by the finger of God I cast out demons, then the kingdom of God has come upon you"); so also Fitzmyer, *Luke,* 2.1159. In order to preserve a strictly future appearance of the kingdom in Luke, some commentators have urged that the force of the present ἐστιν be minimized. After all, in Aramaic future and present forms of the copula are not to be distinguished (cf. W. G. Kümmel, *Promise and Fulfillment,* 34–35). Verse 21b asserts, then, that at some future date the kingdom will come *suddenly* (see, e.g., Mattill, *Last,* 203; cf. Hiers, "Why," 383). Rüstow ("ENTOC," 212) rightly rejects this interpretation because it imports the most important idea (suddenness) into the text; without it, the future reading of the saying becomes a tautology.

[166] This reading of the saying approximates the form taken by the tradition in logion 113 of the Gospel of Thomas: "[Jesus'] disciples said to him, 'When will the kingdom come?' [Jesus said,] 'It will not come by waiting for it. It will not be a matter of saying "Here it is" or "There it is." Rather, the kingdom of the Father is spread out upon the earth, and people do not see it.' " Interestingly enough, while logion 113 supports the reading of ἐντὸς ὑμῶν as "in your midst," the other form of the tradition in logion 3 of the Gospel of Thomas lends support to the translation "inside": ". . . Rather, the kingdom is inside of you, and it is outside of you. When you come to know yourselves. . . ." Nevertheless, this version of Jesus' saying conforms to the tendency of the Gospel of Thomas toward interiorization, and therefore attests *an* early Christian understanding of the saying preserved in Luke 17:21, but not necessarily Luke's understanding of it. Both logia from the Gospel of Thomas presuppose a present rather than future manifestation of the kingdom (that, too, is consistent with the tendencies of that document, however).

range of interpretations![167] A distinctive feature of the Lukan presentation of the kingdom is its association with verbs of proclamation. Fully one-fourth of all Lukan occurrences of the expression "kingdom of God" take this form![168] This phenomenon leads Conzelmann to distinguish between the message of the kingdom and the kingdom itself. While the proclamation of the kingdom takes place in the present, after its initiation by Jesus (16:16), the kingdom itself remains a future entity![169]

This two-sided image of the kingdom, as both present and future, is an aspect of the Lukan portrayal of the kingdom[170] that has evoked various explanations. Several scholars contend that the kingdom itself — not just its "picture" or "message" (Conzelmann) — is present in the person and activity of Jesus. Wieser goes so far as to claim that Luke identifies the kingdom with the person of Jesus. After the ascension, Jesus is present from heaven (as the enthroned king), so that the presence of the kingdom continues in the life of the church![171]

---

[167] Significant studies of Luke's presentation of the kingdom include: Noack, *Gottesreich,* 45–49; Conzelmann, *St. Luke,* 113–19(-125); T. Wieser, "Kingdom and Church in Luke-Acts" (New York: Union Theological Seminary Th.D. dissertation, 1962); E. E. Johnson, "A Study of ΒΑΣΙΛΕΙΑ ΤΟΥ ΘΕΟΥ in the Gospel of Luke" (Dallas: Dallas Seminary Th.D. dissertation, 1968); Farrell, "Perspective" (see, e.g., 21–25, 32–46, 65–72, 83–86); Gause, "Transfiguration" (see, e.g., 73–74, 85, 106, 133–38, 178, 185–86, 193, 204); M. Völkel, "Zur Deutung des 'Reiches Gottes' bei Lukas," *ZNW* 65 (1974) 57–70; O. Merk, "Das Reich Gottes in den lukanischen Schriften," in *Jesus und Paulus,* ed. E. E. Ellis and E. Grässer (Göttingen: Vandenhoeck and Ruprecht, 1975) 201–20; Mattill, *Last,* especially 158–207.

[168] With εὐαγγελίζεσθαι: Luke 4:43; 8:1; 16:16; Acts 8:12. With κηρύσσειν: Luke 8:1; 9:2; Acts 20:25; 28:31. With various other verbs of speaking: Luke 9:11; 9:60; Acts 1:3; 19:8; 28:23. See Merk, "Reich," 204–5. The data lead Merk to conclude that Luke has deliberately formulated this language of kingdom-proclamation. Völkel ("Deutung," 70) explains this transposition into the terminology of proclamation as a corollary of Luke's "individualizing of ecclesiology." The nationally colored salvation hope depicted in Luke 1–2 is definitively liquidated as emphasis shifts to the conversion of the individual. Not Gentiles but believing individuals from both Jewish and Gentile spheres take the place of the Jews. Völkel's reduction of eschatological themes to the status of the individual does not do justice to the persisting collective eschatology in Luke-Acts. Nor may Luke 1–2 be dispensed with so off-handedly.

[169] Conzelmann, *St. Luke,* 117, 122.

[170] On the kingdom as present and future in Jesus' own proclamation, see, e.g., Kümmel, *Promise;* E. P. Sanders, *Jesus and Judaism* (Philadelphia: Fortress, 1985) 150–56.

[171] "Kingdom," 27, 55, 70–74. In Wieser's view, the heightening of the miraculous in the narrative of Acts stems from Luke's "attempt to give expression to the basic theme of Acts, the presence and power of the kingdom" (74). Acts differs from the gospel in that now the kingdom is present *in power.* This approach contrasts with Conzelmann's epochal understanding (in which the kingdom-picture is present during the period of Jesus, but not during the time of the church).

Noack, on the other hand, speaks of two appearances of the kingdom. With Jesus' activity, the kingdom actually exists on earth; it remains present as long as Jesus is on earth. Between resurrection and parousia, however, the church awaits the final manifestation of the kingdom. According to Noack, if the tension between a present and future kingdom in Luke-Acts stems in part from divergent traditions incorporated by Luke, nonetheless he has provided a positive interpretation of that tension.[172] Farrell offers a similar view: Luke perceives the kingdom of God as present in a non-transcendent and non-apocalyptic manner in the person of Jesus, yet Luke emphasizes the present reality of the kingdom precisely in order to strengthen faith in its future manifestation.[173] Gause matches the complexity of kingdom-data in Luke-Acts with a sophisticated, three-level presentation of the kingdom. First, the kingdom is manifest in Jesus' activity, and later in the work of the Spirit. Second, the kingdom will appear at the parousia of the Son of man. Third, the ultimate manifestation of the kingdom is at its consummation, one step beyond the parousia, when the kingdom of God will gather around the exalted Messiah.[174] While the ascension prefigures the *coming* of the kingdom at the parousia, the transfiguration anticipates the established kingdom-in-consummation.[175] With this three-dimensional picture of the kingdom, Luke holds the present and future aspects of the kingdom in tension throughout Luke-Acts![176]

This survey of opinions outlines the dimensions of the problem. If Gause's thesis goes too far in systematizing the data, how may these diverse elements in Luke's presentation of the kingdom of God be assembled, yet without over-simplification or truncation? Given the pivotal role played in this discussion by Luke 17:20–21, as a passage affirming the presence of the kingdom, the issue requires fresh examination. The balance of the section aims to clarify the Lukan conception of the kingdom through a study of the pertinent texts.

It is crucial, at the outset, to adopt an appropriate method for gathering data. The temptation to restrict the probe to passages in which the term appears must be resisted. Rather, the relation of the concept of kingdom to the dynamics of the entire narrative of Luke-Acts must be considered. In particular, the study

---

[172] See the discussion in Noack, *Gottesreich,* 45–49. Noack shares with Conzelmann the denial of the kingdom's presence in the period of the church, but he shares with Wieser the conviction that the kingdom itself (not its "image") is present in connection with Jesus.

[173] "Perspective," 24–25, 46. Farrell understands the Lukan transfiguration account as a proleptic manifestation of the future kingdom, confirming the present, non-glorious appearance of the kingdom and assuring the certainty of the future, apocalyptic manifestation of the kingdom. Merk ("Reich") also stresses the presence of the kingdom in the person and activity of the Lukan Jesus; one sentence in his article does indicate, though, that Merk recognizes the kingdom as still future (with reference to Acts 14:22). Merk does not attempt to integrate the two conceptions.

[174] Gause, "Transfiguration," 135, 185–86.

[175] Ibid., 204–08.

[176] Ibid., 137–38.

must recognize the role played by Jesus' exaltation (resurrection/ascension), as interpreted in Peter's Pentecost speech (especially Acts 2:30–36). Due to the limits of space, I do not attempt a comprehensive survey; instead, I sketch what I perceive to be the most important features in Luke's presentation of the kingdom.

I. The Giving/Receiving of the Kingdom

Although the theme is not unique to Luke, the language of giving and receiving the kingdom is prominent in LukeActs![177] Particularly significant for the dynamics of the narrative are four texts: Luke 1:32–33; 19:11–27 (12, 15); 22:28–30 (29); and Acts 2:30–36. Gabriel announced to Mary that, in fulfillment of scriptural promise, "the Lord God will give to [Jesus] the throne of David his father, and he will rule over the house of Jacob forever; and there will be no end to his kingdom" (Luke 1:32–33). The beginning of Luke's story identifies Jesus as Israel's awaited king; he will receive from God an unending kingdom. The annunciation does not specify just when the coronation will occur. Acts 2:30–36 supplies Luke's answer to that question. By virtue of his resurrection, the crucified Jesus has been exalted to God's right hand (2:33–35). This exaltation constitutes Jesus' taking up the throne of David (2:30).[178]

Luke's composition of the parable of the pounds in 19:11–27 confirms this picture. The introduction (v 11) and the creation of a hybrid story containing the sub-plot of the throne claimant (vv 12b, 14, 15a, 27) enable Luke to use the parable to interpret the impending events at Jerusalem. The throne claimant (Jesus) must journey to a distant country (heaven) in order to receive his kingdom. However, citizens within his domain (Jews of Jerusalem) contest the rightful claim of the king (reject Jesus and crucify him). Their imminent destruction is sure. *This* is the detour by which Jesus will arrive at his throne; the kingdom of God will not put in an immediate appearance, as the approach to Jerusalem had led some to suppose (v 11).[179] These three passages (Luke 1:32–33; 19:11–27; Acts 2:30–36) all presuppose that the kingdom (specifically, sovereign rule over Israel, in fulfillment of the ancient promise to David) is God's to bestow. God has given that kingdom to Jesus, *after* his rejection and passion at Jerusalem; the resurrection and subsequent ascension to heaven represent Jesus' enthronement.

---

[177] The pertinent texts are: Luke 1:32–33; 8:10; 12:32; 18:17, 29–30; 19:12, 15; 22:29; Acts 2:30–36. Luke takes up the image of giving and receiving from Mark in 8:10; 18:17, 29–30. He introduces the motif into the Q passage in 22:29 (διατίθημι). The remaining instances are peculiar to Luke.

[178] And it serves the function of authorizing Jesus' pouring out of the Spirit at Pentecost (2:33b; contrast 2:17, where—and "God" is inserted into the Joel-citation—God is the source of the Spirit).

[179] L. T. Johnson has contested this exegesis of Luke 19:11–27 ("The Lukan Kingship Parable," *NovT* 24 [1982] 139–59). Our own detailed treatment of this passage below will consider Johnson's position.

Luke 22:28–30, in the setting of Jesus' last meal with his apostles, indicates that Jesus confers a share in his rule upon each of the apostles:

> But you are the ones who have remained with me in my trials; and I confer upon you—even as my Father has conferred upon me—a kingdom, so that you may eat and drink at my table, and sit on thrones judging the twelve tribes of Israel![180]

The Lukan presentation of the kingdom is inextricably bound to the motif of Israel. Jesus fulfills Israel's hope as its rightful king, yet his kingship is in large measure rejected by the Jewish people. The apostles supplant the Jewish leaders, who are instrumental in orchestrating Jesus' rejection and crucifixion, as authorized "judges" over Israel![181] While this process of Israel's "restoration" has already begun in Acts, the final establishment of the kingdom remains an eschatological hope![182]

II. Participation in the Kingdom: Division and Reversal

This connection between the themes of kingdom and Israel in Luke-Acts expresses itself in a second category of kingdom texts, those concerning the composition of the kingdom. Indeed, almost half of all occurrences of the term "kingdom" focus on kingdom participation, nearly always in conjunction with the motifs of division and reversal![183] A programmatic series of texts, all linked

---

[180] Although this is Q tradition (cf. Matt 19:28), Luke has reworked it carefully in order to conform it to the dynamics of his story. Luke's version does not specify twelve thrones, because the twelfth apostle (Judas' successor) is yet to be designated. The language of transfer of power (διατίθημι) is present only in Luke.

[181] Cf. Johnson, *Possessions*, 119–20. The motif of judgment exercised over the nations appears, e.g., in Dan 7:22; Wis 3:8; 1 Cor 6:2–3; and cf. the Matthean parallel (19:28).

[182] Cf. Acts 1:6–8; 3:19–26.

[183] I include in this category 4:43–44 (with its close verbal links to 4:16–19); 6:20; 7:28; 8:10; 9:27; 9:60, 62; 10:9, 11; 11:20; 13:28, 29; 14:15[16–24]; 16:16; 18:16, 17 in contrast with 18:24, 25; 19:12, 15; 19:38 [βασιλεύς]; 21:31 (what is ἐγγύς is redemption for believers [21:28], but desolation for Jerusalem [21:20]); Acts 14:22 [θλίψεις implies opposition and division]; and a series of Passion narrative texts revolving around Jesus' kingship: 23:3, 37, 38, 42. These kingdom participation/division texts often use the image of "entrance" (i.e., conditions of entry into the kingdom; e.g., 13:29; 16:16; 18:17, 24–25; 23:42; Acts 14:22). While Luke often employs language of "coming" ("going") into the kingdom, the traditional terminology of the "kingdom coming" is rare (11:20 with the verb φθάνων; 17:20 [but expressing a view requiring correction]; 22:18). Conzelmann notes this avoidance of the language of a coming kingdom in Luke (*St. Luke*, 119). Yet it is not correct to say that Luke avoids such terminology, for he has introduced it himself in the composition of 22:18 (this is part of a section, vv 15–18, formulated in parallel symmetry by Luke; see W. Bösen, *Jesusmahl, Eucharistisches Mahl, Endzeitmahl: Ein Beitrag zur Theologie des Lukas* [Stuttgart: Katholisches Bibelwerk, 1980] 22). Rather, Luke prefers the metaphor of going into the kingdom (largely from the pre-Lukan tradition, but see the Lukan formulation of 16:16; 23:42) to that of the kingdom coming (note Luke's redaction in 9:27). What comes is the Son of man.

through verbal echoes, identifies as the beneficiaries of Jesus' ministry the poor, blind, and lame![184] Luke 14–15 makes this locus of Jesus' activity the wedge separating those who participate in the kingdom, namely sinners who accept the invitation into the kingdom by repenting, and those who exclude themselves, namely Pharisees and others who decline the invitation. The banquet parable in Luke 14:16–24 gives the clearest depiction of this kingdom accompanied by division and reversal. The introduction to the parable provided by Luke (14:15) defines the parable as a kingdom parable:

> One of the [Pharisee's] dinner guests . . . said to [Jesus], "Blessed is that one who will eat bread in the kingdom of God."

Jesus' reply is the story of a banquet in which the invited guests, who were preoccupied with routine affairs of daily life and so declined the invitation, were supplanted by the poor, maimed, blind, and lame. Earlier passages have already singled out precisely these persons as the target of Jesus' ministry![185] In the course of Jesus' ministry, the composition of the kingdom is subjected to a radical role reversal, true to the inspired song of Mary (1:51–53).

It is significant that Luke has an individual servant issue the invitations to the banquet in 14:16–24![186] Moreover, that servant extends the invitation with the words, "[The meal] is already prepared" (14:18). These details suggest that Jesus is the one who has invited people to come to the banquet (14:15 = the kingdom of God), and that kingdom is ready! That is, Jesus' activity of healing and teaching has brought to Israel the blessings and claim of the kingdom of God.

Various texts associate Jesus' activity with the kingdom of God and so confirm this exegesis of 14:16–24. The context of several passages ties the kingdom to Jesus' healings and exorcisms![187] Luke 11:20 interprets the exorcisms of Jesus' ministry as the operation of the advancing kingdom:

> "If by the finger of God I cast out demons, then the kingdom of God has come upon you."[188]

---

[184] The key text is 4:16–21(30). This statement of Jesus' mission drawn from Isa 61:1–2 and Isa 58:6 contains the key words εὐαγγελίζομαι, πτωχός, ἀποστέλλω, τυφλός, and κηρύσσω. Luke 4:43–44, capping the first phase of Jesus' execution of that mission, uses the terms εὐαγγελίζομαι, ἀποστέλλω, and κηρύσσω, and characterizes this activity of Jesus as "declaring the good news of the kingdom of God." Luke 6:20–26 presents the Beatitudes as an illustration of εὐαγγελίζεσθαι τὴν Βασιλείαν τοῦ Θεοῦ; the kingdom [picked up from 4:43] belongs to the poor [πτωχός, picked up from 4:18]. Then 7:18–23 (especially v 22) echoes these earlier texts (τυφλός and πτωχός; εὐαγγελίζομαι), adding to them a pastiche of phrases from Isa 29:18; 35:5–6; 42:18; 26:19; and Sir 48:5. The common thread running through all these texts is the designation of the poor and downcast as the particular focus of Jesus' ministry and as recipients of the benefits of the kingdom.

[185] πτωχός: 4:18; 6:20; 7:22; 14:21. τυφλός: 4:18; 7:22; 14:21. χωλός: 7:22; 14:21.

[186] Luke 14:17, 21, 22, 23; similarly in Gospel of Thomas logion 64. Matthew's version has the host send his servants (two delegations; 22:3, 4).

[187] Luke 4:43; 9:2, 11; 10:9, 11; 11:20; 17:20–21.

[188] The verb here is ἔφθασεν, the aorist of φθάνω. For discussion of the meaning of this

Other texts relate the kingdom to meal imagery, in such a way that the meal fellowship that marked Jesus' public career anticipates the kingdom banquet at the consummation.[189] Finally, Luke brings together the concept of the kingdom and Jesus' distinctive activity of teaching and preaching. Through the proclamation by Jesus and his authorized representatives, the claim and offer of the kingdom impinge upon Israel's story and demand a response.[190]

At this point we finally reach the cutting edge of Luke's presentation of the kingdom. Jesus (and his disciples) have, in their preaching and healing ministry, brought to the lowly within Israel the liberation that is a manifestation of the reign of God. At the same time, they have challenged the privileged and powerful to align themselves with the kingdom-message of Jesus. Nevertheless, Jesus and his representatives repeatedly meet rejection. In fact, it is striking how often kingdom terminology is surrounded by an atmosphere of division and rejection.[191] This completes the reversal motif as it shapes the kingdom language in Luke-Acts. The privileged and acceptable refuse the one who brings access to the kingdom of God; they are in turn excluded, their places awarded to the sinners and downtrodden who respond positively (with repentance) to the invitation to the kingdom.

---

word, see Fitzmyer, *Luke,* 2.922; Kümmel, *Promise,* 105–09; K. W. Clark, "Realized Eschatology," *JBL* 59 (1940) 367–83. The Lukan context, which points to the exorcisms as evidence of *God's* kingdom as opposed to the demonic powers, certainly supports the view that the kingdom has extended its sphere of influence into the present of Jesus' ministry. That does not mean, however, that the full realization of God's kingdom is present fact, in the Lukan conception. Passages such as Luke 21:31 and Acts 14:22 oppose such an interpretation.

[189] Luke associates the kingdom and meal imagery in 13:28–29; 14:15–24; 22:16, 18, 30. Here, of course, Luke draws upon widespread Jewish traditions. Bösen (*Jesusmahl,* 73–76) argues that by linking the eucharistic meal to the meal-praxis of Jesus' ministry, Luke in 22:15–18 stresses the continuity between the church of his own day and the time of Jesus. Moreover, for one who participates in the fellowship of the eucharistic meal, the "*Gottesgemeinschaft*" of the end-time is already anticipated here and now.

[190] The relevant texts are: Luke 4:43; 8:1; 9:2, 11, 60; 10:9, 11; 16:16; Acts 1:3; 8:12; 19:8; 20:25; 28:23, 31. The fact that kingdom-proclamation texts dominate the usage in Acts does not mean that the imminent, future kingdom is no longer affirmed. Rather, the focus of kingdom-activity in the present is the summons to respond to God's saving work in Jesus of Nazareth, in such a way that one may come to enjoy the benefits of the consummation of the kingdom inaugurated by him.

[191] E.g.: 9:27, next to 9:26; 7:28, sandwiched between 7:22–23 and 7:29–35; 11:20, in the midst of the controversies of 11:14–32; 13:28–29 (like 14:15–24, a classic expression of the reversal motif, reworked from Q [Matt 8:11–12 has a similar thrust]); 14:15, followed by 14:16–24; 16:16, anticipating the picture of division and reversal in 16:19–31; 18:16–17 as a foil to 18:24–25 (the failure of the rich man to respond to Jesus' challenge); 19:11–27, especially vv 14, 27; 19:38, followed by the rejection of Jesus' kingship on the part of the Pharisees (19:39), then the prophetic lament over Jerusalem's demise (vv 41–44); cf. also 23:37–38; 9:60, 62; 10:9, 11.

c. Summary

This survey of the passages bearing upon the Lukan conception of the kingdom of God yields the following result. Luke ties the kingdom of God closely to the person and activity of Jesus. In his public ministry, Jesus extends the offer and challenge of the kingdom. Participation in the future kingdom of God is decided on just this basis: has one responded positively to Jesus' summons? In the narrative of Acts, the apostles and the mission endorsed by them continue this work. Jesus himself is, by God's act of conferral, the king of Israel; his enthronement occurs only after rejection at Jerusalem, and takes the form of resurrection and exaltation to the right hand of God. The full realization of the kingdom remains a future event; indeed, the worldwide mission of the church among Jews and Gentiles represents an important component of the formation of the eschatological kingdom. Places at the eschatological banquet are still available wherever that mission advances. Yet, the operation of the kingdom in Jesus and his successors elicits not uniform assent, but rather division: some accept the invitation, others exclude themselves. To the extent, therefore, that persons confront in Jesus the decisive point of access to the future kingdom, Luke portrays a kingdom operative in the person of Jesus, the King-designate who journeys toward his enthronement![192]

In the light of this discussion, the interpretation of Luke 17:20-21 advanced above (section C.2.a.) is seen to make sense![193] To Pharisees who have, in the course of the travel narrative, refused to align themselves with Jesus — hence with the kingdom of God — Jesus discounts all attempts to pinpoint the time or place of the kingdom's arrival. The ground of Jesus' negative reply is not only the theological principle of the Father's sovereign freedom, but also (v 21b) the positive claim that the kingdom of God has already exerted itself in the midst of the questioners, in the person and activity of Jesus. "The kingdom is among you [and you do not discern it!]."

[192] Luke's account of the transfiguration is perhaps to be understood in this way. Luke 9:28-36 fulfills the promise of 9:27 ("There are some standing here who will not taste death before they see the kingdom of God"), giving selected disciples a preview of the glory of Jesus exalted to his throne after the exodus to be accomplished at Jerusalem. This exegesis is supported by the following details:

9:26 — Son of man coming *in glory;*
9:27 — some will *see* the kingdom;
9:31-32 — Moses and Elijah *in glory* (Lukan redaction);
9:32 — they *saw* his [Jesus'] glory.

For discussion of the transfiguration in Luke as the fulfillment of the promise in 9:27, see, e.g., Gause, "Transfiguration"; Farrell, "Perspective," 37-44.

[193] Not that I am arguing for a perfect coherence in Luke's presentation of the kingdom. The diverse traditions incorporated by him resist that kind of leveling interpretive approach. My claim is that Luke-Acts betrays a basic pattern, in which the concept of the kingdom of God serves the functions here identified, and which encompasses most of the Lukan kingdom texts.

3. Eschatological Perspective and Situation in Luke 17:22–18:8

Our detailed examination of Luke 17:20–21 in the context of Luke's presentation of the kingdom of God has uncovered the central role played by Jesus. The public ministry of Jesus, extended in Acts by his followers, provides the decisive point of access to the kingdom. At the same time, the consummation of the kingdom of God is a future event. Luke's juxtaposition of 17:20–21 and 17:22–18:8 achieves that same balance, anchoring the kingdom to the person of Jesus in his present encounter with people, yet casting the spotlight on his future advent in redemption and judgment. Given the extent of 17:22–18:8 relative to vv 20–21, it is inconceivable that vv 20–21 function as an anti-apocalyptic pericope neutralizing the apocalyptic stimuli of the ensuing passage![194] Rather, both sections define aspects of Luke's eschatological perspective. The eschaton is future—delayed yet to be expected at any moment—*and* the mandate of faithful living in the present is determinative for one's participation in the blessings of the end-time.

Within 17:22–37 the same picture emerges. On that future "day" when the Son of man will come suddenly, unmistakably, and ubiquitously, the destiny of all people will be determined on the basis of their conduct during the "days" preceding the End. Those diverted from readiness by the routine affairs of life will come to ruin. Our discussion will therefore elaborate first the portrayal of the "day of the Son of man," then the function of the "days of the Son of man" in vv 22–37, before considering the tension between delay and imminence in 17:22–18:8 as a whole. This tension will offer a glimpse of the correlation between eschatology and setting in Luke.

a. The Picture of "The Day of the Son of Man" in Luke 17:22–37

Luke 17:20–21 (in conjunction with other kingdom texts) speaks of a kingdom present in the activity of Jesus, summoning to decision and so provoking a division among human beings. Luke 17:22–37 supplements this picture by placing division in the context of the eschaton. That is, vv 22–37 focus on the future, final separation effected by the glorious return of the Son of man![195] For disciples, who have accepted the offer of the kingdom, but who wait anxiously for its consummation at the parousia, Jesus' teaching gives the proper orientation to the future![196]

---

[194] This is the view of Sneed, Kaestli, and Gause. See the discussion above, section C.1.

[195] Luke 9:26 also affirmed the continuity between one's response to the ministry of Jesus and the eschatological judgment: "For whoever is ashamed of me and my words, the Son of man will be ashamed of him, when he comes in his glory and that of the Father and the holy angels" (Mark 8:38 par.). Cf. Acts 3:22–23, to be discussed in the next chapter.

[196] In the case of the Pharisees, who have not discerned the offer of the kingdom in Jesus' ministry and so have refused his challenge, Jesus' words concern a proper orientation to the present. It is clearly the instruction of the disciples that fits the situation and needs of Luke's church.

Verses 22–37 depict the "day" of the Son of man as a sudden, inescapable, and ubiquitous invasion of the world to effect a final separation among people. The essential criterion of inclusion among the "saved" is single-minded readiness for the appearance of the Son of man. In contrast, other persons are so absorbed in the routines of life that destruction overtakes them unawares![197]

Verse 24 employs the metaphor of lightning for the Son of man on his day:[198]

> For as the lightning when it flashes shines from [one point] under the sky to [another] under the sky, so will the Son of man be on his day.

This image grounds the imperative of v 23 not to stray after persons who localize the kingdom "there" or "here."[199] That is, the saying assumes that the appearance of the Son of man will be everywhere visible, even as lightning illumines the whole sky. There will be no mistaking the advent of the Son of man in glory.[200]

---

[197] In large measure Luke adopts this picture of the end-time from Q (cf. Matt 24:23, 26–28, 37–41), although he fills out the picture with his own traditions or composition so as to pair Lot with Noah (Matthew has only the Noah illustration), and he provides a different example of separation (snatched from bed [v 34] rather than from the field [Matt 24:40]). Because of the method adopted for this study, it is appropriate to consider the discourse as a whole as a vehicle of Luke's eschatological perspective. Signs of Lukan redaction are present throughout (e.g., vv 22, 23b, 25, 32, 33 [choice of verbs], 37a), and the incorporation of Markan tradition (vv 31, 33) into the Q material also indicates Lukan composition. Moreover, the fact that Luke has included such a strong dose of eschatological medicine toward the close of the travel narrative points to its importance in the gospel. I conclude that Luke 17:22–37 describes to the author's satisfaction features of the end-time. However, the pre-Lukan origin of most of the material does mean that caution must be exercised when the question of Luke's situation is raised. Only when clues to that setting find corroboration elsewhere in Luke-Acts may we legitimately infer correlations with Luke's setting (as opposed to pre-Lukan settings).

[198] The phrase "on his day" is textually uncertain, as it is absent in P75 B D it sa. However, the omission of this phrase is explicable on the grounds of homeoteleuton ($-\pi o \upsilon - \tau o \upsilon$), and the juxtaposition of "days" (v 22) and "day" (v 24) of the Son of man is typical of the entire passage.

[199] Note the γάρ. Matthew's version of the Q saying functions similarly (see Matt 24:26–27).

[200] It is possible that lightning's suddenness or unpredictability is also (implicitly) in view. Certainly, vv 26–30 emphasize the unexpected descent of destruction upon the contemporaries of Noah and Lot. But this theme, if present, is at best secondary in v 24. The sudden and unpredictable arrival of the Son of man is a point already established in the discourse of Luke 12 (vv 36–40, 46). What is new in 17:24 is the emphasis upon the universal, unmistakable character of the parousia. Zmijewski (*Eschatologiereden,* 415) also holds that the conjunction of vv 23 and 24 emphasizes less the suddenness than the universal visibility of the parousia event. Zmijewski argues that vv 23–24 assume the identity of Son of man and Messiah, and therefore polemicize against the belief that the appearance of the Son of man will be after the manner of the appearance of the earthly

The Noah and Lot stories (vv 26–30) sharpen this picture of the universal impact of the coming of the Son of man, adding the hues of catastrophic judgment. Verse 27 and v 29 give emphatic final position to the word πάντας:

> Verse 27b: ". . . and the flood came and destroyed all."
> Verse 29b: ". . . fire and brimstone rained from heaven and destroyed all."

Verses 26 and 30 indicate that the advent of the Son of man will have analogous effects. For people who, like the contemporaries of Noah and Lot, proceed through life oblivious to the catastrophe that looms on the horizon, the Son of man will bring with him destruction. The astonishing feature of these verses is the absence of any connection between the demise of the contemporaries of Noah and Lot and the wickedness of those generations. In fact, no mention is made of their sinfulness. Judgment descends upon them, instead, because they are absorbed in the everyday routines of life (eating, drinking, buying, selling, marrying; vv 27, 28).[201] The note of warning for Jesus' disciples (and Luke's church) is clear: readiness for the parousia is crucial; one need not be wicked to meet judgment. The issue is one of orientation toward the coming Son of man, as opposed to the cares and affairs of this life.[202]

The governing motif from v 29 through the end of the passage is "the day." The day on which the Son of man will be revealed (ἀποκαλύπτεται, v 30) will demand detachment from the things of this life, and it will do so suddenly, with no provision for hesitation, no opportunity for escape (vv 31–33). If one should find oneself on the rooftop when that day arrives, separated from one's belongings, then the wise course is to leave them behind. If that day overtakes one in

---

Messiah. Since Jesus is Son of man *and* Messiah, there can be no local Messiahs, only false messianic pretenders, before the parousia of the Son of man (416).

[201] Of course, it must be conceded that the sinfulness of the flood generation and Sodom were proverbial in Luke's day. It is significant, though, that the stories carry an especially potent punch for Luke's readers because they link destruction to lack of preparation and immersion in daily routines. J. Schlosser ("Les Jours de Noé et de Lot. A propos de Luc, XVII,26–30," *RB* 80 [1973] 13–36) surveys the Jewish interpretive tradition relative to Noah and Lot (in which the contemporaries of Noah and Lot become the type of the sinner, and their destruction the type of God's punishing judgment), and concludes that, at least in a primitive layer of the tradition, Luke 17:26–30 insisted on the certainty of judgment for sins, rather than the suddenness of the eschatological catastrophe (35). Schlosser does not, however, consider the absence of any catalogue of vices in the passage, and his guess about the pre-Lukan function of the tradition does not affect our reading of Luke's use of it.

[202] Obviously, the Noah and Lot stories open up the problem of the relationship between the "days" and "day" of the Son of man, for the conduct of Noah's and Lot's contemporaries in the days leading to judgment forms a negative model for the behavior of Luke's generation of believers living in the period before the Son of man. To this theme we will return in the next subsection.

the field, then the attempt to return to the household from which one is separated will prove disastrous (v 31).[203] Lot's wife is the negative role model (v 32): on such a day, to turn back (εἰς τὰ ὀπίσω) is to invite disaster.[204] That day reverses the customary strategies of life preservation (v 33): only those who are willing to leave life behind will find it. The paraenetic force of all these sayings is that the eschatological perspective — the standpoint of the day of the Son of man — forever rules out "business as usual." The disciples (Luke's fellow believers) are to live in such orientation toward the kingdom and away from the cares of life, that they will be ready — and willing — to abandon all on that day when the Son of man comes. Only so will they live "into" the benefits of the consummated kingdom.

Verses 34-35 assume a sudden and unforeseen intrusion of the eschatological day, rounding out the picture with a graphic depiction of the division effected by the eschaton. Of two men sleeping in a bed at night,[205] one will be taken[206] and the other left behind (v 34). Of two women grinding at the mill, one will be taken and the other left behind (v 35). The preceding Noah and Lot allusions indicate that the fate of being taken denotes rescue, while being left behind means destruction. When the Son of man comes, an irrevocable division of humanity will occur. The division provoked by Jesus' mission (continued by his followers) is set in concrete at the eschaton.

Luke places in climactic position the enigmatic Q saying, "Where the body [corpse] is, there the eagles will also be gathered" (v 37b; cf. Matt 24:28). By introducing this saying with the disciples' question, "Where, Lord?," Luke apparently connects the image of carrion with the fate of those left behind.[207]

---

[203] It is no accident that Luke has relocated to this place the Markan tradition recorded in Mark 13:15-16 (while Luke includes Mark 13:14b in 21:21). In the context of the approaching destruction of Jerusalem, the prescription of flight is appropriate (Mark 13:14b; Luke 21:21). However, the context of the eschaton renders all escape attempts futile; Mark's injunctions to "stay put" do fit the situation envisaged in Luke 17, however, and so Luke incorporates them in v 31.

[204] This motif picks up the warning of Jesus (9:60) that "no one who puts his hand to the plow and looks εἰς τὰ ὀπίσω is fit for the kingdom of God." Unlike Matthew's version (6:33), Luke 12:31 does not urge seeking God's kingdom as a priority concern (πρῶτον, Matt 6:33), but as an absolute imperative. The kingdom of God and the coming of the Son of man alike require single-minded commitment and readiness. Next to this requirement, all else is to be abandoned.

[205] The night imagery should not be pressed, so that one concludes Luke expects the parousia to occur at night (e.g., Strobel, "Dieser"). By the same logic, one could insist that the next verse locates the parousia during the daytime. The point in each case is not the time of the day, but the sudden, unforeseen, and inescapable nature of the separation.

[206] Zmijewski (*Eschatologiereden,* 505) suggests that this "being taken up" (παραλημφθήσεται) connotes salvation conforming to the pattern of Jesus' exaltation (ἀνάλημψις).

[207] The sequence is: (1) . . . and the other will be left; (2) Where?; (3) where the body is, there the eagles, too, will be gathered.

That is, persons not seized from their worldly existence and thrust into the benefits of kingdom life will find destruction as certainly as the dead body is found by the eagle (vulture). The comparison suggests the certainty and universality of judgment for those who are not taken into salvation.

Using a variety of images, Luke 17:22-37 presents the day of the Son of man as an inescapable event, which will disrupt the normal course of things suddenly, ubiquitously, and unmistakably. It will mean a final separation of humanity by God,[208] and only an alert manner of living oriented toward the eschaton will equip one for its onset. The urgent tone of this paraenetic instruction is evident, but just when will this sudden arrival of the Son of man occur? Apart from the necessity to be ready for its appearance at any moment, does the discourse offer additional clues?

b. The Picture of the "Days of the Son of Man" in Luke 17:22-37

Already the Q tradition presupposed a period of time ("the days of Noah"; cf. Matt 24:37) preceding the parousia. Luke elaborates this theme, juxtaposing the "day" and "days" of the Son of man in vv 22/24; 26/27 ("day" implicit); 28/29-30. This feature of the discourse, coupled with Luke's insertion of v 25 ("But first the Son of man must suffer many things and be rejected by this generation"), balances the portrayal of last events with a corresponding emphasis on the period that stretches out before the End.[209]

Verse 22, which is almost certainly from Luke's hand,[210] presupposes a period of time of sufficient duration and difficulty that believers will yearn

---

[208] Taking God as the agent behind the passives παραλημφθήσεται and ἀφεθήσεται in 17:34-35.

[209] Zmijewski (*Eschatologiereden*, 530-31) concludes that the emphasis on the post-Easter *Zwischenzeit* in Luke 17:22-37 shows a weakening of imminent expectation in Luke. As will become clear in the subsequent discussion, this view is not the only way to interpret the function of the "days" in the discourse and in Lukan eschatology.

[210] Several details support this assertion. First, the εἶπεν πρός with the accusative is a Lukan stylistic peculiarity. By my count, Luke uses a form of λέγω with πρός and the accusative one-third of the time in Luke, with the percentage increasing to 50% in Acts (88 instances of λέγω + πρός + acc. in Luke; 30 in Acts; 177 instances of λέγω + the dative in Luke; 30 in Acts). Matthew and Mark do not employ this expression (similar data for λαλέω + πρός + acc.). Second, the verb ἐπιθυμέω, while by no means a favorite Lukan term, does occur four times elsewhere in Luke-Acts (Luke 15:16; 16:21; 22:15; Acts 20:33), only 11 other occurrences in the New Testament. Third, the expression "one of the days" is common in Luke (5:17; 8:22; 17:22; 20:1; cf. "one of the Sabbaths" in 24:1 and Acts 20:7); Lukan redaction is probably to be credited with the usage in 5:17; 8:22; and 20:1. More generally, the phrase "one of the [plural noun]" appears in Luke 5:3, 12; 12:6, 27; 13:10; 15:15, 19, 26; 17:2, 15; 22:47; and Acts 23:17. These data, together with the fact that v 22 serves to introduce the discourse (specifying the audience, true to Luke's form), lead to the conclusion that Luke has composed v 22.

for "just one" of the days of the Son of man:[211]

> [Jesus] said to the disciples, "Days will come when you will desire to see one of the days of the Son of man, and you will not see [it]."

The phrase "days will come" is a common designation in the prophetic literature for a future time of judgment and distress.[212] Such an era has come; it represents the past and present of Luke's church. The coming of the Son of man has been fervently awaited, yet has delayed. During this difficult period of waiting, the temptation has arisen to seek the Son of man in specific locales. Because of the nature of his coming, however (depicted in vv 24–37), such temptations are to be shunned (v 23). Verse 25, likely also from Luke,[213] injects the passion of the Son of man into the sequence of events that must precede the parousia. To be sure, the suffering and death of Jesus at Jerusalem thus become another "delaying moment";[214] but that is true only from the perspective of the story line. Like 19:11–27, this verse explains to the disciples in the story that the glorious parousia stands on the far side of rejection by this generation. The emphasis is not so much on the path through suffering to glory[215] as on rejection by this generation, a culpable rejection which finds its answer in the parousia yet to come. For Luke and his readers, however, Jesus' death occurred long ago.

---

[211] Cf. Grässer (*Problem*, 170), who states that v 22 presupposes a long time of waiting. The prevalent opinion seems to be that the phrase "one of the days of the Son of man" should be read in terms of the use of "days of the Son of man" in v 26. That is, the "days of the Son of man" are the period of time preceding the day of the Son of man (Flender [*Luke*, 94–96] and Zmijewski [*Eschatologiereden*, 401–02] add the observation that these days are the period of Jesus' enthronement in hidden fashion. The day of the Son of man will make public what is true only invisibly during the days of the Son of man.) However, I perceive the function of "days of the Son of man" to be different in vv 22 and 26. Verse 26 does indeed use the expression in analogy to the "days of Noah" to refer to the period of time preceding the End. In v 22, however, this meaning clashes with the sense of the verse: the disciples are not longing to see one of the days from the period before the End! (The interpretation of Flender and Zmijewski requires that the verse read: "You will long to see the Son of man enthroned, during the period before his parousia.") Kümmel (*Promise*, 38) and Conzelmann (*St. Luke*, 124) are probably correct in identifying the days of the Son of man in v 22 as the time of salvation initiated by the parousia. Nevertheless, going beyond Conzelmann (*St. Luke*, 124), who interprets the plural usage as an indication that Luke views the eschaton as a succession of events distinct from one another, I am inclined to see in the phrase "one of the days" an indirect reference also to the depth of testing and extent of waiting experienced by believers: the "days will come" when they will be so hard-pressed and anxious for redemption, that they will be eager for just one of the days of bliss.

[212] Though in the present tense; see, e.g., Amos 4:2; Jer 7:32; 16:14; Zech 14:1. Luke has employed the expression also in Luke 5:35 and 21:6.

[213] That is, as a Lukan reformulation of Mark 8:31, used elsewhere by Luke (9:22).

[214] So, e.g., Schneider, *Parusiegleichnisse*, 45.

[215] So, e.g., Zmijewski, *Eschatologiereden*, 408–10.

Therefore, v 25 reassures Luke's generation that the divinely willed course of
history has been proceeding according to plan: Jesus knew that his glorious
parousia would have to wait. Nothing is amiss! At the same time, the note of
warning is clear: for those who live during the "days before the day," aligning
oneself with the Son of man is everything.

Verses 26–30 highlight the dangers of the interim before the parousia.
Immersion in the day-to-day affairs of life represents the chief threat for
believers, turning them away from life's proper orientation, the kingdom of
God.[216] Why did the generation of Noah and the fellow citizens of Lot fall victim
to sudden destruction?

Verse 27: "They were eating, drinking, marrying, and being married until that day. . . ."
Verse 28: "They were eating, drinking, buying, selling, planting, building."

Diverted by daily activities from being ready, they met their doom. Because it
will be just so in the days of the Son of man, i.e., the period leading up to the
parousia (vv 26, 30), the dangers of behavior that has lost the edge of
eschatological expectancy lie open before Luke's community. Unless believers
remain alert and prepared, and unless they orient life toward the kingdom of
God, the End will be their end.[217]

Luke 17:22–37, then, urges the necessity of eschatological faith. The need
to be expectant and ready is all the greater during a protracted time of waiting
for the day of the Son of man. Delay (the present experience of the church) and
imminent expectation (the present obligation of the church) go hand in hand.
Living during the "days of the Son of man," Luke and his community must be
kept ready and waiting.

c. Persevering Hope in the Situation of Delay: Luke 18:1–8 and the Setting of Luke-Acts

This tension between living hope and the situation of delay is the central
motif in Luke 18:1–8; indeed, the parable of the persevering widow and the unjust
judge—together with the introduction and application supplied by Luke—
affords a clear glimpse of the Lukan setting. In its Lukan form,[218] the parable

---

[216] To use the terminology of 12:31, which occurs in a passage making a sir ar point.

[217] The insistence of this passage that the cares and activities of life pose the most
serious threat to the believer is not unique in the Lukan corpus: cf. Luke's interpretation
of the parable of the sower, especially 8:14; 9:57–62; 12:16–21, 22–34, 45–46; the excuses
offered in 14:16–24; 18:18–30. Possessions are particularly lethal, to judge from 16:19–31
and Acts 5:1–11.

[218] The original parable probably comprised vv 2–5 (so, e.g., Bultmann, *Synoptic Tradition,* 175, Grässer, *Problem,* 36–37; Grundmann, *Lukas,* 346). Luke is likely responsible
for the composition of vv 6–8, which fit the parable to its present context and shift the
emphasis from the judge's conduct to the vindication that rewards those who persevere in

gives prominence to the themes of perseverance (the widow serves as a model of faith for believers), delay (the reluctance of the judge to vindicate the widow), and assurance of speedy vindication. The application of the parable, in particular (vv 6–8), emphasizes the motif of imminent vindication.[219] While the behavior of the judge in the parable, consonant with the experience of Luke's readers, raises the question of interminable delay, the argument *a minori ad maius* permits the conclusion that God will vindicate his elect ἐν τάχει.[220] In other words, the situation of delay does not cast doubt on the validity of hope in an imminent eschaton, though it does sorely test eschatological faith. The present experience of delay, coupled with the certainty of vindication (soon!), demands that the disciples (Luke's fellow believers) be unceasing in prayer and persevering in expectation. The widow models this behavior, and the parable's introduction ("it is necessary to pray always," v 1) and application ("his elect who cry to him night and day," v 7) reinforce this example. Delay and living faith oriented toward the parousia go hand in hand. Luke's conclusion to the parable, however, raises the haunting question: "Nevertheless, when the Son of man comes, will he find faith[221] on earth?" This climax to the unit 18:1–8 balances consolation with warning, and in so doing supplies the final corrective to the Pharisees' question in 17:20. The decisive question is not "When comes the kingdom?," but rather "What will the Son of man find when he comes?" Will persevering, expectant faith still be found among believers?[222]

---

prayer. The introductory words in v 6 ("And the Lord said. . . .") are characteristic of Luke's writing, and the language of v 7 (prayer "night and day") echoes Luke 2:37; Acts 26:7. Verse 8b forms an inclusio with 17:20, thereby linking the parable in chapter 18 to the discourse about the coming of the kingdom of God/Son of man. Moreover, the ceaseless prayer of v 7 corresponds to the clearly Lukan introduction of the parable in v 1. Fitzmyer prefers to include v 6 with the original parable (*Luke,* 2.1176), on the ground that the parable seems to require a comment on the judge's conduct.

[219] Note the way in which the twofold ἐκδίκησιν (vv 7, 8) extends the remark of the judge (v 5): ἐκδικήσω αὐτήν.

[220] Verse 8a ("I say to you that he will effect their vindication speedily") dictates the translation of the difficult v 7b: "And will he delay over them (i.e., their vindication)?" The idea of God's patience with the elect is foreign to the text.

[221] Or "that faith [which prompts persistent prayer]": Fitzmyer views the definite article with πίστις as anaphoric (*Luke,* 2.1181).

[222] Fitzmyer sees this connection between 18:8b and 17:20 (*Luke,* 2.1181), even though he contends that the bond between 17:20–37 and 18:1–8 is "tenuous" (1175–76). Schneider (*Parusiegleichnisse,* 75–77) views 18:7b–8a, which denies further delay, as pre-Lukan, and v 8b as from Luke. He concludes that Luke has sought to dampen the imminent hope expressed in vv 7b–8a by placing v 8b in the emphatic final position. With this expansion, ἐν τάχει loses its culminating position in the discourse. This understanding of the relationship between vv 6–8a and 8b is not persuasive. To be sure, the parable (and entire discourse of 17:20–18:8) now closes on a paraenetic note, which has particular force because of the continuing experience of delay. However, imminent hope is not dampened thereby: v 8b

Luke 18:1–8 indicates that Luke's eschatological perspective has made room for delay. The protracted period preceding the eschaton is now history for Luke, however. Although he cannot know the precise time, he upholds expectant faith that prays, despite delay, for the Lord's return. However, the parable, as Luke has told it, permits a more concrete description than this of the correlation between eschatology and setting in the third gospel. Luke 18:1 mirrors a setting in which delay has resulted in disillusionment and despair:

> [Jesus] told a parable to them, to the effect that they should always pray, and not lose heart [μὴ ἐγκακεῖν].

The negative injunction, which comes from Luke's own hand, has meaning only in a situation where discouragement is a present threat to faith. Luke's community has experienced a delay in the fulfillment of the end-time promise, and the twin dangers of "life as usual" (17:26–30) and a loss of eschatological faith demand a response. Luke's answer, too, has two sides: reassurance that the long awaited consummation may be expected soon (18:7–8a), and a sharp warning about the negative consequences of a life stripped of expectant faith (17:26–37; 18:1, 8b).

Behind the concluding paraenesis of 18:8b lurks the real possibility of a loss of faith.[223] The context defines that faith as a persevering trust and expectancy in God's fulfillment of his promise to vindicate his own. The inference lies close at hand that Luke's community provided him with examples of just such a failure of eschatological faith. Life between promise and fruition, if prolonged, threatens to obscure the promise and undermine hope of its realization. Luke's perspective on the future was forged in such a climate. His composition of 17:20–18:8 betrays his concern to undergird expectant faith, expressed in a vigilant mode of life, against the inertia of the "long haul." The goal of the discourse is to foster persevering faith that holds fast to the inherited future hope against the empirical evidence.

---

opens with reference to the coming of the Son of man, and the question has urgency, in the first place, precisely because that coming may be at any moment.

[223] Zmijewski (*Eschatologiereden,* summarized on pp. 537–39) has also read Luke's situation between the lines of 17:20–37. He discovers a community that has confronted the problematic of duration and delay in three aspects: (1) the emergence of intra-church *Auseinandersetzungen;* (2) external threats to faith; and (3) the danger of *Verweltlichung.* The last two elements resemble my own proposal; however, Zmijewski's development of the first aspect is not persuasive. He concludes from Jesus' correction of the Pharisees' question in 17:20–21 that Luke's church knows certain "Pharisaic tendencies," i.e., a false Pharisaic position with respect to the kingdom's coming (pp. 383–84, 390). The vagueness of the thesis matches the dearth of evidence for it; Zmijewski reads too much into Luke's introduction of Pharisees as the audience for vv 20–21.

D. JERUSALEM AND JESUS' KINGSHIP IN RELATION TO ESCHATOLOGY: THE PARABLE OF LUKE 19:11-27

Luke places the hybrid parable of the pounds/throne claimant (Luke 19:11-27) in the last phase of the travel narrative in such a way that the parable interprets the ensuing Jerusalem narrative[224] as the human rejection/divine confirmation of Jesus' kingship, and defines the relation of those Jerusalem events to eschatology. In its Lukan form, the parable distinguishes the arrival of Jesus at Jerusalem from the end-time appearance of the kingdom, yet identifies the rejection of Jesus by the leaders of Israel (by "this generation"; cf. 17:25) as a repudiation of the kingship of Jesus—which is itself the decisive fact of the eschatological kingdom.

Verse 11 is critical to an understanding of the function of the parable of 19:12-27 in the narrative. At the same time, Luke tips his hand here with rare transparency. That Luke has composed 19:11 is almost universally acknowledged, and for good reason. The vocabulary is Lukan: προστίθημι;[225] παραχρῆμα;[226] μέλλω;[227] ἀναφαίνω;[228] and so is the style.[229] As is his custom elsewhere, Luke employs a question or supposition to "set up" eschatological instruction[230] (or, more generally, teaching in parables).[231] Moreover, the inclusio of vv 11, 28—which brackets the parable with mention of the approach to Jerusalem—points to Lukan composition of both verses.

With the introductory genitive absolute, Luke explicitly ties vv 11-27 to the preceding story of Zacchaeus—specifically, to the assertion of 19:9-10. The notice, "as they were listening to these things," refers back to Jesus' response interpreting Zacchaeus' repentance: "Today salvation has happened in [for] this house, because he, too, is a son of Abraham. For the Son of man came to search out and save that which is lost." The claim that salvation has occurred for Zacchaeus[232] gives rise to the idea that end-time hopes are on the verge of

---

[224] That is, the approach to Jerusalem (19:28-40); Jesus' lament over the city (19:41-44); the Jerusalem ministry of teaching and debate (19:45-21:38); the passion narrative (22:1-23:56); and the resurrection and ascension narratives (Luke 24:1-Acts 1:11).

[225] Of eighteen New Testament occurrences, thirteen are in Luke-Acts.

[226] Seventeen of nineteen New Testament occurrences are in Luke-Acts.

[227] Luke-Acts contains 47 of 112 New Testament uses of this verb.

[228] Luke 19:11; Acts 21:3 only in the New Testament.

[229] E.g., the genitive absolute (ἀκουόντων δὲ αὐτῶν ταῦτα) and the causal use of διά plus the articular infinitive (cf. Luke 2:4; 6:48; 8:6; 9:7; 11:8; 18:5; Acts 4:2; 8:11; 12:20; 18:2, 3; 27:4, 9; 28:18).

[230] Cf. Luke 12:40; 17:20; 21:7; Acts 1:6.

[231] See note 150 above, and note 247 below.

[232] In conjunction with the identification of Zacchaeus as a "son of Abraham," recalling Luke 3:8, where the context brings together the motifs of repentance, salvation (using the related noun, σωτήριον), and "children of Abraham." Significantly, 3:9 proceeds to the image of an axe positioned for the tree's destruction.

realization.[233] In view of Jesus' proximity to Jerusalem, the supposition is reasonable: "Now the kingdom of God is going to be manifest!" The literary context of vv 12–27 shows how Luke understands the parable and defines the function it is to serve in the narrative.

Unlike Matt 25:14–30, the Lukan form of the parable focuses on kingship, not stewardship.[234] Luke achieves this transposition through insertion of the motif of the throne claimant in vv 12, 14, 15a, 27:[235]

> A certain man of high birth went into a distant region to receive for himself a kingdom [kingly rule], and [then] to return. . . . But his [fellow] citizens despised

---

[233] In fact, the Lukan perspective is that salvation is already decided before the end-time, by virtue of one's response to Jesus. In 19:1–10, salvation comes to Zacchaeus' household precisely because Jesus—with his invitation— has come. The parallelism of vv 5 and 9 establishes this point:

Verse 5: ". . . for today I must stay in your house."

Verse 9: ". . . today salvation has come about for [in] your house. . . ."

This identification of Jesus and σωτηρία is reminiscent of Luke 2:30, in which Simeon, having met the infant Jesus, affirms "my eyes have seen your salvation [σωτήριον]." Both kingdom- and salvation-language in Luke-Acts are bound to Jesus' person and his invitation (cf. also Acts 4:12); nevertheless, neither kingdom nor salvation is reduced to present experience, without eschatological remainder. The decisive point is the connection between present response to Jesus and participation in final salvation/kingdom of God.

[234] Johnson ("Kingship") appropriately labels Luke 19:12–27 the "Lukan Kingship Parable." Actually, the central section of the Lukan parable still revolves around faithful fulfillment of the task assigned to the servants. The narrative context, together with the beginning and ending of the parable, guides the reader to the theme of the throne claimant.

[235] The origin of this theme is variously estimated. Fitzmyer considers it probable that Luke has himself composed these verses (*Luke*, 2.1231); so also Schneider, *Parusiegleichnisse*, 40–41. F. D. Weinert, however ("The Parable of the Throne Claimant [Luke 19:12, 14–15a, 27] Reconsidered," *CBQ* 39 [1977] 505–14), not only views this motif as stemming from an originally independent parable but also ascribes that parable to Jesus himself. Several indicators point to Lukan composition: the coherence of this motif with the narrative context (cf. especially 19:38); the presence of Lukan vocabulary (e.g., εὐγενής [Luke 19:12; Acts 17:11; elsewhere only in 1 Cor 1:26]; μακρός [Luke 15:13; 19:12; 20:47]; elsewhere only in Matt 23:14; Mark 12:40; cf. Luke's use of the adverb μακράν, amounting to 5 of 10 New Testament instances]; ὑποστρέφω [Luke-Acts contains 33 of 37 occurrences]; πολίτης [Luke 15:15; 19:14; Acts 21:39; elsewhere only in Heb 8:11]; πρεσβεία [Luke 14:32; 19:14 only in the New Testament]; ἐπανέρχομαι [Luke 10:35; 19:15 only in the New Testament; note especially the similar grammatical construction]); the coherence of the motif with the place of the ascension and enthronement in Luke's story. These details make it likely that Luke is responsible for the weaving of the throne-claimant theme into the parable of the pounds, even if it may have originated as an independent parable. Memory of Archelaus' attempt to acquire the title of king, and of the Jewish delegation opposing him (cf. Josephus, *Ant.*, 17.11,1–2), may have provided Luke with a model for this element of the parable. Whatever its origin, the present form of the parable plays an important interpretive role in Luke's story.

him and sent a delegation after him, with the message, "We do not want this one to rule over us." And it happened, when he had received the kingdom and returned, that he said . . . "But [as for] my enemies, who did not want me to rule over them, bring [them] here and slaughter them before me."

This plot sandwiches the parable (from Q) dealing with servants' accountability for their performance during the absence of their master. The central section of the parable (19:13, 15b–26), in a manner consistent with 12:35–48, envisages the delay of the parousia and urges faithful, energetic obedience in the interim.[236] Most interpreters have seen in this emphasis upon delay a correction of the supposition in v 11. That is, in this parable Jesus dampens the expectation of some that his approach to Jerusalem signals an imminent appearance of the kingdom; rather, they must anticipate a protracted delay.[237]

According to this reading of the function of 19:11–27 in the narrative, the kingship interlude (the throne claimant) is an allegorical depiction of Jesus' rejection at Jerusalem and subsequent enthronement (resurrection/ascension). Not until after his kingship is repudiated by the Jewish leaders at Jerusalem (the delegation in the parable) will Jesus' reign as king be established by his resurrection and exaltation to God's right hand (Acts 2:30–36). At his return (the parousia), the King (Jesus) will call his servants (disciples) to account for their conduct during his absence and punish those who opposed his claim upon the throne (unbelieving Israel and its leaders, responsible for Jesus' crucifixion).

Eschatology and Situation in Luke 19:11–27

Despite recent criticism, this explanation of the literary function of 19:11–27 is correct.[238] Luke employs the parable of the pounds/throne claimant to counter a particular eschatological expectation associated with Jesus' approach to Jerusalem. This is so only from within the story, however.[239] Luke's readers

---

[236] This is also the force of the phrase "distant region" (εἰς χώραν μακράν) in v 12. Matthew's formulation is different (Matt 25:19: "after a long time" [μετὰ δὲ πολὺν χρόνον]), but the function is similar. A journey into a remote region (so Luke) necessarily involves a prolonged absence. Luke's wording, however, is particularly apt given his emphasis on the ascension to heaven (Luke 24–Acts 1).

[237] This is the conventional reading of the parable: e.g., Kaestli, *Eschatologie,* 39; Grässer, *Problem,* 116–17; Noack, *Gottesreich,* 48–49; Gause, "Transfiguration," 144; Bartsch, *Wachtet,* 109; Conzelmann, *St. Luke,* 113; Schneider, *Parusiegleichnisse,* 41–42; Fitzmyer, *Luke,* 2.1232; Weinert, "Claimant," 506.

[238] Johnson ("Kingship"), building on the suggestion of D. L. Tiede (*Prophecy,* 79), has challenged the conventional reading of the parable. See Excursus 2 below for an assessment of Johnson's interpretation. His conclusions are to be rejected, although the method he espouses is to be embraced. He insists that "before looking to what Luke may have wanted to teach a (putative) community by a single pericope . . . the exegete needs to look first to the role that passage plays in the literary composition as a whole" ("Kingship," 143; cf. Johnson, "Cautious").

[239] Cf. my earlier comment on Luke 17:25, section C.3.b. above.

would recognize this as a datum of history: Jesus met death, not the kingdom, at Jerusalem.[240] The Lukan Jesus, shortly before the enthusiastic affirmation of his kingship (19:38), and within the hearing of the crowd traveling with him, empties his approach to Jerusalem of all end-time expectation.[241] Luke thereby assures his readers that Jesus was not in for a surprise, that all proceeded according to plan. It is not legitimate, however, to infer that Luke here applies the delay motif to counter apocalyptic enthusiasm that connects the destruction of Jerusalem with the end-time.[242] Rather, from the vantage point of Luke's community, when delay was fact, the parable's delay motif serves to shore up eschatological faith in a situation when the failure of the promised end-time to materialize has apparently disconfirmed such hopes. The fact of delay does not challenge the credibility of eschatological faith; instead, it raises the question of faithfulness during the time of waiting. As in 12:35–48 and 17:22–37, Luke turns the experience of delay against those who have been lulled into complacency. Luke's readers may expect to be called to account for their service between ascension and parousia. Once again Luke offers eschatological paraenesis, exhortation to a faithful lifestyle based on a proper eschatological perspective.

At the same time, the parable in 19:11–27 interprets the coming events at Jerusalem as a repudiation of Jesus' rightful claim to be king over Israel.[243] The leaders of the Jewish people will, as early as 19:39 and then throughout the Jerusalem narrative, show that they scorn Jesus' status as king.[244] The plot of the parable removes all ambiguity concerning the destiny that awaits Jesus' "rebellious citizens." They have voluntarily chosen to have no part in Jesus' eternal reign, which is constitutive of the kingdom of God.

EXCURSUS 2: A CRITIQUE OF L. T. JOHNSON'S EXEGESIS OF LUKE 19:11–27

Against the usual view, Johnson maintains that delay is not an important element of Luke's version of the parable. In fact:

> Everything gets carried out with dispatch. The "getting of the kingdom" is not an unrealized event of the future, but one already accomplished in the story (Lk. 19:15).[245]

[240] Stressed with particular sharpness by J. T. Sanders, "The Parable of the Pounds and Lucan Anti-Semitism," *TS* 42 (1981) 660–68, 665–66.

[241] Similarly, immediately after 19:38, Jesus encounters rejection of the acclamation and announces Jerusalem's future destruction because it did not acknowledge the "time of its visitation" (19:39–44).

[242] So, e.g., Kaestli, *Eschatologie*, 39.

[243] The content of angelic promise in Luke 1:32–33, seemingly disconfirmed by the crucifixion, yet substantiated by God's raising Jesus from the dead and exalting him to his right hand.

[244] Thereby cementing the division that has been developing in response to Jesus' teaching ministry during the travel narrative, and anticipating the final separation effected in Acts, with the Jewish leaders' rejection of the apostles' mission to Jerusalem.

[245] "Kingship," 143–44.

Moreover, the faithful servants of the parable receive as their reward not a future oversight of possessions but a present exercise of power over cities within the king's realm (19:17, 19). They play a leadership role within the kingdom already gained by the nobleman.[246] This feature of the parable contradicts a reading of it as a parousia parable.

Johnson also questions the customary interpretation of Luke's introduction of the parable (v 11), which sees it as advancing views to be refuted in the parable itself. Neither Luke's language here nor his habitual practice in introducing parables compels this conclusion, Johnson argues.[247] As it turns out, the content of 19:11 reveals that Luke intends to confirm the supposition. To be sure, the adverb παραχρῆμα is rightly emphasized in the common interpretation; however, it need not be seen as disconfirmed and so pointing forward to the Lord's distant return.[248] Johnson rests his case primarily on the meaning of the verb ἀναφαίνω, however. He concludes from a survey of its use in Philo that it "is not impossible" that Luke intended the meaning: "the Kingdom of God was going to be *declared.*"[249] Examination of Luke's conception of the kingdom yields the finding that, subsequent to this parable, Luke brings together the kingdom of God and the kingship of Jesus. Jesus is acclaimed as king in 19:38, and the theme of Jesus' kingship surfaces again in 23:2-3, 37-38, 42; (cf. 22:29). The story line of Luke-Acts confirms the expectation of 19:11: Jesus is proclaimed king (19:38) and exercises his rule through the apostles in the restored Israel.[250] Johnson summarizes his reading of the parable:

---

[246] Ibid., 144.

[247] Ibid., 146. Luke uses the verb δοκέω in its full range; it need not connote false suppositions. Johnson contends that Luke has Jesus on only one occasion (18:9) tell a parable explicitly to refute an understanding of his audience. Johnson finds (146-47) an implicit, subtle rebuff in 16:14-31, regards the parable of the Good Samaritan as subverting, but not strictly refuting, the implicit understanding of the questioner (10:28-37), characterizes the parable of the rich fool as a response (but not a rebuttal) to an inappropriate request (12:13, 16-21), and sees the parable of the Great Banquet as shifting the focus of attention from the future kingdom to the present of Jesus' ministry, but not as a rebuttal of the guest's exclamation (14:15, 16-24). Of Luke 15:1-3 in relation to the parables of 15:4-32, Johnson claims that each parable is "clearly intended by Luke" not to refute the perception of scribes and Pharisees that Jesus receives and eats with sinners, but rather to confirm it (147-48). In my judgment, Johnson has, in fact, assembled the evidence that undermines his argument. Even if Luke does not often explicitly correct a viewpoint through a parable, he does direct parables (implicitly) against a belief, attitude, or expectation on the part of his audience. Johnson has forced the evidence to fit his theory.

[248] Ibid., 148-49.

[249] Fitzmyer (*Luke,* 2.1234) rightly rejects Johnson's translation of ἀναφαίνεσθαι. Luke's other use of the verb (Acts 21:3: "catching sight of") and the preponderance of the extra-biblical evidence line up squarely against Johnson's view. See BAG, 62; LSJ, 124-25.

[250] "Kingship," 158-59. Johnson views 22:28-30 as fulfilled in the course of the narrative of Acts (see his full development of this argument in *Possessions*).

Who is the nobleman who would be king, and who in fact gets βασιλεία, so that he cannot only exercise it, but share it with his faithful followers? Jesus, who will immediately be hailed as king, dispose of βασιλεία, grant entrance to the thief, and, as risen Lord, continue to exercise authority through his emissaries' words and deeds. Who are the fellow citizens who do not wish to have this man as their ruler, who protest it, and then, defeated, are slaughtered before the king? The leaders of the people who decried the proclamation of Jesus as King, who mocked him as such on the cross, who rejected his mission as prophet, who persecuted his Apostles and who, at last, found themselves "cut off from the people." Who are the servants whose use of possessions is rewarded by ἐξουσία within the domain of this king? The Twelve, who have been schooled in service (22:28), and whose βασιλεία over the restored Israel is exercised and expressed in the ministry of word and table-service. . . . When will all this occur? In the course of the story Luke is telling, beginning *immediately* with the messianic proclamation of Jesus in 19:38.[251]

Johnson's approach to Luke 19:11-27, while provocative and based on a commendable devotion to the function of the passage within its narrative context, meets with telling objections. First, the verb ἀναφαίνω does not bear the meaning here which it must have if the exegesis of Johnson is to stand.[252] Luke 19:11 ascribes to Jesus' audience[253] the expectation that the kingdom of God (not Jesus' kingship) was going to appear in the immediate future. The ground for that expectation was Jesus' impending arrival at Jerusalem—together with Jesus' words about salvation already effected in relation to the tax collector Zacchaeus. Luke's composition of vv 11-12 leaves no doubt that the parable is prompted by that expectation.[254] Does the parable itself confirm or disconfirm such suppositions? It is at this point, second, that Johnson fails to give due weight to the phrase εἰς χώραν μακράν, with which Jesus opens the parable. This expression answers to both geographical and temporal aspects of the expectation voiced in v 11. Proximity to Jerusalem does not signal the arrival of God's kingdom, for Jesus must first be awarded his kingly status elsewhere.[255] In addition, that kingship is confirmed not immediately but after a long journey.[256] The presence

---

[251] "Kingship," 158 (emphasis his).

[252] See above, footnote 249.

[253] Johnson (ibid., 145) correctly observes that Luke gives an uncharacteristically vague description of Jesus' audience in 19:11-27. The reader does not know just who is possessed by the thoughts expressed in v 11: the nearest candidate for the antecedent of αὐτούς in v 11 is πάντες in v 7. Johnson infers that Luke's "failure to make *this* audience clearer to his reader leads one to think that the group to whom the parable was spoken was meant to consist in all those with Jesus on the way to Jerusalem, with the parable addressing each segment in diverse ways, and Luke's readers most of all" (145; emphasis his).

[254] Note the causal use of διά with the articular infinitive (v 11), and the οὖν of v 12.

[255] Obsessed with his concern to show that the journey into a distant country does not imply temporal delay, Johnson does not consider this side of the issue.

[256] The juxtaposition of the belief in an immediate manifestation of the kingdom and a journey to a distant land does (against Johnson) imply a delay. Johnson places considerable weight on the observation that the story proceeds "with dispatch": the nobleman

of the motif of long journey/return, alongside the narrative's (twofold; vv 11, 28) mention of proximity to Jerusalem, suggests, against Johnson, that the parable corrects the expectation voiced in v 11.[257]

This counter-proposal also runs aground because, for all its attention to the flow of Luke's narrative, it neglects the role played by the ascension narratives, as interpreted by Peter's Pentecost speech (specifically, Acts 2:30-36). That key juncture in Luke's story, in which Jesus' resurrection and ascension constitute his coronation, accords well with the imagery of the throne claimant. Like the nobleman, Jesus must journey into a distant land (heaven) in order to receive his kingly power. As Johnson himself admits,[258] "not everything fits exactly." The order of events in the parable does not conform perfectly to the sequence of Luke's narrative.[259] Nevertheless, in the prevalent understanding of the place of 19:11-27 in Luke's overall narrative, the range of agreement, with respect to narrative development, theme, and theological perspective, is striking. Through the composition of vv 11 and 28, and the insertion of the throne claimant into the parable of the pounds, Luke has made of this passage an apt vehicle of his literary purposes. Luke 19:11-27 both interprets the decisive turn in the story which the arrival of Jerusalem represents, and clarifies the relation of the Jerusalem narrative to the end-time.

E. LUKE'S PROGRAMMATIC STATEMENT ON ESCHATOLOGY: THE DISCOURSE OF LUKE 21:5-36

Luke presents his eschatological perspective with greatest clarity and elaboration in the eschatological discourse of Luke 21:5-36, which amounts to

---

receives his rule without delay, returns at once, and rewards/punishes the behavior that occurred while he was away. If, however, Luke has inserted the throne-claimant motif into the parable of the pounds (which already presupposes delay), then the fact that he does so in the most cursory fashion is not to be pressed as evidence that the parable contains no delay motif.

[257] I have already pointed out the weakness in Johnson's contention that Luke only rarely uses a parable to correct the perspective of Jesus' audience. Johnson's narrow focus on parable introductions, moreover, leads him to overlook the analogy with other Lukan introductions to eschatological teaching, which often corrects the viewpoint articulated (e.g., 17:20-21; 21:5-6; Acts 1:6-8).

[258] Ibid., 158.

[259] The lack of harmony should not be exaggerated, however. (1) It is not self-evident that the promise of Luke 22:28-30 is fulfilled in the Acts narrative, losing all eschatological content. If *eschatological* rule over Israel's tribes (22:28-30) corresponds to the parable's reward of authority over cities (19:17, 19), then this facet of the problem of sequence evaporates. Following faithful performance of their assigned duties during the Lord's absence, the servants (apostles) receive their reward at the parousia. (2) If v 27 does not refer to the destruction of Jerusalem but rather end-time destruction (representing exclusion from God's people; cf. Acts 3:22-23) of unbelieving Israel, then it is no longer problematic that punishment of Jerusalem follows the master's return (parousia).

a programmatic statement on the subject of last things in relation to history. My analysis of the discourse will unveil two primary literary motives guiding its composition. First, Luke arranges and adapts his traditional material in order to clarify the sequence of phases in the eschatological drama. History (events which, from Luke's vantage point, are past) and eschatology (culminating events still lying in Luke's future) are brought into the proper interrelationship. Second, Luke places this phase-clarification motif at the service of his governing pastoral motive, which comprises a further appeal for vigilance (cf. Luke 12 and 17) and correction of misconceptions about the course of eschatological events. My thesis is that Luke incorporates parousia delay into his eschatological program, but does so in order to persuade his readers that they now live in the time of imminent expectation. Luke's community has found the experience of delay and duration to be an obstacle to living eschatological faith. By pointing to history as history and last things as last things, and by elucidating the connection between the two, Luke aims to restore credibility to imminent hopes in his own situation.

Luke 21 affords the best clue to Luke's eschatological view, because here his redactional activity is transparent as nowhere else in the eschatological sections of Luke-Acts. Although most scholars have assumed that Luke 21 represents redaction of Mark 13 (perhaps with the inclusion of additional traditions), dissenting voices are occasionally heard. Such exegetes as L. Gaston and A. Salas discover in Luke 21 a pre-Lukan eschatological discourse, to which Luke has added Markan elements.[260] Our picture of Luke's redaction of the speech will vary widely depending upon the approach taken to the question of sources.[261] While my interest is in Luke's version of the discourse and in its place in his whole narrative (not in the pre-Lukan forms of the discourse), the importance of this passage and the pivotal role played by redactional analysis in its interpretation require a preliminary glance at the issue of sources underlying Luke 21.

1. Sources in Luke 21:5–36

Conzelmann based his view of Luke's "de-eschatologizing," in large measure, on Luke's redaction of Mark 13.[262] Conzelmann assumed that Mark was Luke's sole source in Luke 21; any divergences from Mark he attributed to Lukan

---

[260] Gaston, *Stone;* Salas, *Discurso Escatologico Prelucano: Estudio de Lc. XXI, 20–36* (Real Monasterio de el Escorial: Biblioteca < <La Ciudad de Dios, > > 1967).

[261] Although Salas appears to be an exception: when he turns from reconstruction and interpretation of the pre-Lukan discourse to Luke's redaction of it, he begins to sound much like Conzelmann (see especially *Prelucano,* pp. 215–23)! This results from a narrow (emendation) application of redaction criticism (pp. 215–16), and attention to Luke's treatment of Mark (not a feature of Gaston's approach).

[262] See *St. Luke,* 125–32.

redaction.[263] Proponents of the proto-Luke hypothesis, on the other hand, maintain that Lukan redaction in the discourse is to be seen in his incorporation of Markan elements into his proto-Lukan framework, rather than in the inclusion of non-Markan traditions within a Markan framework.[264]

The appeal to a proto-Lukan source underlying Luke 21 is beset with insuperable difficulties. In the first place, this view must assume extensive overlap between Mark and proto-Luke. According to Gaston, for example, Luke 21:5-7 must be assigned to proto-Luke because these verses have in Luke a different setting and audience from those in Mark.[265] Luke 21:5-7, however, is an editorial rewriting of Mark: nearly half of the words in Luke are present in Mark's version, and all the divergences are explicable in terms of Lukan redaction.[266] Second, removal of the material clearly derived from Mark does not, as Taylor claims,[267] leave a more intelligible text. So Gaston must transpose 21:10-11 before v 25 in order to yield a coherent discourse.[268] Third, those apparent contradictions within the discourse[269] to which advocates of proto-Luke make appeal are

[263] Ibid., 125. Conzelmann rejected the hypothesis that Luke drew upon a non-Markan source in Luke 21 on the ground that this approach "misunderstand[s] both the extent and the individuality of Luke's revision" (p. 125). Cf. Kaestli, *Eschatologie,* 41-42.

[264] See Gaston, "Sondergut und Markusstoff in Luk. 21," *TZ* 16 (1960) 162-72; *Stone,* especially pp. 244-56; Salas, *Prelucano;* V. Taylor, "A Cry from the Siege: A Suggestion Regarding a Non-Marcan Oracle Embedded in Lk. XXI 20-36," *JTS* 26 (1924-25) 136-44; P. Winter, "The Treatment of His Sources by the Third Evangelist in Luke 21-24," *Stud Theol* 8 (1954) 138-72. Gaston claims that his analysis of Luke 21 does not presuppose the proto-Luke theory, but is a "study in special Lukan material" (*Stone,* 254). In fact, however, Gaston's entire discussion is built on the reconstruction of a written source, which includes Luke 19:37-44, 47-48; 21:5-7, 20, 21b, 22, 23b, 24, 10-11, 25-28, 37-38, and into which Luke has inserted material from Mark 13 (pp. 255-56). The important point is that (whatever name is given the source theory employed) Gaston gives priority in interpretation to the pre-Lukan, non-Markan (and pre-Markan) discourse. In similar fashion, Salas identifies a pre-Lukan, non-Markan (and pre-Markan) discourse encompassing Luke 19:41-44; 21:20, 21b, 22, 23b, 24, 25, 26a, 28, 34-36. He differs from Gaston in allowing Luke's handling of the Markan materials fitted into this discourse to shape the discourse's interpretation.

[265] "Sondergut," 162-72: 168; *Stone,* 355-65.

[266] See W. Nicol, "Tradition and Redaction in Luke 21," *Neotestamentica* 7 (1973) 61-71, 62-63.

[267] "Cry," 137-38. Taylor argues that the four Markan passages in Luke 21:20-36 (21:21a, 23a, 26b-27, 29-33) are loosely connected to their present context, and that the sequence of thought is better if they are excised. The remaining material (vv 20, 21b, 22, 23b-26a, 28, 34-36), in Taylor's judgment, forms one unit (pp. 138-39).

[268] A transposition that Gaston acknowledges (*Stone,* 357) to be the weakest aspect of his reconstruction.

[269] Especially the tension between vv 16 (". . . they will put some of you to death") and 18 ("not a hair of your head will perish"), and the seam between vv 20 and 21: grammatically, αὐτῆς and αὐτήν in v 21 must have 'Ιουδαίᾳ as antecedent; the sense requires that Jerusalem (v 20) be the antecedent.

explained just as well by the insertion into Mark of other traditions accessible to Luke as by the insertion of Markan elements into a non-Markan base. Finally, this approach fails to recognize the extent, coherence, and distinctiveness of Luke's redaction of Mark 13. Significant features of Luke 21 not derived from Mark betray typical Lukan formulation and, as Conzelmann correctly perceived, a definite compositional plan.[270] This assertion will find corroboration in my analysis of the discourse below.

It is perhaps an exaggeration to contend[271] that Mark is Luke's only source in this discourse.[272] Nevertheless, given clear evidence for Lukan redaction in the discourse, the extent of non-Markan traditions employed by Luke should not be overstated.[273] Discussion of sources underlying Luke 21 should not overlook

---

[270] St. Luke, 125; cf. Kaestli, Eschatologie, 41–42; Nicol, "Tradition;" Zmijewski, Eschatologiereden, 54, 311. Zmijewski concludes that Luke has adapted his only literary source, Mark, according to a definite plan (311), and emphasizes the unity of Luke 21:5–36 as a Lukan discourse-composition. A methodological flaw shared by the analyses of Taylor ("Cry") and Salas (Prelucano) is restriction of the pre-Lukan discourse to vv 20–36 (like Gaston, Salas includes Luke 19:41–44 as well). The coherence and perspective of vv 5–36 as a single discourse thus fall from view.

[271] As do Zmijewski (Eschatologiereden, 311) and Conzelmann (St. Luke, 125).

[272] Nicol (summarized in "Tradition," 68) suggests that Luke has added non-Markan traditions to his Markan source in Luke 21:11b, 18, 21b, 22, 23b, 24, 25, 26a, 34–36. Nicol proposes a Palestinian, pre-siege setting for this oracle (with the exception of vv 34–36).

[273] Even Salas concedes that Luke has left his stamp on the style and vocabulary of the entire discourse (Prelucano, 50–54). Salas lists several examples: (1) ἄχρι οὗ (v 24; cf. Acts 7:18; 27:33); (2) καὶ οἱ ἐν μέσῳ (v 21; cf. Acts 28:9 [an erroneous reference]); (3) προσέχετε ἑαυτοῖς (v 34; cf. Luke 12:1; 17:3; Acts 5:35; 20:28); (4) πάντα etc. (vv 22, 24, 35, 36; Luke favors the use of πᾶς and ἅπας); (5) genitive absolute constructions (vv 26, 28; see Cadbury, The Style and Literary Method of Luke [Cambridge: Harvard University, 1920] 133–34); (6) ἄστρον (v 25; cf. Acts 7:43; 27:20); (7) ἐκφύγω (v 36; cf. Acts 16:27; 19:16); (8) a series of typical Lukan words: ἐπέρχομαι (v 26; cf. Luke 1:35; 11:22; Acts 1:8; 8:24; 13:40; 14:19); ἐπαίρω (v 28; cf. Luke 6:20; 11:17; 16:13; 18:13; 24:50; Acts 1:9; 2:14; 14:11; 22:22; 27:40); διότι (v 28; cf. Luke 1:13; 2:7; Acts 13:15; 18:10; 20:26; 22:8); δέομαι (v 36; cf. Luke 5:12; 8:28, 38; 9:38; 10:2; 22:32; Acts 4:31; 8:22, 24, 34; 21:39); ἐφίστημι (v 34; cf. Luke 2:9, 38; 4:39; 10:40; 20:1; 24:4; Acts 4:1; 6:12; 10:17; 11:11; 12:7; 24:13, 20; 23:11, 27; 28:2); πίμπλημι (v 22; cf. Luke 1:15, 23, 41, 57, 67; 2:28; 5:7, 26; 6:11; Acts 2:4; 3:10; 4:8, 31; 5:17; 9:17; 13:9, 45; 19:29). Salas also enumerates constructions unusual for Luke, a much less impressive catalog (pp. 54–58): (1) ἐπὶ πρόσωπον (v 35; contrast Acts 17:26 and Gen 7:23, where the object of ἐπί appears in the genitive case); (2) ἐπὶ τῆς γῆς (vv 23, 25, 35 [v 35 is incorrectly included in the list]; cf. Luke 4:25; 5:11; 6:49; 8:27; 12:49; 22:44; 23:44 — ἐπὶ τὴν γήν — and Luke 5:24; 18:8 — ἐπὶ τῆς γῆς); (3) the anomalous threefold ἔθνη, ἐθνῶν, ἔθνων in v 24 (Cadbury [Style, 83–90] has shown that Luke avoids repeating words in a passage); (4) the use of φόβος with ἀποψύχω in v 25 is unusual for Luke, who ordinarily uses φόβος with a variety of common verbs; (5) βιωτικος is found only in v 34 in Luke-Acts (cf. τοῦ βίου in Luke 8:14); (6) the use of πίμπλημι (v 22) to describe fulfillment of scripture is atypical for Luke, who customarily employs πληρόω. Of the items on this list, (1) and (2) tend to cancel each other, and (3) tends to undercut (6) — Salas fails to note that Luke uses πληρόω in v 24.

Luke's use of the Greek Bible, particularly in vv 20-24.[274] In any case, both Lukan redactional alterations of Mark *and* Luke's incorporation of other traditions into the Markan discourse constitute valid evidence for the Lukan eschatological perspective. Lukan redaction is not limited to editorial activity[275] but is to be witnessed in all his compiling and compositional work, through which he draws upon traditions available to him to create a coherent discourse set in the temple in the final days of Jesus' ministry at Jerusalem. It is, finally, the plan implicit in the entire discourse (whatever the origins of the traditions embedded in it) that discloses the Lukan eschatological perspective.

2. Eschatological Phase Clarification in Luke 21:5-36

After Luke 13:34-35 and 19:39-40, 41-44, the eschatological discourse in Luke 21 stands as the third and decisive pronouncement of Jerusalem's impending fate.[276] Verses 5-6 and 20-24 announce the coming devastation of the temple and holy city, as prophesied in scripture (v 22). Luke's radical recasting of the Markan discourse setting and audience transforms it from private instruction of select disciples to a public statement, addressed primarily to the disciples but audible also to the people of Jerusalem, concerning the approaching catastrophe.[277] The Markan Jerusalem narrative presents a gradual narrowing of

---

The repetition of ἔθνη in v 24 is indeed striking, but may be an indicator of Lukan emphasis rather than non-Lukan origin. Compared to the evidence for Luke's compositional work in vv 20-36, the data pointing to a pre-Lukan source are meager.

[274] Cf. Dodd, "Fall;" F. Flückiger, "Luk. 21,20-24 und die Zerstörung Jerusalems," *TZ* 28 (1972) 385-90; Salas, *Prelucano*, 48-50. Salas maintains that the author of the pre-Lukan discourse used the LXX: v 20: ἐρήμωσις (cf. Jer 4:7; 7:34); v 21: ἐκχωρείτωσαν (cf. Num 17:10); v 22: ἡμέραι ἐκδικήσεως (cf. Hos 9:7; Jer 26:10); v 24: καὶ αἰχμαλωτισθήσονται (cf. Ezek 30:17); v 25: συνοχὴ ἐθνῶν ἐν ἀπορίᾳ ἤχους θαλάσσης (cf. Ps 64:8). These scriptural allusions are perhaps better ascribed to Luke than to a pre-Lukan source.

[275] Contrast Conzelmann, *St. Luke;* Salas, *Prelucano*, 215-16.

[276] Luke 23:28-31 gives the final statement. The passages in chapters 13, 19, and 23 have in common the tone of the lament, while Luke 21, insofar as it addresses the subject of Jerusalem's destruction, takes the form of a prophetic oracle. Of course, Luke includes further passages explaining the demise of Jerusalem, notably the parable of the pounds/throne claimant (19:11-27).

[277] Luke 20:45: "While all the people were listening, he said to his disciples. . . ." Luke addresses the eschatological instruction contained within the discourse as a whole primarily to the disciples, hence to all within Luke's community (cf. F. Keck, *Die öffentliche Abschiedsrede Jesu in Lk 20,45-21,36* [Stuttgart: Katholisches Bibelwerk, 1976] 322-23). Lukan redaction in 21:12-19 confirms this interpretation. While Mark's version of this pericope oscillates between the 2nd person plural (Mark 13:9, 11, 13a) and the 3rd person (singular and plural; Mark 13:10, 12, 13b), Luke renders the entire passage in the 2nd person plural. Jesus' eschatological teaching (specifically, encouragement for the time of persecution and mission) is consistently addressed to his hearers—and to Luke's own community. Nicol ("Tradition," 64) notes the extensive revision by Luke of his Markan

Jesus' audience: 12:37b, large crowd; 12:43, Jesus' disciples; 13:1, one of his disciples; 13:3, Peter, James, John, and Andrew. The transition in Mark to private instruction (13:3, κατ' ἰδίαν) is accomplished by means of a scene change from the temple to the Mount of Olives (13:1-3). The picture is altogether different in Luke. True to his pattern for the Jerusalem ministry (namely, public teaching in the temple by day; lodging at the Mount of Olives by night; Luke 21:37; cf. 19:47; 20:1), Luke omits the Markan scene change. As a result, the questions and discourse of chapter 21 occur entirely within the temple, as semi-public teaching and prophecy. Likewise, no shift in audience occurs in Luke (τινων λεγόντων, v 5; ἐπηρώτησαν, v 7; all Mark's references to the disciples are eliminated).[278] Luke again emphasizes in his general summary (21:37-38; cf. 19:47-48; 20:45) that all the people (πᾶς ὁ λαός) heard Jesus' teaching. Insofar as the eschatological discourse in Luke touches upon the destiny of Jerusalem, this is a prophetic oracle delivered by Jesus within the hearing of the people of Jerusalem. Given the imminent rejection of Jesus by Jerusalem (cf. 19:11-27, 39-40, 41-44), in fulfillment of scriptural prophecy, the fate of the holy city is sealed. From the vantage point of Luke's community, there can be no misunderstanding: the destruction of Jerusalem (now past) was foreseen by Jesus and happened in accord with scripture.

Yet the discourse may not be reduced to this theme, important as it is in the Lukan narrative. In composing the speech, Luke has expended considerable energy to elucidate the relationship between the destruction of Jerusalem and the eschaton. In fact, this eschatological phase clarification is the dominant feature of Luke's redaction in the discourse. Lukan phase clarification is especially apparent in the adjustment of the eschatological program to include parousia delay.[279] Luke revises Mark 13 extensively in order to incorporate a delay motif.[280]

---

source in 21:12-19: only 24 of 98 words in Luke are present also in Mark. Nicol is persuaded, however, that Luke follows Mark here, since the general order of the Lukan pericope corresponds completely with Mark (65). Nicol accounts for the deviation from Mark in this pericope by pointing out that "this is the only pericope dealing with the church and [Luke] is more interested in the church than in the descriptions of the last things. Now he has the opportunity to exhort, encourage, and comfort. . . ." Nicol's formulation is in need of revision (what happened to vv 34-36? If Luke is relatively uninterested in the description of last things, why has he devoted so much space—and so much redactional work—to that subject?), but it does highlight the role in the discourse of paraenesis and encouragement of Luke's community.

[278] Consequently, when Jesus is addressed as διδάσκαλε (v 7), the title is probably placed (as is customary in Luke) on the lips of one outside the circle of disciples—in contrast to Mark 13:1. For a different view, see Keck (*Abschiedsrede*, 22, 56-57, 67-69, 321).

[279] With respect to this dimension of Lukan redaction in chapter 21, then, Conzelmann's analysis is correct.

[280] Zmijewski appropriately observes that this tendency, already discernible in Mark 13 (*Eschatologiereden*, 565-66), is taken up also by Luke; however, Zmijewski exaggerates the continuity between Luke and the *Urkirche*. See the discussion, pp. 565-72.

A series of significant alterations of Mark 13 achieves this assimilation of parousia delay. First, Luke replaces συντελεῖσθαι in Mark 13:4 with γίνεσθαι (21:7), a change which—in conjunction with Luke's omission of πάντα (Mark 13:4)— suggests that the temple destruction prophesied in 21:6 is not of one piece with the eschatological completion.[281] Second, Luke expands the content of the message to be brought by deceivers in Jesus' name, to include the assertion: ὁ καιρὸς ἤγγικεν (v 8).[282] In place of Mark's pessimistic prophecy, "They will lead many astray" (Mark 13:6), the Lukan Jesus issues the directive concerning these preachers of imminence: "Do not go after them." Why? Imminent expectation is not yet appropriate to the situation, for many world-shaking events must happen first. This is the burden of a third set of redactional changes. Luke inserts ταῦτα, πρῶτον, and εὐθέως in 21:9b (εὐθέως replacing Mark's οὔπω) to reinforce the point that the events so far prophesied occur at some distance from the End (τὸ τέλος). The period of turmoil coming to a head in the Jewish War and the fall of Jerusalem[283] is not the end-time. Fourth, by adding a temporal reference in v 12 (πρὸ δὲ τούτων πάντων), Luke further accents this delay in eschatological consummation.[284] This modification places the onset of the time of persecution and testimony (vv 12-19) *before* the international and heavenly portents of vv 9-11. Luke thus distances the phase of persecution/testimony (= the time of the early church, as narrated in Acts[285]) from the End. Fifth, Luke reworks Mark

[281] Since Luke elsewhere shows no aversion to the use of συντελέω (Luke 4:2, 13; Acts 21:27; half of all New Testament occurrences), the change seems especially significant here. Similarly, Luke's deletion of πάντα, one of his favorite words, is revealing. Zmijewski (*Eschatologiereden*, 79) observes of the modification to γίνεσθαι, that these events at Jerusalem continue to have eschatological significance but do not, for Luke, belong to the end-time, strictly speaking.

[282] Farrell ("Perspective," 112-13) sees a link between this piece of Lukan redaction and Mark 1:14-15. He suggests that some in Luke's community "are using the Markan Gospel contrary to the way Luke thought it should be understood and that Luke is attempting to bring out the viewpoint which he thought Mark intended. In other words, Luke is attempting to clarify the Markan traditions in the new setting in which he finds himself" (113). This last statement is a valid description of one aspect of Luke's interpretive project. The specific inference is less certain, however. Luke has inserted the claim that ὁ καιρὸς ἤγγικεν into a section of the discourse revolving around the destruction of the temple (v 7), a past event for Luke's readers. By contrast, Luke omits Mark's second reference to messianic deceivers (Mark 13:21-23) when the context is the last phase before the eschatological climax. It is unlikely, therefore, that "apocalyptic enthusiasts" who wrongly interpret Mark's gospel form part of Luke's setting.

[283] Luke's alteration of Mark's "wars and rumors of wars" (13:7) to "wars and insurrections [ἀκαταστασίας]" (21:9a) is probably designed to conform the prophecy to the character of the events leading to the fall of Jerusalem. So also Nicol ("Tradition," 64).

[284] Because of this expansion of the Markan text, Mark's "this is the beginning of the woes" (13:8) is no longer applicable and is accordingly omitted by Luke. Nicol ("Tradition," 64) is therefore unduly puzzled by the omission of this Markan phrase.

[285] The identification of the period envisaged in vv 12-19 and the time of the church

13:13b to suppress the eschatological note: ὁ δὲ ὑπομείνας εἰς τέλος οὗτος σωθήσεται becomes ἐν τῇ ὑπομονῇ ὑμῶν κτήσεσθε (κτήσασθε) τὰς ψυχὰς ὑμῶν.[286] Luke's redaction shifts the focus of attention away from the End that calls for saving endurance to the active quality of endurance that delivers from danger under the duress of persecution. Sixth, Luke 21:24 extends the eschatological program to include a period of Gentile domination of Jerusalem ("until the times [καιροί] of the Gentiles are fulfilled";[287] contrast καιρός in v 8). At the conclusion of this period of Gentile dominance—but not before—the eschaton will appear on the horizon.[288] Finally, Luke excises Mark's reference to the "shortening of the days" (13:20), without which none would be saved.

In view of such an impressive collection of revisions, there can be no doubt that the Lukan eschatological discourse accommodates a delay in the completion of the eschatological scenario. However, against the view of Conzelmann that the delay motif implies Luke's removal of the end-time to the remote future, I will now show that the parousia delay serves just the opposite function in Luke's situation—namely to emphasize that the parousia, delayed until the present

---

in Acts is demonstrated in Excursus 3 below. As will become clear in the next chapter, this identification is crucial to a proper reading of eschatology in Acts.

[286] κτάομαι is a Lukan term: five of seven New Testament occurrences are in Luke-Acts.

[287] Kaestli (*Eschatologie*, 50) suggests that the expression "times of the Gentiles" indicates the period of Gentile domination of Jerusalem, but also that of God's saving activity among them (i.e., the Gentile mission). Cf. Farrell, "Perspective," 178 n. 1; Geiger, *Endzeitreden*, 207; Robinson, *Weg*, 51; Borgen, "Heilsgeschichte," 184. However, the content of verse 24—note the threefold repetition of ἔθνη—points only to Gentile subjugation of Jerusalem. The notion of Gentile mission is absent (so also Fitzmyer, *Luke*, 2.1346–47). Verses 12–19 and 20–24 therefore depict overlapping penultimate phases in the eschatological drama. The fall of Jerusalem initiates a new phase, namely the "times of the Gentiles"; the era of Gentile subjugation of Jerusalem will come to an end only with the final events of the end-time (vv 25–28). Events foretold in vv 12–19 find fulfillment beginning in the Acts narrative but continue through and beyond the fall of Jerusalem (thus overlapping the καιροὶ ἐθνῶν). Chance ("Jerusalem," 379–85) concedes that Luke does not mention Jerusalem's future restoration following the "times of the Gentiles," yet regards such an expectation on Luke's part as "logical." The existence of Jewish parallels where the temple's desolation is followed by restoration leads Chance to surmise that Luke 21:24c implies such restoration. However, Luke's handling of the Joel citation in Acts 2 contradicts this picture of an "implicit, logical" Lukan hope for Jerusalem's physical restoration. Luke omits from Joel 3:1–5 only that section which localizes salvation in Jerusalem and Mount Zion; he exploits the passage because it links salvation to "calling upon the name of the Lord [Jesus]" (Acts 2:21). Nowhere does Luke presuppose a final restoration of Jerusalem and temple that would somehow bypass the fundamental Lukan soteriological pattern (which is bound to Jesus; cf. Acts 3:22–23; 4:9–12).

[288] Despite important material differences, therefore, Luke 21:24 has a similar function in the discourse to that of Mark 13:10 (omitted in Luke 21). In each case an era focused on Gentiles precedes the eschatological climax.

time, is now to be regarded as imminent. Luke achieves this revision of the eschatological time-frame by means of a thoroughgoing phase clarification operation, of which the delay motif is but the first step.

Luke's recasting of Mark 13:14-20 in Luke 21:20-24 is especially revealing. Luke "historicizes" the account to conform it to the (now past) event of Jerusalem's destruction. Several scholars have noted the rich use of LXX materials in 21:20-24, and certain inconsistencies with the actual course of events (66-70 C.E.), and concluded that, far from giving a prophecy after the event, Luke 21:20-24 antedates the Jewish War.[289] Flückiger deems it *"undenkbar"* that, had Luke known the historical outcome, he would have composed his discourse solely on the basis of scriptural prophecies.[290] Flückiger's objection may in fact be a clue to the function of vv 20-24 in Luke's eschatological discourse. This is precisely history recast in terms of prophecy, history portrayed as fulfillment of scriptural prophecy. Luke makes the point explicitly in v 22. In other words, the Lukan Jesus, in vv 20-24, gives a prophetic oracle of judgment (composed after the event) against Jerusalem and "this people."[291] From Luke's perspective, however, prophetic judgment has become historical event.

Luke has shaped his sources to correct any misconception that the fall of Jerusalem—now history—was to have been the end-time event. The expansion of v 8 (ὁ καιρὸς ἤγγικεν. μὴ πορευθῆτε ὀπίσω αὐτῶν) following the question about the timing of the temple destruction (v 7) expressly warns against identifying the fall of Jerusalem, with the temple in ruins, as an event of the eschaton. Moreover, Luke's redaction of Mark 13:7a, b both conforms the language to the Jewish War (ἀκαταστασίας, 21:9)[292] and distances this event from the End (addition of πρῶτον, οὐκ εὐθέως for οὔπω). Further, the temporal indicator of v 12 (πρὸ δὲ τούτων πάντων) has the effect of placing the phase of persecution/testimony and of the Jewish War (vv 12-24) prior to the final events. Luke, in sum, has shaped the Markan discourse in order to demonstrate that the fall of Jerusalem was not to be seen as the end-time event.[293]

At the same time, Luke does not sharply demarcate the destruction of Jerusalem from the true end-time events (which begin with the cosmic signs of vv 25-26 and culminate in the advent of the Son of man and the redemption of believers [vv 27-28]). Conzelmann's insistence upon this separation between

---

[289] Dodd, "Fall;" Gaston, *Stone,* 358-65; B. Reicke, "Synoptic Prophecies on the Destruction of Jerusalem," in *Studies in New Testament and Early Christian Literature,* ed. D. E. Aune (Leiden: Brill, 1972) 121-34, 124-28; Flückiger, "Zerstörung"; cf. I. H. Marshall, *Commentary on Luke* (Grand Rapids: Eerdmans, 1978) 770-74.

[290] "Zerstörung," 390.

[291] See the discussion above of Luke's transformation of the discourse setting and audience.

[292] So also Nicol, "Tradition," 64; Kaestli, *Eschatologie,* 44. See note 283 above.

[293] Cf. Geiger, *Endzeitreden,* 170, 249-55. Geiger holds (252) that Luke consistently separates historical and eschatological events, and (249) that he looks back on the destruction of Jerusalem as a strictly historical event.

vv 24 and 25 has been justly rejected by, among others, Flender and Zmijewski.[294] In contrast to Mark 13:24, where explicit time indicators situate vv 24–27 (cosmic signs and parousia) after the events of the preceding passage,[295] Luke 21:25 has the simple connective καί. The final eschatological events —cosmic signs and parousia (21:25–28) —are thereby *distinguished but not separated* from the event of Jerusalem's destruction. For Luke and his community, the chronological distance separating the fall of Jerusalem (past) and the eschaton (future) was not something that needed to be shown: it was a datum of history. Luke's task, in clarifying the relation of Jerusalem's demise to the parousia, was to correct a mistaken identification of the two, yet without severing their connection. At an unspecified (and unspecifiable) time following the fall of Jerusalem —but not in the remote future —the eschaton will overtake Luke's community.

This reading of the discourse is confirmed by the function of vv 9–11 in Luke 21. By adding to v 11 φόβητρά τε καὶ ἀπ' οὐρανοῦ σημεῖα μεγάλα ἔσται,[296] Luke employs vv 9–11 to provide an overview of the entire eschatological scenario.[297]

---

[294] Flender, *Luke,* 103–04; Zmijewski, *Eschatologiereden,* 95. Zmijewski repeatedly emphasizes the *"sachliche Verbindung"* in Luke between history and eschatology. His own approach, however, concedes too much to the position of Conzelmann. Because Zmijewski fails to distinguish between the situation implicit in Jesus' career within the discourse and Luke's own situation, he misses the *zeitliche* connection that Luke also maintains between the fall of Jerusalem and now-imminent end-time events. Against Zmijewski (319), it must be argued that events are eschatological in Luke not simply because they are part of God's plan which is being worked out (history becomes eschatology), but also because the era of the church and of Jerusalem's destruction does chronologically precede— by an unknown, *but not indefinite* interval —the final events of history.

[295] Even as the phrase "in those days" (Mark 13:24) also locates the events of vv 24–27 within the period of affliction.

[296] Again, Nicol's puzzlement over this "inexplicable" addition ("Tradition," 64) is unwarranted. "Signs and wonders" is a favorite Lukan expression (although φόβητρα is a *hapax legomenon*); cf. especially Acts 2:19.

[297] The noun ἀκαταστασία in v 9 being, however, the only allusion to the Jewish War/destruction of Jerusalem (cf. Geiger, *Endzeitreden,* 169; Fitzmyer, *Luke,* 2.1336). Robinson (*Weg,* 47–51) and Fitzmyer (*Luke,* 2.1334–37), however, distinguish between the cosmic signs of vv 9–11 and those of vv 25–26, and refer vv 9–11 as a whole to the period preceding the fall of Jerusalem. According to this reading, the question of v 7 controls the section through v 11. In its Lukan form ("When will these things be, and what is the sign [indicating] when these things are about to happen?"), the question is restricted to the timing of the destruction of the temple. Nevertheless, v 9b (". . . for these things must happen first, but the End is not immediately"), coupled with the new beginning in v 10 ("Then he said to them . . ."), sets off vv 10–11 as an advance beyond the preceding verses. Verses 10–11 trace the scenario up through the τέλος (v 9). At this point, Fitzmyer's argument falters, for the absolute use of "the End" is unlikely to refer to Jerusalem's end, as Fitzmyer asserts (2.1335).

All that follows, including mission/persecution (vv 12-19) and the fall of Jerusalem (vv 20-24), constitutes a course of events moving toward the consummation. Yet, Lukan phase clarification emphasizes the penultimate quality of vv 12-24 (πρὸ δὲ . . . , v 12).

The results of the investigation so far may be summarized as follows. From the vantage point of Luke's own community, vv 12-19, depicting the time of mission/ persecution to be narrated in Acts,[298] and vv 20-24, portraying prophetic judgment against Jerusalem, together define a series of events that is for the most part past. Luke distinguishes this penultimate phase from a final phase—the eschatological period itself—the content of which is a set of cosmic wonders preceding a sudden, universal parousia of the Son of man (21:25-27, 34-36). Verses 12-24, while not portraying end-time events,[299] link the recent past of Luke's church to the awaited parousia. The outcome of this phase clarification is that Luke places his own community within the closing chapter of the period before the End. There they are to await an imminent parousia which, while its timing remains unknown and undecipherable, will assuredly come in a decisive manner for "all who dwell on the face of the earth."[300] When the world-shaking events of vv 25-26 begin to occur—and there will be no missing them—then the arrival in glory of the Son of man, bringing with him redemption of the faithful, will follow in short order (vv 29-33).

Further confirmation of this understanding of the eschatological view expressed in Luke 21 is supplied by two additional redactional observations. First, the use of ἐγγύς and ἐγγίζω in the discourse not only suggests a coherent compositional plan,[301] but also highlights Luke's phase clarifying activity. In Luke 21:8 ἤγγικεν characterizes false teaching: the End was not to be seen in close proximity to the ruin of the temple. Luke 21:20 employs ἤγγικεν to refer not to the eschaton but to Jerusalem's destruction ("desolation," ἐρήμωσις). Not until 21:28 does ἐγγίζω have a positive content with respect to final events. Here the nearness of redemption (ἀπολύτρωσις)[302] forms a sharp contrast to the imminent

---

[298] See Excursus 3 below.

[299] From the perspective of Luke's community, the view (which Luke corrects) that the end-time was to have arrived, but did not, in the cataclysmic events of 66-70 C.E., may have led to a despairing abandonment of eschatological hopes in Luke's own time. Such a development is certainly consistent with Luke's occasional heightening of eschatological expectation, with his emphasis on the need for vigilance, and with his whole program of phase clarification, as described in this section.

[300] Dupont ("La Parabole du Figuier qui Bourgeonne," *RB* 75 [1968] 526-48) rightly perceives that the teaching of the parable of the fig-tree (and all the trees!) in Luke 21:29-31 becomes applicable, for Luke, only when the cosmic signs of vv 25-28 occur (536). Dupont inaccurately describes Lukan eschatology, however, when he claims that the end-time signs are pushed back to the indefinite future and that Luke is wary of short-term eschatological expectations (535-36).

[301] So Zmijewski, *Eschatologiereden,* 56.

[302] Answering the hopes of Anna and other expectant Jews who looked for Jerusalem's

desolation of Jerusalem prophesied in v 20. Finally, Luke preserves a twofold ἐγγύς from Mark's version of the parable of the fig-tree (Luke 21:30, 31), yet specifies in the second instance that it is the kingdom of God that is near. The careful repetition of ἐγγίζω and ἐγγύς in the Lukan discourse indicates that Luke has endeavored to be clear about what is and what is not to be seen as valid future expectation.

Second, Luke's treatment of Mark 13:15-18, 21-23 has brought the Markan discourse into harmony with his own distinction between penultimate and final events. In its Markan context, Mark 13:21-23 depicts a second appearance of deceivers (cf. 13:5-6) subsequent to the section on tribulations (13:14-20, which Luke "historicizes"). Luke removes any possible confusion of phases in the eschatological program and preserves a close connection between the fall of Jerusalem and the parousia by relocating his version of Mark 13:21-23 to his eschatological discourse in chapter 17 (v 23). The effect in Luke 21 is to eliminate the deceivers from the final period before the end-time itself—an especially important move because of the content of their deception (ὁ καιρὸς ἤγγικεν). Luke also rewrites Mark 13:15-18 with a view to "tidying up" the sequence of historical and eschatological events. Mark 13:15-16 stands in a certain tension with vv 14, 17-18: are the people in Judea to stay put (vv 15-16) or flee (vv 14, 17-18)? The former strategy suggests a sudden event for which no preparation is possible, the latter an event that may be avoided by flight. Luke resolves this tension by bringing Mark 13:15-16 forward to Luke 17:31, where the admonition is appropriate in light of Luke's portrayal there of a sudden, inescapable parousia. Luke 21, on the other hand, is left with the reformulated call for flight/avoidance of Jerusalem (Mark 13:21-23), a warning appropriate to the destruction of Jerusalem here in view.[303] In other words, Luke has carefully revised Mark to portray two distinct (though related) events—the one chronologically prior and avoidable (Jerusalem's destruction, emphasized in Luke 21), and the other still future, inescapable, and sudden (the parousia, emphasized in Luke 17).[304] This finding reinforces the thesis that Luke clarifies the phase sequence of the eschatological program by distinguishing penultimate events (past and present for Luke's community) and final events (imminent future for Luke and his readers).[305]

λύτρωσις (2:38). Ironically, the "consolation of Israel" (2:25) has found fruition in the Christian story (21:28) even as Jerusalem itself experienced ἐρήμωσις instead of λύτρωσις.

[303] Cf. Nicol ("Tradition," 67), who observes that Luke omits Mark 13:15-16, 19-20 because they refer to the consummation, not to the events of 70 C.E. which he is describing in Luke 21:20-24.

[304] Cf. Flender (*Luke,* 13), who explains the differing audiences in Luke 17 and 21 by their respective content. Chapter 17 emphasizes the suddenness and unexpectedness of the onset of the parousia, while chapter 21 focuses attention on the time preceding this sudden End. Similarly Grundmann, *Lukas,* 378.

[305] Cf. the similar conclusions reached by L. Hartman, "A Linguistic Examination of

3. "That you may stand before the Son of man": Pastoral Motives Informing Luke 21:5-36

Eschatological phase clarification is not for Luke an end in itself. This "revisionist history" is not a theoretical project, but rather serves a governing pastoral motive.[306] In a fashion anticipated by the paraenetic tenor of Luke 12:35-48 and 17:20-18:8, Luke 21 approaches the problem of eschatology with an eye to the ethos of the Lukan community. Luke's interest in eschatological phase clarification corrects a faulty reading of the eschatological timetable that has rendered imminent future hope suspect in his own situation. By concluding the discourse with an appeal for readiness in view of the sudden, inescapable arrival of "that day" (vv 34-36), Luke indicates the importance of pastoral motives in his composition of the discourse and states the goal of the project: ". . . that you[307] may be able to escape all these things that are about to happen, and to stand before the Son of man" (21:36).

The first dimension of Luke's pastoral motive in the discourse consists in the correction of an inaccurate understanding of the relation of future (eschatology) to past (history). The redactional features of 21:8-9[308] show Luke instructing his readers that hope for an imminent consummation was out of place in connection with the fall of Jerusalem (now past). Verse 12 ("but before all these things . . .") makes the same point with respect to the period of Christian witness and persecution which Luke will narrate in Acts. Indeed, an imminent End becomes applicable—but then decisively so—only with the beginning of the cosmic signs portrayed in vv 25-26 (cf. v 11). Nevertheless, the End—though postponed—does not recede into the distant future. Faith must remain eschatological faith,

---

Luke 21,13," in *Coniectanea Neotestamentica* 19 (1963) 57-75. Hartman maintains that Luke distinguishes between events that are "typical of the eschatological period as a whole and those that will characterize the final phase of that period" (73). Similarly, Creed, *Luke*, 253: "The contemporary situation has made it necessary for Luke to impose an interpretation upon his sources which will distinguish for his readers between fulfilled and unfulfilled prophecy." Farrell ("Perspective," 102-03) comments: "It is this Lukan situation which appears to be most significant for the shaping of Luke's thought. . . ." Where Mark saw the destruction of Jerusalem as a part of the End, Luke, Farrell contends, "expresses more precisely that the destruction of Jerusalem is an event during the eschatological period inaugurated by Jesus, but before the End itself" (107). This analysis agrees with my own reading of the discourse, with the single difference that I am reserving the term "eschatological" for the period of the End *per se*.

[306] Emphasized also by Wilson ("Lukan") and Farrell ("Perspective," 164-65, 171). Geiger (*Endzeitreden*, 260-61) notes that pastoral motifs are consistent in Luke 17 and Luke 21, but views the role of paraclesis as more pronounced in Luke 21. He conjectures that Luke 21 has been more thoroughly shaped by the present situation of Luke's community than has Luke 17.

[307] It is noteworthy that Luke has cast 21:12-19 and 21:34-36, the pericopae of paraenesis and consolation, entirely in the 2nd person plural. See footnote 277 above.

[308] Discussed above, section E.2.

for the consummation of history may occur at any moment. It will announce its arrival with world-shaking events that provoke fear in people without faith (vv 25-26), but expectation of imminent redemption in those whose eschatologically charged faith has remained intact (v 28). Not only the absence of any indicators of temporal separation between vv 24 and 25,[309] but also the assertion of v 32, taken up from the tradition, make clear that Luke expects the eschaton sooner rather than later (certainly not in the indefinite future): "Truly I tell you, this generation will not pass away before all has occurred."[310]

Luke's project involved more than ideational revision, however. Its true target was the ethos of the Lukan community, a by-now familiar theme. So Luke's second pastoral motif in Luke 21 takes the form of an exhortation to vigilance and readiness.[311] The culmination of the discourse has precisely this function:

> But take heed to yourselves lest your hearts be weighed down with dissipation and drunkennesss and cares of this life, and that day come upon you suddenly like a snare. . . . But watch at all times, praying that you may have strength to escape all these things that will take place, and to stand before the Son of man (21:34, 36).

Comparison of vv 34-36 with the paraenetic section of 1 Thess 5:1-11[312]

[309] Verse 25 begins with the conjunction καί. See the discussion above, section E.2.

[310] Luke adjusts Mark's "all these things" (ταῦτα πάντα; 13:30) to "all things" (πάντα; 21:32). Luke's version removes all doubt about the scope of events promised to "this generation." The universal denouement will happen before the present generation has run its course. Heaven and earth will disappear from the scene at that moment (v 33), but Jesus' word (and, by implication — cf. v 28 — his faithful community) will stand. Of course, various attempts to evade this reading of v 32 are scattered through the literature. For example, Conzelmann (St. Luke, 131) claims that " 'this generation' means here humanity in general. . . . The saying is no longer a declaration that the End is near at hand." M. Meinertz (" 'Dieses Geschlecht' im Neuen Testament," BZ 1 [1957] 283-89) surveys the uses of "this generation" in the New Testament and concludes that the expression (with Deut 32:5 as the starting point) becomes a technical term signifying the people Israel in its wickedness, not the contemporary generation (285). The moralistic character of the phrase has priority over the chronological in the New Testament (286). Thus γενεά and λαός are to be viewed as parallel terms. The insight that the phrase "this generation" ordinarily has a negative connotation in the gospels — pointing to a collectivity deserving of judgment — is valid. It does not follow, however, that the chronological force of the expression evaporates, as it must for Conzelmann's view to stand.

[311] As in Luke 12:35-48 and 17:20-18:8.

[312] The vocabulary common to the two passages includes: (1) "day of the Lord," 1 Thess 5:2; "that day," Luke 21:34; (2) suddenly (αἰφνίδιος), 1 Thess 5:3 and Luke 21:34; (3) come upon (ἐφίστημι), 1 Thess 5:3 and Luke 21:34; (4) escape (ἐκφύγω), 1 Thess 5:3 and Luke 21:36; (5) drunkenness (μεθύω and μέθη), 1 Thess 5:7 and Luke 21:34. Cf. also γρηγορῶμεν (1 Thess 5:6, 10) and ἀγρυπνεῖτε (Luke 21:36); and the imagery of thief (1 Thess 5:2, 4; also Luke 12:39) in relation to that of a snare (παγίς, Luke 21:35). Verse 35 in Luke 21, which has no part in this shared imagery and language linking the two passages, may come (after ὡς παγίς, at least) from Luke himself. The verse emphasizes the universal and inescapable nature of the end-time events.

shows that Luke has tapped traditional paraenetic material pertaining to the parousia in this concluding section. Not only its climactic position in the discourse, but also the way in which it takes up themes from the earlier eschatological passages,[313] indicates, however, that Luke has made this piece of paraenesis his own. The goal of the Lukan eschatological discourse, therefore, is a pastoral and paraenetic one: to enable Luke's readers to stand before the Son of man on his day. Despite hardships suffered during the time of mission and persecution (vv 12-19),[314] Christians may be sure that deliverance will be complete (vv 18-19), effected through their very endurance. Despite the passage of time, Luke's readers must persevere in faith (cf. 18:1-8) and must remain vigilant (cf. 12:35-48; 17:22-37). For the parousia will indeed come — suddenly, swiftly, and inescapably, though unpredictably — on the heels of a set of remarkable events of cosmic proportion. Luke cautions his church not to be lulled into complacency; they stand in the time when the End draws near. Promised penultimate events[315] have been realized — or, in the case of the "times of the Gentiles," are approaching realization. Only the cosmic signs and final appearance of the Son of man (vv 25-27; cf. Acts 2:19-20) await fulfillment in Luke's situation. Luke has shaped the discourse of Luke 21:5-36 in order to equip his community for those certain and approaching events in which the history of God's saving activity among his people will come to a climax and he will exercise his sovereign judgment over the entire world.

EXCURSUS 3: LUKE 21 AND THE NARRATIVE OF ACTS

The so-called "eclipse of the eschaton" in Acts, as described by Gaventa (for chapters 3-28), will prove to be less problematic when we note the methodical way in which the author of Luke-Acts has linked his narrative in Acts to the eschatological discourse of Luke 21. Events in Acts take on the character of fulfillment of prophecy; moreover, this literary device enables us to fit the narrative of Acts into the Lukan eschatological program, defined programmatically in Luke 21. The correspondence between the narrative of Acts and Luke 21, especially vv 12-19, is demonstrated by numerous verbal echoes in Acts

---

[313] Dissipation and drunkenness: cf. 12:45; cares of this existence: cf. 17:26-30; 8:14; sudden, unexpected advent of the End: cf. 12:35-48; 17:24-35; call for alertness: cf. 12:35-48; 17:22-37.

[314] In my judgment, Maddox is correct to argue that this section of the discourse corresponds more closely to the period of church activity narrated in Acts than to the concrete experiences of Luke's community in the present. For other assessments of the role of persecution in the Lukan setting, see, e.g., S. Brown, *Apostasy and Perseverance in the Theology of Luke* (Rome: Biblical Institute, 1969); G. Braumann, "Das Mittel der Zeit, Erwägungen zur Theologie des Lukasevangeliums," *ZNW* 54 (1963) 117-45.

[315] That is, the time of testimony and persecution (vv 12-19, fulfilled in the narrative of Acts) and the fall of Jerusalem (vv 20-24) and its temple (vv 5-6).

of this portion of the eschatological discourse.[316] These links are summarized in the table below.

Luke 21:12-19	Narrative of Acts
v 12 παραδιδόντες εἰς . . . φυλακάς	Fulfillment — Frequent imprisonments in Acts: 16 occurrences of φυλακή
v 12 ἀπαγομένους ἐπὶ βασιλεῖς καὶ ἡγεμόνας ἕνεκεν τοῦ ὀνόματός μου	Representative fulfillment in 9:15-16 and its realization in the subsequent narrative — τοῦ βαστάσαι τὸ ὄνομά μου ἐνώπιον . . . βασιλέων . . . ὅσα δεῖ αὐτὸν ὑπὲρ τοῦ ὀνόματός μου παθεῖν
v 14 ἀπολογηθῆναι	Fulfillment — 8 occurrences of ἀπολογέομαι in Acts
v 15 ἐγὼ γὰρ δώσω ὑμῖν στόμα καὶ σοφίαν ᾗ οὐ δυνήσονται ἀντιστῆναι ἢ ἀντειπεῖν ἅπαντες οἱ ἀντικείμενοι ὑμῖν	Representative fulfillment in 6:10 — οὐκ ἴσχυον ἀντιστῆναι τῇ σοφίᾳ καὶ τῷ πνεύματι ᾧ ἐλάλει
v 16 θανατώσουσιν ἐξ ὑμῶν	Representative fulfillment in the deaths of Stephen and James
v 18 θρὶξ ἐκ τῆς κεφαλῆς ὑμῶν οὐ μὴ ἀπόληται	Echo in 27:34 — Paul's words of encouragement: οὐδενὸς γὰρ ὑμῶν θρὶξ ἀπὸ τῆς κεφαλῆς ἀπολεῖται

From the Corresponding Phase in the Eschatological Program in Luke 21:8-11, which presents an overview of the entire course of events leading up to the eschaton:

v 11 σεισμοὶ μεγάλοι	Partial fulfillment in 16:26 σεισμὸς μέγας
v 11 κατὰ τόπους λιμοί	Partial fulfillment in 11:28 λιμὸν μεγάλην μέλλειν ἔσεσθαι ἐφ' ὅλην τὴν οἰκουμένην

---

[316] Maddox (*Purpose*, 116) has observed this correspondence: "The passage may not be addressed directly to the situation of Luke's contemporaries at all. Instead, Luke's reference in v. 12-19 seems to be to the period leading up to the Jewish War, which is more or less the same as the period covered by Acts." So also Farrell, "Perspective," 124–32; Chance, "Jerusalem," 365–66; Zmijewski, *Eschatologiereden*, 220–21; cf. Keck, *Abschiedsrede*, 11–12.

The data indicate that the events narrated in Acts fall squarely within the period portrayed in Luke 21:12–19, that is, the time of persecution and testimony. Since Luke's form of the discourse explicitly rejects any assertion of an imminent consummation throughout this penultimate phase (cf. v 8: ὁ καιρὸς ἤγγικεν), it should come as no surprise that an imminent parousia recedes from view in the narrative of Acts. Imminent expectation would be as ill-timed in Acts (which stands in the penultimate phase of eschatological fulfillment) as Jesus pronounces it to be in Luke 21:8. This correlation of Luke 21 with the narrative of Acts is basic to a correct reading of the eschatology of Acts (the subject of our next chapter).

3
Eschatology and Situation in Acts

The Book of Acts has played the part of the chameleon in recent study of Luke's eschatology. According to the majority of commentators, the second of Luke's two volumes betrays a blunting of the eschatological edge of earliest Christianity. Maddox assesses the extent of eschatology in Acts as "only slight,"[1] and Schneider concludes that "das Parusie-Thema tritt in der Apostelgeschichte gegenüber dem dritten Evangelium auffallend zurück."[2] Scholars have parted company, however, in defining the relation of this diminution of eschatology in Acts to the eschatological perspective of Luke's gospel — and to his project taken as a whole. For scholars aligned with Conzelmann,[3] these observations about Acts are consistent with the evaluation of eschatology in the third gospel. The eschaton retreats in importance even as it recedes into the remote future, both in Luke and in Acts. The very fact of Acts constitutes decisive proof, according to this view, that Luke no longer thinks eschatologically.[4] For other scholars, who discern a living imminent hope in Luke's gospel, Acts poses a serious problem. S. G. Wilson concludes from the divergent data in Luke and Acts that it is necessary to distinguish the eschatological perspectives expressed in the two volumes:

> The eschatology of Acts follows much the same pattern as Luke's gospel, with the important exception that we do not find any example of imminent expectation such as we found in the Gospel. . . . Luke's eschatology does not appear to be the same in the Gospel and Acts. In the Gospel there is a tension between the delay and imminent expectation; in Acts there is no imminent expectation.[5]

Wilson decides that Luke wrote Acts long after the gospel; in the interim, his views changed.[6] B. Gaventa follows a similar approach but draws the line

---

[1] *Purpose*, 129–30.

[2] Schneider, *Apostelgeschichte*, 1.336. Cf. Franklin, *Christ*, 27.

[3] That is, Vielhauer, Käsemann, Haenchen, Grässer. See the discussion in chapter one above.

[4] See Käsemann, "Problem," 28–29; Vielhauer, "Paulinism," 47.

[5] Wilson, "Lukan," 343, 347.

[6] Ibid., 347. It should be noted that neither Maddox nor Schneider, both of whom agree with Wilson's portrayal of eschatology in Acts, accepts his twin conclusions that Acts comes from a later time and reflects a different eschatological posture vis-à-vis the gospel (see Maddox, *Purpose*, 130–32; Schneider, *Apostelgeschichte*, 1.336).

differently—either between chapters two and three of Acts or between chapters three and four. Eschatological hope is central in Acts 1–3[7] but is "eclipsed" in the remainder of the narrative.

Advocates of imminent future expectation in Acts have also registered their dissenting minority opinion. F. O. Francis, on the basis of the controlling function of the Joel citation in Acts 2:17–21 for the entire narrative of Acts, argues that all manifestations of the Spirit in Acts are eschatologically charged.[8] R. H. Smith, too, contends that the hope for an imminent consummation remains alive in Acts.[9] The ending of Acts, in particular, has "eschatological overtones."[10] Mattill claims that the eschatological atmosphere created by numerous passages in Acts has been overlooked because of a persistent failure to translate the verb μέλλω with its proper imminent force (Acts 10:42; 17:31; 24:15, 25).[11] The Western text of Acts 28:31 accurately conveys the "contagious Naherwartung" of Acts, "for the whole world is about to be judged."[12]

The Book of Acts may not be as rich in explicitly eschatological material as is the gospel; nevertheless, the pivotal role of Acts in the assessment of Lukan eschatology is now obvious.[13] This chapter of the dissertation will focus attention on four passages of special importance for the subject of Luke's eschatological perspective: Acts 1:3–11; 2:17–21; 3:12–26; and 28:17–31.[14] I will advance the thesis that an apparent soft-pedaling of imminent future hope is exactly what we should expect to find in Acts, given the chronological position within the eschatological program that Luke assigns the events narrated in Acts.[15] The narrative situation presupposed throughout Acts corresponds to the penultimate phase before the final eschatological period (the destruction of Jerusalem and the completion of the "times of the Gentiles" [Luke 21:24] intervene between the two). Accordingly, hope for an imminent parousia is never appropriate during the narrative of Acts. Nevertheless, Luke places this phase of mission and persecution (cf. Luke 21:12–19) within an eschatological context. Because these events constitute the fulfillment of promises announced long ago for the "last days" (Acts 2:17–21), culminating events still awaited by Luke and his readers acquire an additional measure of certitude. In Luke's situation—as distinguished

---

[7] Gaventa, "Revisited," 34–35, 38: the analysis is unclear, for Acts 3 is aligned sometimes with the eschatological chapters 1–2, sometimes with the uneschatological Acts 4–28.

[8] "Eschatology."

[9] "Exegesis" and "History."

[10] "History," 897–98.

[11] Mattill, *Last,* 41–49.

[12] Ibid., 54.

[13] Similarly, Schnackenburg, "Aussagen," 262: the paucity of statements regarding the parousia in Acts does not lessen its significance in Luke's theology.

[14] The theme of future judgment appears in such passages as Acts 10:42; 17:31; 24:25 (cf. 24:15); however, these texts disclose no information about the timing or nature of end-time judgment and so do not figure in the discussion here.

[15] See Excursus 3 above.

from the situation within the story—imminent hope remains relevant, indeed crucial. This message of Luke for his day has come to light already through the analysis of the third gospel. Nothing in Acts contradicts that message.

A. THE ASCENSION NARRATIVE OF ACTS 1:3-11

To [the apostles] Jesus also presented himself alive, after he had suffered, with many proofs—appearing to them over forty days, and talking about the kingdom of God. And while he was eating with [them], he charged them not to depart from Jerusalem but to await the promise of the Father "which you heard from me, that 'John baptized with water, but you will be baptized with [the] Holy Spirit in a few days.' " Therefore, when they had come together, they asked him, "Lord, are you going to restore the kingdom to Israel at this time?" But he said to them: "It is not for you to know times or seasons which the Father has set by his own authority. Nevertheless, you will receive power—when the Holy Spirit has come upon you—and you will be my witnesses in Jerusalem, and in all Judea and Samaria, and to the farthest reaches of the earth" (1:3-8).

In a manner reminiscent of Luke 19:11 and 21:7, Acts opens (1:6) with a question from Jesus' disciples concerning the timing of the eschatological fulfillment: κύριε, εἰ ἐν τῷ χρόνῳ ἀποκαθιστάνεις τὴν βασιλείαν τῷ Ἰσραήλ; Jesus' talk about the kingdom (v 3) and the promise of the Spirit (v 5) appear to evoke this query.[16] The question of verse 6 has two components, the first concerning the *timing* of kingdom restoration, the second concerning the *nature and scope* of the kingdom. Correspondingly, Jesus' reply (vv 7-8) contains two elements, offering both correction and promise. In response to the disciples' question about the immediacy of the kingdom, Jesus denies the possibility of knowledge of the chronology of the consummation:[17] "It is not for you to know times or seasons. . . ." (v 7). This posture of agnosticism is consistent with the eschatological view expressed in Luke 12:35-48. Although God has established the chronology of coming events (ἔθετο), it necessarily eludes human

---

[16] Joel 3:1-5 (LXX) assigns a prominent role to the Spirit in the end-time events, an association upon which Luke capitalizes in Acts 2. Cf. Francis, "Eschatology"; S. G. Wilson, "The Ascension: A Critique and an Interpretation," *ZNW* 59 (1968) 269-81, 278. Other texts portraying an end-time outpouring of the Spirit include Isa 44:3; Ezek 36:26-27; 37:14; 39:29; T. Levi 18:11.

[17] This is likely a Lukan formulation of Mark 13:32, which Luke omits from his version of the eschatological discourse (Luke 21); cf. Haenchen, *Acts,* 143. Especially striking is the absence of any mention of Jesus' ignorance of the timing of kingdom restoration. Evidently Luke's Jesus, unlike his disciples, knows the "timetable"; for Luke to attribute ignorance to Jesus on this point would mitigate the consoling and warning force of Luke 12:35-48; 17:20-18:8; and 21:5-36. The combination of the motifs of kingdom and restoration makes the eschatological quality of vv 6-8 unmistakable, although Haenchen's assertion that "from Malachi 3.23 LXX onwards, ἀποκαθίστημι is a technical term in eschatology" (p. 143 n. 2; cf. A. Oepke, "ἀποκαθίστημι, ἀποκατάστασις," *TDNT* 1.388) may conclude too much from too little evidence.

discernment. At the same time (v 8), Jesus redefines the content of "restoration of the kingdom to Israel":

ἀλλὰ λήμψεσθε δύναμιν ἐπελθόντος τοῦ ἁγίου πνεύματος ἐφ᾽ ὑμᾶς καὶ ἔσεσθέ μου μάρτυρες ἔν τε Ἰερουσαλὴμ καὶ (ἐν) πάσῃ τῇ Ἰουδαίᾳ καὶ Σαμαρείᾳ καὶ ἕως ἐσχάτου τῆς γῆς.

Verse 8 repeats the promise of the Spirit (v 5) in Lukan language[18] and links to that promise a programmatic prophecy-mandate: the disciples will be Jesus' witnesses ἕως ἐσχάτου τῆς γῆς,[19] in a mission program commencing in Jerusalem and advancing by stages to its final destination. The subsequent narrative represents both obedience to this mandate and fulfillment of this prophecy of the risen Jesus.

If the question of Acts 1:6 recalls the related queries of Luke 19:11 (implicit) and 21:7, the same is true of the reply. In all three cases, imminent or immediate end expectation is declared inappropriate to the situation at hand. The explicit eschatological assertion of Acts 1:3-8 is that—in this setting on the eve of the world mission—the End is not to be expected at once, indeed, that Jesus' disciples must remain uncertain about the answer to the question "when?" A period of mission throughout the world will precede the End. Haenchen infers from this that Luke aims the same message to his own situation: "Luke is the spokesman of a new age. He has decisively renounced all expectation of an imminent end."[20] However, it is hazardous to assume that Luke equated the situation at this point within his story with the situation now confronting his contemporary church.[21] When the world mission has reached fruition, in fulfillment of promise, the matter of the timing of the consummation may receive a new answer. The triumphant conclusion of Acts, with Paul preaching the gospel freely at Rome,[22] and the path leading openly to the Gentiles, may not represent final fulfillment of the prophecy of Acts 1:8,[23] but it does serve as a bridge to

---

[18] Cf. the formulation in Luke 24:49.

[19] This phrase, which is borrowed from Isa 49:6, recurs in Acts 13:47. The worldwide mission of the church, as narrated in Acts, thereby receives a double investment of authority: to the voice of scripture is added Jesus' own word.

[20] *Acts,* 143. Cf. Schnackenburg ("Aussagen," 255), who argues that Acts 1:6-8 dismisses imminent expectation, but not the coming of the kingdom itself. Luke does not just reject a false imminent hope; he also, at the same time, upholds the "Tatsächlichkeit" of the parousia.

[21] Schnackenburg ("Aussagen," 254) dismisses the suggestion that the conversation in Acts 1:6-8 is to be understood in terms of the situation reported in the narrative: "Aber ein blosser Rückblick auf die damalige Situation der Jünger ist mit Sicherheit auszuschliessen." Rather, the question of the disciples stems from a perspective current in Luke's own situation. But apart from reference to the redactional nature of the question in v 6, Schnackenburg offers no argument to buttress his "certain" judgment.

[22] Despite the condition of house arrest.

[23] In "Der Ausdruck ΕΩΣ ΕΣΧΑΤΟΥ ΤΗΣ ΓΗΣ (Apostelgeschichte 1:8) und sein alttestamentlicher Hintergrund" (in *Studia Biblica et Semitica,* ed. W. C. van Unnik and A. S. van der Woude [Wageningen: Veenman and Zonen, 1966] 335-49, 336-37), W. C. van

Luke's own day, when the church stood even closer to that goal. Verses 7-8 also assert that restoration of the kingdom to Israel will include participation of the nations. The subsequent narrative makes clear that Gentiles will come to enjoy the realization of the "hope of Israel."[24]

In a fashion corresponding to Luke 21:12-19 ("but before all these things," v 12), Acts 1:3-8 indicates that the End will not arrive until a period of mission has taken the Christian witness to the corners of the earth. An imminent End is out of the question at this place in the story; however, Luke's church stands in a different relation to the Gentile mission (now largely a past accomplishment) from that in which the church stands in the Acts narrative (only the ending of Acts brings the reader to the threshold of a world mission focused on the Gentiles).

When we move beyond v 8 we come to the account of the ascension (Acts 1:9-11),[25] another event with a significant eschatological dimension.

> And when he had said these things, as they were watching, he was lifted up, and a cloud concealed him from their eyes. And while they were looking intently toward heaven—as he departed—behold, two men stood before them in bright clothing. They said, "Men of Galilee, why do you stand looking toward heaven? This Jesus who has been taken up from you into heaven will come in the same way that you saw him going into heaven" (1:9-11).

Unnik argues, against what he terms a consensus of recent German scholarship (e.g., Haenchen, *Acts*, 143-44 n. 9; Conzelmann, *Apostelgeschichte*, 22), that ἔσχατον τῆς γῆς refers, in Acts, to Rome. Only PsSol 8:15 appears, at first glance, to support this identification. Even this piece of evidence is shaky, van Unnik holds, for if Pompey was in Spain from 77 to 72 B.C.E., the author of PsSol may have used ἔσχατα γῆς with reference to Spain, that is, to "the farthest limit of the earth" (p. 347). Survey of the use of the expression ἕως ἐσχάτου τῆς γῆς in both Greco-Roman literature and the Septuagint leads van Unnik to conclude that the meaning "bis zum äussersten Ende der Welt" is well established. Luke envisaged, then, a world mission to the remotest reaches of the earth, that is, to the whole world without exception. Van Unnik also notes that ἕως with the singular ἐσχάτου occurs only here and in the LXX: Luke evidently borrowed the phrase from the LXX. Confirmation of the view that ἕως ἐσχάτου τῆς γῆς in Acts 1:8 means "to the farthest reaches of the world" is supplied by the ending of Acts. Luke gives his writing an open-ended conclusion; this final episode brings the reader to the dawn of a new era, that of the Gentile mission (v 28: salvation will go out to the Gentiles, and *they* will hear!). Rome is not the culmination of the mission but rather a new point of departure.

24 This redefinition of the salvation awaited by pious Israel, anticipated in Luke 1-2 (see chapter two above), will come to a climax in the final episode of Acts, with Paul at Rome. My discussion of Acts 28:17-31 will clarify the status of Israel's salvation hopes in Luke-Acts. The themes of eschatology and Israel are inextricably interwoven; there can be no eschatological completion without a decisive answer to the end-time hopes of Israel.

25 For discussion of the relationship between the ascension accounts in Luke 24 and Acts 1, see Wilson, "Ascension"; P. A. van Stempvoort, "The Interpretation of the Ascension in Luke and Acts," *NTS* 5 (1958-59) 30-42; G. Schille, *Apostelgeschichte*, 75-76.

The language with which Luke narrates Jesus' ascension points the disciples (and Luke's readers) ahead to Jesus' parousia.[26] That event will occur with the same certainty that already attends the exaltation of Jesus, an accomplished fact. The disciples' prolonged skyward stare is, however, inappropriate to the situation at hand, for Jesus' final words to his assembled followers (1:7-8) outlined a period of mission which necessarily precedes the End and instructed them to return to Jerusalem to await the gift that will empower the mission (1:4). In addition, the message of reassurance which verse 11c affords ("[this Jesus] will come in the same way that you saw him going into heaven") appears to imply the presence of doubt that the departed Jesus will return. If so, the correlation established by vv 9-11 between Jesus' ascension and his return is no accident. Affirmation of Jesus' present status as exalted Lord (and Christ, 2:36) serves to reinforce expectation of his parousia. In view of the delayed parousia which will enable the worldwide mission of the church (1:6-8), eschatologically oriented faith has evidently been shaken.[27] Luke undergirds hope in Jesus' return by employing the ascension as a pledge.

Acts 1:3-11 makes no specific assertion regarding the timing of Jesus' return. It does, however, indicate that the parousia will not be immediate:[28] a delay in service of the worldwide mission will conform the course of history to scriptural promise (to which Jesus has added his authoritative voice).[29] Haenchen goes too far, however, when he claims that Luke's narrative of the ascension reflects the author's belief that the eschaton will occur only in the remote future.[30] In Haenchen's view, the heaven-directed stare of 1:10 connotes a paralysis induced by expectation of an immediate parousia. The two "heavenly" men declare this posture to be ill-timed. Haenchen assumes that Luke in this passage is depicting the disciples as a model of the church in his own situation. Luke's church, too, should focus its energies on the ongoing life and activity of the church immersed in the world, and should disavow the mistaken expectation of an imminent parousia of the Son of man. In assessing Haenchen's position, it is important

---

[26] Cf. Lohfink, *Himmelfahrt,* 262: Luke could not narrate the parousia in Acts 28. "So benutzt Lukas zu Beginn seines Zweiten Buches die Perikope, mit der er die Zeit Jesu beendet hatte, um mit ihrer Hilfe nun auch den Abschluss der Zeit der Kirche vorwegnehmend zu markieren und auf die Parusie auszublicken." Cf. also Schnackenburg, "Aussagen," 255.

[27] Cf. my exegesis of Luke 18:1-8 in chapter two above. My reading of the setting underlying Luke's account of the ascension has many points of contact with the exegeses of Franklin ("Ascension") and Wilson ("Ascension"). However, as will soon become clear, I find Wilson's two-front bifurcation of Acts 1:3-8 and 1:9-11 unpersuasive.

[28] That is, from the standpoint presupposed at this place in the story, as distinct from Luke's later setting. Schnackenburg ("Aussagen," 258) regards the "delay problematic" as implicit in Acts 1:7, 11.

[29] This finding agrees with the reading of Luke 21:5-36 presented in chapter two above.

[30] See Haenchen's analysis of this pericope in *Acts,* 150-52.

to recognize that the setting within the narrative (post-ascension, pre-Pentecost) requires not hope for an imminent parousia but preparation for activity. Moreover, Luke would not advocate a policy of passive waiting for his community.[31] Nevertheless, the opinion that delay remains the governing motif in Luke's own future expectation overlooks the crucial difference in time and setting that separates Luke from the events which he narrates at the outset of his second volume.

Wilson's attempt to correlate the eschatological statements of this passage with the Lukan setting is more carefully nuanced than is that of Haenchen.[32] Wilson agrees with Haenchen that Acts 1:6-8 affirms that the End will be delayed: Pentecost heralds the universal mission of the church rather than the End.[33] Wilson further assents to Haenchen's inference that Luke addresses this piece of dialogue to members of his own church who still cling to hope for an imminent End.[34] Luke opposes a "fervent renewal of Apocalypticism."[35] Nevertheless, Wilson differs from Haenchen in understanding Acts 1:11 as Luke's answer to disappointed parousia hopes — which had resulted in "a denial that the End would come at all."[36] According to this reconstruction, Luke is waging in vv 6-8 and v 11 a battle on two different fronts (*"praesumptio"* and *"desperatio"*). Luke takes the middle road in order to correct both false extremes to which some of his contemporaries had succumbed.[37]

Wilson correctly insists that Luke's narrative treatment of eschatological issues pursues practical, pastoral — rather than theoretical — goals.[38] This hypothesis has the additional strength of recognizing that Acts 1:6-11 contains both the motif of delay and the affirmation of parousia hope. Like Haenchen, however, Wilson fails to consider that Luke's own setting is not identical to that presupposed within his narrative. Expectation of an imminent consummation is inappropriate at this juncture in the story, for delay — opening up a time of mission — is the order of the day. Luke and his community live, though, on the far side of a series of events which have fulfilled scripture (and the promise of the risen Lord as well) and brought the eschaton itself closer to realization.[39] In

---

[31] Eternal vigilance — yes! But this means continual readiness accompanying faithful fulfillment of duties (cf. the exegeses of Luke 12:35-48 and 17:22-37 in chapter two above).

[32] See "Ascension," especially pp. 277-81.

[33] Ibid., 279.

[34] Ibid.

[35] Ibid.

[36] Ibid., 277. This half of Wilson's hypothesis accords with the position I am advancing in this study.

[37] Ibid., 280.

[38] Ibid., 280-81. See also the discussion of Wilson's general approach in chapter one above.

[39] The pivotal role of scripture in shaping Luke's eschatological perspective surfaces here. Scripture prophesied both the extension of salvation to the ends of the earth (Isa 49:6, alluded to or cited in Acts 1:8 and 13:47) and the incorporation of Gentiles within the

such a situation, persevering hope in Jesus' return—not in the distant future but at an imminent, while unspecified point in time—becomes especially important. Luke's narration of Jesus' final episode with his followers and his ascension into heaven serves to undergird just such eschatological faith.

B. THE JOEL CITATION OF ACTS 2:17-21 IN RELATION TO THE ESCHATOLOGICAL PERSPECTIVE OF LUKE-ACTS

R. Zehnle has persuasively argued that Peter's Pentecost dicourse in Acts 2 serves as a programmatic inaugural address for the Acts narrative—much as Luke 4:16-30 functions in the gospel.[40] Since the programmatic force of the Pentecost speech is concentrated in the Joel citation in 2:17-21, which in fact defines the contours of the speech as a whole, the eschatological perspective conveyed in Luke's use of this scriptural promise is especially significant for the present study.[41]

1. The Literary Function of the Joel Citation in Acts

The Joel citation (Joel 3:1-5 LXX) has both programmatic and prophetic functions in the Acts narrative. The course of events in Acts thus represents the fulfillment of God's ancient promise: the outpouring of the Spirit (with its universal scope), manifested in an age of prophecy; signs and wonders; and, most importantly, the offer of salvation to all who call upon the name of the Lord (Jesus). Scriptural prophecy,[42] therefore, serves not only to interpret the

---

restored Israel (Amos 9:11-12, quoted in Acts 15:16-18). The course of history remains incomplete until these promises of God find fulfillment. To the extent, therefore, that Luke narrates in Acts the process of fulfillment of these prophecies, the world mission represents an advance toward the eschatological goal. Of course, it is for Luke the divine will, not any eschatological charge latent within these events, that moves history toward its end.

[40] Zehnle, *Peter's Pentecost Discourse* (Nashville: Abingdon, 1971) 95, 128, 130-31.

[41] For discussion of the programmatic function of the Joel citation, see Francis, "History," and B. J. Hubbard, "The Role of the Commissioning Accounts in Acts," in *Perspectives on Luke-Acts,* ed. C. H. Talbert (Danville: Association of Baptist Professors of Religion, 1978) 187-98, 194-95. Zehnle regards Peter's speech in Acts 2 as the "epitome of Lukan theology" (*Pentecost,* 61-70), in contrast to Acts 3:12-26, where Luke transmits primitive traditions (71-94). While this formulation does not do justice to Luke's role in composing Acts 3 (see the next section of this chapter), it does correctly recognize the crucial part played by Acts 2:14-41 in the narrative, and as a vehicle of Luke's theological view.

[42] On the pivotal role of scripture in shaping the speeches of Acts, see C. H. Dodd, *According to the Scriptures: The Sub-Structure of New Testament Theology* (Digswell Place: Nisbet, 1952); J. W. Doeve, *Jewish Hermeneutics in the Synoptic Gospels and Acts* (Assen, Netherlands: Koninklijke, 1954); B. Lindars, *New Testament Apologetic: The Doctrinal Significance of the Old Testament Quotations* (Philadelphia: Westminster, 1961); and especially M. Rese, *Alttestamentliche Motive in der Christologie des Lukas* (Studien

event just narrated (Acts 2:1-13), but also to point the reader forward to the worldwide mission that will unfold in the "last days" preceding the "day of the Lord." These preliminary observations set our agenda for discussion of the literary function of the Joel citation in the narrative of Acts.

a. Authentication of the Pentecost Event

The immediate purpose of the Joel citation within the story is to explain the ecstatic speech of the gathered community on the day of Pentecost.[43] The prophecy does not merely link the speech to the preceding account, however; it also gives divine authentication to a surprising and otherwise ambiguous occurrence. For the Jews and proselytes who form the audience in the narrative, Peter quotes scripture as a positive response to the onlookers' puzzlement (2:7, 12), even as he has mentioned the time of day (2:15) to counter the mockers' skepticism. Further, for Luke's readers, the prophecy from Joel demonstrates beyond doubt that these founding events of the church came to pass both by divine initiative and in a manner consistent with the divine plan, announced long ago by the prophet.[44]

By means of the vehicle of prophecy (promise) and fulfillment,[45] therefore, Luke draws out, both for his readers and for the participants in his drama, the true meaning of Pentecost (2:1-13). These developments have their origin and authentication in the God who speaks (λέγει ὁ θεός) through the mouth of the prophet Joel.[46] What appears, on the surface, to be sudden, inexplicable, and unprecedented is actually the planned realization of ancient promise.[47]

---

zum Neuen Testament 1; Gütersloher, 1969), and D. Juel, "Social Dimensions of Exegesis: The Use of Psalm 16 in Acts 2," *CBQ* 43 (1981) 543-56. Juel finds the use of scripture in Acts to be "closer in perspective to rabbinic than to Qumran exegesis" (555). He argues (against Lindars, *Apologetic,* 44) that this form of biblical interpretation is not primitive, but depends on a long interpretive tradition. Concerning the social setting of this mode of interpretation, Juel conjectures that "the 'apologetic' form of exegesis may point . . . to a new social setting in which structures have been solidified and in which opposition from 'the Jews' is less a threat to the survival of the group. The most important function of such biblical interpretation, in fact, may be internal" (555).

[43] This point is emphasized by U. Wilckens, *Die Missionsreden der Apostelgeschichte* (3d ed.; Wissenschaftliche Monographien zum Alten und Neuen Testament 5; Neukirchener, 1974) 32; and C. H. Giblin, "Complementarity of Symbolic Event and Discourse in Acts 2,1-40," in *Studia Evangelica* 6 (Berlin: Akademie, 1973) 189-96. Cf. Rese's classification of the use of the Joel passage in Acts as "hermeneutische" (*Motive,* 52).

[44] Luke highlights the divine initiative that prompts each turning point in his story. See, e.g., Acts 1:24-26; 2:1-4; 8:26, 29; 9:3-6, 10-16; 10:3-6, 10-16, 19-20, 44; 13:2-4; 16:6-10.

[45] A fulfillment which will, so to speak, be repeated at crucial moments of transition throughout the narrative (cf. Acts 4:8, 31; 10:44; 13:9).

[46] Cf. also Acts 2:33, which names Jesus as the direct author of these events (God having given to Jesus the promise of the Holy Spirit).

[47] Cf. Hubbard, "Commissioning," 194-95. F. Mussner ("In den letzten Tagen," *BZ* N.F.

b. Programmatic, Prophetic Description of the Worldwide Mission

The Joel citation looks forward as well as backward. In fact, it furnishes Luke with a programmatic description of the church's mission "to the end of the earth,"[48] under the power and direction of the Holy Spirit.[49] In fulfillment of the prophecy that "your sons and daughters shall prophesy" (v 17; cf. v 18), Luke portrays recurring prophetic activity in the church (11:27–28; 13:1–3; 15:32; 21:9, 10–11). It is of particular interest that Luke mentions both female (21:9) and male prophets in the course of his account, as prophesied by Joel. The promise of visions and dreams[50] (v 17) finds actualization throughout Acts, notably in crucial moments of transition such as the Cornelius episode.[51] Luke thereby emphasizes God's continuing guidance of the mission and depicts even surprising, revolutionary developments as the fulfillment of ancient promise.

The "wonders and signs" of the last days (v 19) begin to occur in the divinely empowered mission activity of the apostles (and others). Luke repeatedly describes this activity with the terms σημεῖον (4:16, 22; 8:6, 13) and σημεῖα καὶ τέρατα (2:43; 4:30; 5:12; 6:8; 14:3; 15:12). Only the heavenly wonders named in the Joel prophecy (vv 19c, 20a) go unfulfilled in Luke's account;[52] these elements

---

5 [1961] 263–65) goes even further in linking the Joel quotation to the preceding Pentecost events. Mussner regards the cosmic signs accompanying the day of the Lord (Acts 2:19–20) as already fulfilled in Pentecost (264). According to this reading, the cosmic signs are the "Sturmesbrausen vom Himmel" and the "Feuerzeugen." This identification has a certain appeal. Nevertheless, the content of v 20a cannot be subsumed under the Pentecost events. On the contrary, the cosmic (heavenly) wonders are yet to occur ("before the day of the Lord"). This holds as well for the signs on earth below (stressed by Luke via expansion of the LXX text, at the expense of the parallelism of the Joel passage): these signs God will accomplish through the hands of the apostles (and others) in the *subsequent* narrative.

[48] Acts 1:8 outlined the expanding circle of this mission, also in programmatic fashion.

[49] Cf. Hubbard, "Commissioning," 194–95.

[50] Luke's inversion of these two lines of the LXX text is usually explained as a copying mistake (so, e.g., T. Holtz, *Untersuchungen über die alttestamentlichen Zitate bei Lukas* [Berlin: Akademie, 1968] 12) or with reference to the relative ages of the men who receive the Spirit, if indeed the transposition is even noticed (generally it is not mentioned). It seems likely, however, that by inverting the lines Luke sought to accent the "visions" rather than the "dreams" (thus bringing "visions" — together with their "young men" — into first position). Visions, not dreams, are the primary vehicle of divine revelation in Acts (alongside, of course, angels and the Spirit). Cf. Hubbard ("Commissioning," 192, 194), who finds the prophesied dreams in Acts by defining them as visions occurring at night. See note 51 below.

[51] See the brief treatment by Hubbard ("Commissioning," 192–94). He argues that each of the "commissioning accounts" in Acts, with the possible exception of 22:12–16, occurs in a vision. Five of the visions happen at night and so should be classified as dreams (12:6–7; 16:9; 18:9; 23:11; 27:23).

[52] Rese (*Motive,* 50) rightly recognizes that Luke brings the signs and wonders of the end-time (Joel 3) into connection with God's actions in Jesus (Acts 2:22). It does not

remain intact as a continuing component of the end expectation (cf. Luke 21:25-26).

Finally, the principle of salvation for the Gentiles is anticipated in the Joel prophecy *as employed by Luke*.[53] Because he closes his quotation with Joel 3:5a (and only alludes to Joel 3:5b in Acts 2:39), Luke avoids the restriction of the promised salvation to the Jews (Joel 3:5b). Indeed, when Luke returns to Joel 3:5b in Acts 2:39, he corrects it by bringing out, with the help of Isa 57:19, the universal character of the promise.[54] In the course of his story, Luke will narrate the process by which the Gentiles join the πᾶς who call upon the name of the Lord and so come to participate in the Lord's salvation (Acts 2:21). Although both Jervell and Dupont exaggerate the extent to which the Gentile mission governs this passage,[55] it is certain that Luke perceived this later development as the fulfillment of God's promise, announced even now at the outset of the worldwide mission through the prophet Joel. To a limited degree and in an anticipatory manner, therefore, the Joel citation serves as a scriptural warrant for

---

necessarily follow, however, that Jesus' ministry is thereby characterized as the end-time event that fulfills Joel 3. The presence of δυνάμεις ("mighty deeds") alongside σημεῖα and τέρατα in Acts 2:22 speaks against too hasty an identification of the "signs and wonders" of v 19 and those of v 22. Moreover, both in Joel 3:1-5 LXX and in Luke-Acts, the end-time events occur only subsequent to the outpouring of the Spirit. The presence of "wonders and signs" in Acts 2:22 with reference to Jesus' ministry, then, should be understood as a literary device which underlines the continuity between the activity of the church after Pentecost and the earthly ministry of Jesus (while, at the same time, a distinction is drawn between them [δυνάμεις]). The insertion of ἄνω and κάτω apparently serves to heighten the contrast, or distinction, between the heavenly portents of the end-time (which do not yet find fulfillment in the narrative) and the earthly marvels (which Luke does narrate). The latter σημεῖα, comprising the work of the church in its world mission, are thereby placed within an eschatological frame of reference.

[53] Cf. Rese, *Motive*, 50. J. Dupont, in numerous articles, has emphasized the universal scope (embracing Gentiles) of the Pentecost narrative and discourse. See, e.g., "The Salvation of the Gentiles and the Theological Significance of Acts," the title essay in *The Salvation of the Gentiles* (New York: Paulist, 1979) 11-33; "The First Christian Pentecost," p. 58 in the same volume. Jervell likewise insists on the importance of the motif of the Gentile mission already in Peter's Pentecost speech ("Divided," 57-58). E. J. Epp (*The Theological Tendency of Codex Bezae Cantabrigiensis in Acts* [Cambridge: University, 1966]) discerns a universalizing, anti-Judaic tendency in the Western text—the Joel citation being no exception (*Tendency*, 68-69)—but concedes that even the B-text of Acts 2:17-21 manifests "possible adumbrations of a future universalism" (75).

[54] Cf. Rese, *Motive*, 50; Lindars, *Apologetic*, 38. Rese comments (*Motive*, 48) that Luke's omission of Joel 3:5b has too often gone unnoticed. Luke's handling of Joel 3:5 is one of the most telling objections to the increasingly popular thesis that Luke expected Israel's restoration on the far side of the eschatological events that he mentions explicitly. See further the discussion of "Israel and Eschaton," section D.3. below.

[55] Jervell, "Divided," 57-58; Dupont, "Salvation," 22-23; and "Pentecost," 58.

the Gentile mission. Salvation will come to all, Jew and Gentile alike (cf. Acts 10:34-35, 47; 11:17-18), who call upon the name of the Lord, but to no others (cf. Acts 4:9-12): all in fulfillment of God's promise.

The title κύριος thus plays a pivotal role in Peter's Pentecost speech. Verse 21 ties participation in God's salvation to "calling upon the name of the κύριος." The rest of the discourse (through its climax in v 36) identifies this κύριος as none other than Jesus. Through this skillful blending of scriptural passages — with the transition from the Joel citation to Peter's kerygma about Jesus turning on the identity of the κύριος mentioned in Joel 3:5a[56] — Luke establishes, at the inception of the church's mission, that the mission to the "end of the earth," with its summons to faith in Jesus as Lord and Christ, fulfills the prophecy of Joel for the "last days."

2. The Joel Citation and Lukan Eschatology

Luke interprets the prophecy of Joel 3:1-5 LXX as an announcement that salvation would come to all who call upon Jesus as Lord. The subsequent narrative reports the way in which the opportunity to call upon Jesus as Lord is systematically extended to all people.[57] The entire narrative thus constitutes a decisive fulfillment of scriptural promise. It is all the more striking that the Joel citation — in the form in which it appears in Acts — typifies this era of fulfillment as the "last days" (ἐν ταῖς ἐσχάταις ἡμέραις; v 17). The world mission of the church makes its way in an eschatological frame of reference, defined for the reader by this prophecy from Joel.

a. The Prophecy from Joel Sets the World Mission in Relation to the Eschaton

In a manner analogous to the eschatological discourse of Luke 21:5-36, Acts 2:17-21 gives an overview of the course of events leading to the eschaton.[58] The power of the Spirit will be unleashed in prophetic activity, revelation through dreams and visions, and the performance of signs (vv 17-19b). The day of the Lord itself will be preceded by heavenly wonders (vv 19a, 19c, 20; corresponding

---

[56] Cf. Juel, "Dimensions," 544.

[57] It reports, as well, their divided response. Salvation comes to all who respond affirmatively; repudiation of the apostolic preaching results in exclusion from God's people (Acts 3:22-23).

[58] Because Luke draws upon Joel 3, the precision of Luke 21 is missing. For example, Acts 2 makes no mention of the destruction of Jerusalem (Luke 21:20-24), nor of the coming of the Son of man (Luke 21:27). Acts 2:17-21 differs from the discourse of Luke 21, moreover, in the way in which the period of the church (as narrated in Acts) is portrayed. In Luke 21:12-19 the twin motifs of testimony and persecution prevail, while in Acts 2:17-19b the empowerment of the Spirit is the controlling theme. It scarcely requires comment that Acts 2:17-21, as a piece of scriptural prophecy, does not, like Luke 21, clarify the sequence of phases in the eschatological drama. But see the discussion, section B.2.b. below.

to Luke 21:25-26). Verse 21 links participation in salvation—in view of the impending day of the Lord—to invocation of the name of the Lord (Jesus). Like Luke 21, therefore, Acts 2:17-21 locates the time of the church and its mission squarely within the eschatological program.[59] Although the "last days" of Acts 2:17 stretch out over a period of several decades (and Luke looks back over this history), that expression itself and the content of the entire Joel prophecy point the reader through the narrative to its eschatological culmination.[60] History has moved into its final chapter.

b. The Prophecy from Joel Locates Luke's Own Church in the Unfolding Eschatological Program

On the one hand, the Joel citation in Acts 2 places the spotlight on divine promises that have come to fulfillment in connection with Pentecost and the ensuing mission activity of the church. On the other hand, the prophetic portrayal of cosmic signs that will precede the "day of the Lord" (v 20) represents unfulfilled prophecy, even in Luke's day. The Joel quotation thus locates Luke's community within the unfolding eschatological program by enabling a distinction to be drawn between prophecy already fulfilled and prophecy still awaiting fulfillment.[61] Inasmuch as both sets of events are subsumed under the rubric "the last days," it would be mistaken to speak of a divorce between history and eschatology in Luke-Acts. Fulfillment of events promised for the last period of history (past for Luke's readers) serves to undergird trust in the fulfillment of events promised for the end-time itself (still future for Luke's readers).

In view of Luke 21:25-28, Acts 2 indicates that the climactic "day of the Lord" will be preceded by a set of unmistakable cosmic occurrences. While the onset of these wondrous events may not be pinpointed, the inextricable connection between them and the previously fulfilled prophecies for "the last days" suggests a time sooner rather than later. Although imminent hope was not appropriate at the moment when Peter was inspired to quote the prophet Joel (events prophesied by Joel had yet to be fulfilled in the course of the narrative), Luke himself looks back upon a mission that has fulfilled all these predicted developments. Only the supramundane events prophesied also by Jesus (Luke 21:25-27) are still outstanding as the "eschatological remainder." Acts 2:17-21 makes no explicit assertion about the timing of the End, other than to locate it subsequent to the developments narrated in Acts. Luke's use of the Joel prophecy is certainly consistent with living imminent hope, however.

---

[59] Similarly, Acts 1:6-8 offered the worldwide mission as Jesus' answer to the question of the timing of kingdom restoration.

[60] For detailed consideration of the expression, "in the last days," in Acts 2:17, see Excursus 4 below.

[61] This is, of course, implicit (not explicit) in Luke's use of the passage from Joel. However, my inference is consistent with Luke's clarification of phases in Luke 21:5-36 (see the discussion in chapter two, section E.2.).

c. The Prophecy from Joel Indicates that the Decisive Eschatological Issue —
Access to the Future Kingdom — Is Decided Now on the Basis of Response to
the Mission Proclamation of Jesus as Lord.

Luke 17:20—18:8 linked fortunes at the eschaton to the nature of one's
present life in response to Jesus.[62] In similar fashion, Luke's use of the Joel
prophecy in Acts ties participation in salvation—with the day of the Lord
looming ominously on the horizon—to one's affirmation of Jesus as Lord. The
mission activity of the apostolic church in Acts extends to all people the opportunity to experience salvation by summoning them to repentance and to faith in
Jesus' Messiahship and Lordship.[63]

The mission to the "end of the earth" is determinative of the individual's[64]
destiny at the eschaton. Access to the future kingdom hinges on acceptance of
the Christian proclamation about Jesus, and on a manner of life that accords
with such faith.[65] Therefore, there is finality to the mission and the response of
both Jews and Gentiles to it.

3. Eschatology and Situation in Acts 2:17-21

Analysis of the Joel citation in Acts 2 has shown that no positive indicator
of the timing of the End is present. However, the translation of the "last days"
of the Spirit into an era of history interposed between Pentecost and eschaton
does not have as a necessary corollary the abandonment of imminent expectation in Luke's situation. On the contrary, by tapping this prophecy from Joel and
placing it at the head of the church's mission in Acts, Luke provides for the past
and present work of his church an eschatological frame of reference, and on two
levels.

First, Luke confirms the credibility of continuing eschatological faith, in his
own day, by emphasizing the present realization of all aspects of the Joel
prophecy except those reserved for the end-time itself. Those aspects as yet
unfulfilled will assuredly have their day as well. Second, the urgency of the
mission activity of Luke's church is transparent, given the pivotal role played by
the mission proclamation in opening up access to eschatological salvation.
Where Jesus is preached (as Lord), and where that message is received, the
eschatological outcome is established already here and now. When God completes his saving activity in the world,[66] people will take their place in God's

---

[62] See the discussion in chapter two, section C.3.

[63] Luke will display the negative side of the coin in Peter's next speech, Acts 3:12-26.
See the discussion below, section C.1.

[64] See the discussion of "individual eschatology" in Luke-Acts, Excursus 1 above.

[65] Recall the treatments of Luke 12:35-48 and 17:20-18:8, in chapter 2 above.

[66] And this cosmic scope remains intact in Luke-Acts: "individual eschatology" does not
replace it! See the discussion, Excursus 1 above.

kingdom because they have lived believing, faithful, and vigilant lives in the interim.

Luke and his community find themselves in the "last days" preceding the "day of the Lord." Luke would have his readers acknowledge what is at stake in this final era in God's history with his people. The mission summons to repentance and faith, obedient to the directive of the risen Lord, forms the closing chapter of that history which leads on to the end-time itself. And the eschatological verdict will affirm the results of the work that the church is now performing.

EXCURSUS 4: "IN THE LAST DAYS" (ACTS 2:17): TEXT-CRITICAL OBSERVATIONS AND INTERPRETATION

The phrase ἐν ταῖς ἐσχάταις ἡμέραις in Acts 2:17 has provoked extensive discussion, both because of the text critical issues raised by the verse and because of its relation to Lukan eschatology. Haenchen's reading of Lukan eschatology led him to discount the weight of the external evidence and advocate the originality of μετὰ ταῦτα (B 076 sa^mss): "In Lucan theology the last days do not begin as soon as the Spirit has been outpoured!"[67] F. Mussner countered that Acts 2:17–21 has an eschatological thrust even if μετὰ ταῦτα is original.[68] In view of the weighty external attestation of the reading ἐν ταῖς ἐσχάταις ἡμέραις, the majority of commentators favor it as original. The reading of B is then probably explicable as an assimilation to the LXX text.

Although the eschatological character of Luke's[69] alteration of the LXX has

---

[67] *Acts*, 179. See the more detailed treatment in "Schriftzitate." For similar assessments of the relation of Acts 2:17 to Luke's eschatology, cf. also Wilckens, *Missionsreden*, 33; Grässer, "Parusieerwartung," 119–22 ("Der redaktionelle Eingriff des Lukas in das alttestamentliche Zitat in Apg 2,17 hat keinerlei sinnverändernde Wirkung: Pfingsten ist das kirchengründende Datum, nicht das eschatologische" [p. 122]); Conzelmann, *St. Luke*, 95; Kaestli, *Eschatologie*, 63–64; Dupont, "Les discours de Pierre dans les Actes et le chapitre XXIV de l'évangile de Luc," in *L'Evangile de Luc*, ed. F. Neirynck (Bibliotheca Ephemeridum Theologicarum Lovaniensium XXXII, 1973) 329–74, 347.

[68] Mussner, "In den letzten Tagen," *BZ* N.F. 5 (1961) 263–65, 263. Cf. Rese, *Motive*, 52; Zehnle, *Pentecost*, 117, 123; K. Lake and H. J. Cadbury, *The Acts of the Apostles*, vol. 4 of *The Beginnings of Christianity*, ed. F. J. Foakes Jackson and K. Lake (London: Macmillan, 1933) 20; C. S. C. Williams, *The Acts of the Apostles* (London: Black, 1957) 66–68; F. F. Bruce, *Commentary on the Book of Acts* (London: Marshall, Morgan, and Scott, 1954) 68–69.

[69] But see Holtz, *Untersuchungen*, 8. Observing that Luke does not otherwise use the expression "in the last days," and that later writings commonly employ the phrase as a ready formula for the end-time (cf. James 5:3; 2 Tim 3:1; 2 Pet 3:3; Did 16:3; Barn 4:9; 12:9; 16:5; 2 Clem 14:2), Holtz argues that a later scribe, not Luke himself, has changed μετὰ ταῦτα to ἐν ταῖς ἐσχάταις ἡμέραις (though without changing the meaning!). Nevertheless, the occurrence of the phrase "in the last days" in Isa 2:2—indeed, in connection with "all the nations"!—suggests that Luke may well have borrowed the expression from Isa 2:2. There is no need to resort to post-Lukan scribal activity.

not gone uncontested,[70] a further observation confirms both the reading "in the last days" and its eschatological import in Acts 2.[71] Luke, after all, selected the Joel citation — which is but an excerpt from an extended passage in Joel regarding "the day of the Lord"[72] — as the opening statement in Peter's first mission discourse. Moreover, he cited not only those elements (Acts 2:17–18) that pertain to the preceding Pentecost event (2:1–13), and not only the statement (2:21) that ties salvation for all to the name of the Lord,[73] but also the intervening verses (Joel 3:3–4; Acts 2:19–20), which speak directly of end-time events. Indeed, precisely here Luke's editorial hand is most evident: he adds ἄνω, κάτω, and σημεῖα to the LXX text, surely a sign that he regards this part of the Joel prophecy as important.[74]

I conclude that the reading "in the last days" should be adopted in Acts 2:17, and, further, that Luke has likely inserted the phrase in order to establish as

---

[70] Conzelmann, e.g., concedes that "in the last days" is the correct reading, yet denies that, for Luke, the phrase carries the same eschatological meaning as in its original context in Joel (*St. Luke,* 95).

[71] The sequence of dialogue in Acts 1:4–8 also corroborates Luke's understanding of Joel 3:1–5 LXX as prophecy for the end-time. In Acts 1 Jesus' mention of the promise of an imminent Spirit-baptism (vv 4–5) gives rise to the question (v 6): "Lord, do you at this time restore the kingdom to Israel"? In Joel 3 the outpouring of the Spirit is followed by the restoration of the fortunes of Judah/Jerusalem and by judgment upon the nations. It is not inconceivable that Luke composed the dialogue of Acts 1:4–8 in the light of the course of events prophesied in Joel 3. Acts 1:7, then, corrects the disciples' preoccupation with the timing of the End, without denying the eschatological implications of the outpouring of the Spirit (even as Acts 1:8 corrects the disciples' conception of the "restoration of the kingdom," without denying that Israel is indeed restored through the world mission of the church). Cf. Jervell, "Divided"; and see the discussion, section C.2.a.III below.

[72] See C. H. Dodd, *Scriptures,* 62–63.

[73] Thereby preparing for the proclamation of the Lord *Jesus* (Acts 2:22–36) and for the summons to repentance (2:38).

[74] Rese (*Motive*) and Lindars (*Apologetic*) capitalize on divergences from the text of the LXX to gain insight into the purposes of the NT author. Rese discovers in Acts 2:17–21 numerous instances in which Luke has changed the LXX text either to fit it to the narrative context or to conform it to his theological conceptions (*Motive,* 48–51). On the other hand, Holtz (*Untersuchungen*) prefers to attribute variations from the LXX to a text-form different from that which is extant (hence to Luke's *Vorlage*), or to a copying mistake, whether by Luke or by a later scribe (*Untersuchungen,* 8–12, 166–67). In assessing Holtz's study, Rese correctly observes (*Motive,* 216) that Holtz, because of his concern to emphasize Luke's faithfulness to the OT text which he cites, has underestimated the role played by Luke in shaping the quoted text. Of course, conclusions regarding Lukan composition on the basis of divergences from the LXX must be advanced with caution. Nevertheless, in the case of Acts 2:17–21, the appearance of a cluster of variations (especially the addition of "and they will prophesy" in v 18 and "signs" in v 19) which coincide with the narrative context or with Luke's theological emphases indicates that Luke's role in shaping the text of the Joel citation should not be minimized.

eschatological the context of the world mission about to be narrated. Certainly, the "last days" stretch out over several chapters—and decades—in Acts (and beyond). Luke's point, however, is not that the mission of the church is itself an eschatological phenomenon (an event of the End), but rather that it represents the decisive activity of God among people in the period that precedes the eschaton of history.

C. THE FUNCTION OF ACTS 3:19-26 IN LUKAN ESCHATOLOGY

The first mission speech of Peter in Acts (chapter two) places the worldwide mission mandated by Jesus (1:8) within an eschatological frame of reference (2:17-21), then proceeds, on the basis of Jesus' resurrection and enthronement (as Christ and Lord), to summon Peter's Jewish audience at Jerusalem to repentance and faith in Jesus (2:22-41). In view of the approaching "day of the Lord," participation in God's salvation is promised to everyone who accepts the apostolic call to repentance and faith (2:21; cf. v 40). In his second speech (3:12-26), Luke's Peter defines what is at stake in the response of Jews to the church's mission. God's blessing, in fulfillment of the covenant with Abraham, will come to those who respond with repentance and faith; those, however, who reject the message are evicted from the people of God. As in Peter's Pentecost sermon, a Christological claim has decisive soteriological consequences, but in this case the fulcrum is the identification of Jesus as the prophet like Moses (vv 22-23).[75] Embedded within this discourse is a series of eschatological statements (vv 19-21) for which the most diverse interpretations have been advanced. Accordingly, the goal of this section will be to elucidate the eschatological viewpoint that is conveyed in Acts 3:19-26, with vv 19-21 as the focus. First, however, I will consider in detail the strategic role played by Peter's entire speech within the narrative of Acts.

1. The Literary Function of Acts 3:12-26

Like the Pentecost speech, Peter's sermon in chapter three looks both backward and forward. Peter first supplies his audience with a pair of interpretive lenses through which they may view the healing related in 3:1-10.[76] Verses

---

[75] The best recent discussion of Luke's portrayal of Jesus as the prophet like Moses, together with the soteriological implications of that portrayal, is provided by P. F. Feiler in his Ph.D. dissertation, "Jesus the Prophet: The Lucan Portrayal of Jesus as the Prophet like Moses" (Princeton: Princeton Theological Seminary, 1986).

[76] Cf. Schneider, *Apostelgeschichte*, 1.313. For a provocative treatment of the healing in Acts 3:1-10, and of its interpretation in Peter's speech, see M. D. Hamm, "This Sign of Healing, Acts 3:1-10: A Study in Lucan Theology" (St. Louis: St. Louis University Ph.D. dissertation, 1975); note also the compressed treatment in "Acts 3:12-26: Peter's Speech and the Healing of the Man Born Lame," *PerspRelStud* 11 (1984) 199-217. Hamm argues that the healing in 3:1-10 is for Luke an "emblem" of the restoration of Israel, which the balance of Acts narrates. Hamm suggests that the healing of the temple beggar constitutes

12-16 attribute the healing of the lame beggar at the temple to faith attached to
the name of Jesus, the killed and resurrected ἀρχηγὸς τῆς ζωῆς. This latter theme
of Jesus denied and killed, yet vindicated by God through resurrection, displaces
the act of healing (and its explanation) as the center of attention (vv 15, 17–18)
in the speech. Nevertheless, the kerygma is itself but the springboard for the
summons to repentance which is the actual burden of the speech (v 19).[77] The
ignorance of God's purpose (vv 17–18) in which Jerusalem Jews repudiated
God's "holy and righteous one" (v 14) will not excuse continuing rejection of
him, for God has made clear through prophetic testimony that the Christ would
suffer, and God has now fulfilled that prophecy (v 18). After the resurrection
(vv 13 [ἐδόξασεν], 15 [ἤγειρεν]), all ambiguity has evaporated. God's initiative in
Jesus' ministry—and in his crucifixion and resurrection—is now transparent.
Accordingly, those who have rejected Jesus have no choice but to repent (v 19),
if they would remain God's people (vv 22–23).

Peter's speech, therefore, also looks forward to the ensuing narrative. Peter
here defines what is at stake in the worldwide mission that is beginning. Acts
3:12–26 sets the paradigm for the rest of the story: participation in the blessings
of God (promised to Abraham) comes to those who repent (vv 19, 26), but those
who fail to attend to the voice of the Mosaic prophet[78] will find themselves
rooted out of the people of God (vv 22–23).

Luke begins to chronicle this negative side of the coin in chapter four. Again
the healing of the lame beggar—and now in light of its interpretation in
3:12–16—forms the backdrop for the action (4:7, 9–10, 14, 16). The true bone of
contention, however, is the apostles' preaching "in Jesus the resurrection from

---

an eschatological sign, that is, a sign that the promise of an end-time restoration of Israel
and of a new exodus has begun to be fulfilled (223–24). Luke, therefore, "appears more
interested in portraying the inauguration of the Reign of God in the ministries of Jesus
and the church" than in the final manifestation of the kingdom, whether imminent or
distant (218). I will argue that 3:12–26, along with other passages in Luke-Acts, holds up
the present situation of response to the message (faith *and* faithfulness) as the decisive
moment in which participation in the kingdom is determined (cf. also the emphasis on
inaugurated eschatology in W. S. Kurz, "Acts 3:19–26 as a Test of the Role of Eschatology
in Lukan Christology," in 1977 SBL *Seminar Papers,* ed. P. J. Achtemeier [Missoula:
Scholars, 1977] 309–23; and on the present fulfillment of eschatological blessings in Feiler,
"Prophet," 252–61). However, this observation should not lead one to underestimate, as
Hamm does, the continuing significance of end-time expectation in Luke-Acts (rightly
perceived by Feiler, "Prophet," 258; Farrell, "Perspective," 193–94).

[77] G. Lohfink ("Christologie und Geschichtsbild in Apg 3,19–21," *BZ* N.F. 13 [1969]
223–41) has correctly noted the central role of repentance in this passage (240–41); cf. also
Schneider (*Apostelgeschichte,* 1.327); F. Hahn ("Das Problem alter christologischer Überlieferungen in der Apostelgeschichte unter besonderer Berücksichtigung von Act 3,19–21,"
in *Les Actes des Apôtres,* ed. J. Kremer [Leuven: University, 1979] 129–54, 137).

[78] Who speaks through his commissioned apostles. Cf. Acts 26:23, and especially Luke
10:16, a formulation unique to Luke: "One who hears you hears me, and one who rejects
you rejects me. And one who rejects me rejects the one who sent me."

the dead" (4:2).[79] The confrontation between the apostles and the Jewish leaders at Jerusalem escalates in the course of Acts 4–5. Peter reiterates what is at stake in the confrontation; salvation is inextricably bound to the name of Jesus, the resurrected one:

> Let this be known to you all and to all the people of Israel, that this man stands before you well by the name of Jesus Christ the Nazarene—whom you crucified, (yet) whom God raised from the dead. He is the stone that was rejected by you builders, (but) that has become the cornerstone. And salvation is not in anyone else; for there is no other name given among people under heaven by which we must be saved (4:10–12).

As the story unfolds, the Jewish leaders at Jerusalem take their place outside the boundaries of restored Israel. Gamaliel interprets for his fellow members of the Sanhedrin the import of what is occurring: "For if this plan or this work is of human origin, it will be thrown down, but if it is of God [and the reader knows that it is of God!], you will not be able to destroy them, (and) perhaps may even be found opposing God!" (5:38b–39a). Far from hearing the prophet like Moses (through his commissioned apostles), the leaders of the people attempt twice to silence the apostles (4:17; 5:40), imprison them, and finally execute Stephen. Later they seek to bring Paul to a similar fate. The Jewish leaders show themselves to be θεομάχοι. Nothing less than irrevocable exclusion from the people of God—with a corresponding transfer of leadership over Israel (cf. Luke 22:28–30)—is being narrated.

Peter's speech in Acts 3, therefore, defines the soteriological parameters along which the mission proceeds. Israel is being restored, but only by being divided,[80] and the criterion of participation in restored Israel is the nature of one's response to the apostles' preaching. Refusal of the message results in removal from the people of God.

Acts 3:19–26 also develops the positive side of the coin, and it is here that the eschatological statements appear (vv 19–21).

> Repent, therefore, and return, in order that your sins may be erased, so that seasons of refreshing may come from the face of the Lord, and he may send the Christ appointed for you, Jesus, whom heaven must receive until the times of the restoration (establishment) of all things that God spoke through the mouth of his holy prophets from of old.

---

[79] R. F. O'Toole ("Some Observations on ANISTĒMI, 'I Raise,' in Acts 3:22,26," *Science et Esprit* 31 [1979] 85–92, 91) rightly concludes from 4:1–2 that the "raising up" of 3:22, 26 likely includes reference to Jesus' resurrection. Cf. also Schneider, *Apostelgeschichte*, 1.330; Hamm, "Sign," 178–80.

[80] Jervell's work is, of course, particularly successful in bringing out this feature of the narrative, though in one-sided fashion (see especially "Divided"). For a more balanced treatment of this theme, see Feiler, "Prophet," 47–107. The course of events in Acts represents the fulfillment of Simeon's prophecy at the outset of the two-volume work (Luke 2:34).

Whatever the precise meaning of these verses,[81] they certainly make the point that repentance carries with it positive benefits. Refreshment, or respite (ἀνάψυξις), and the return of Jesus as Christ for Israel (ὑμῖν), follow repentance. Verses 25–26 link acceptance of the prophet like Moses (and his messengers) to the foundational covenant with Abraham.[82] God's promise to Abraham, which included blessing for all families of the earth,[83] finds fulfillment in the church's mission, through which God now blesses those who turn from their sins:[84]

> You are sons of the prophets and of the covenant which God granted to your fathers, when he said to Abraham, "And in your seed all the families of the earth will be blessed." When God had raised his servant, he sent him to you first, blessing you when each (of you) turns from your sins (Acts 3:25–26).[85]

Since repentance is the aim of the apostles' preaching,[86] and its effect, the promise to Abraham[87] is realized before the reader's eyes as Luke narrates the formation of God's people out of those who respond in affirmation and repentance to the mission of the church.[88]

---

[81] See the discussion below.

[82] This passage thus picks up the motif of Luke 1:55, 70–75. The verbal contacts between Luke 1:70–75 and Acts 3:19–26 are striking: Luke 1:70 and Acts 3:21b are nearly identical (cf. also Acts 3:24); "our fathers," Luke 1:72 (also 1:55) and Acts 3:25 ("your fathers" is better attested); "covenant," Luke 1:72 and Acts 3:25. The noun διαθήκη occurs in the Lukan corpus only in Luke 1:72; 22:30; Acts 3:25; 7:8 (see Schneider, *Apostelgeschichte,* 1.329 n. 121). Whatever sources Luke may have tapped in these sections (see, e.g., C. H. Scobie, "The Use of Source Material in the Speeches of Acts III and VII," *NTS* 25 [1979] 399–421), it does seem clear that Acts 3:19–26 recalls Zechariah's prophetic speech (Luke 1:68–79) by design. The worldwide mission definitively fulfills the covenant with Abraham, thereby bringing to fruition the promise and hope raised at the start of the gospel.

[83] The departure from the LXX text, which reads "all the nations" (πάντα τὰ ἔθνη), is explicable as an assimilation of the quotation to the narrative context, in which Jews are being addressed. So also Schille, *Apostelgeschichte,* 130. Schneider (*Apostelgeschichte,* 1.329 n. 126) sees in the modification an indication of Luke's knowledge of the LXX (see Pss 21:28; 95:7).

[84] Significantly, Luke in v 26 repeats the key verb from the scripture citation, so reinterpreting the blessing promised through Abraham in terms of repentance/forgiveness, actualized in the apostolic mission in Acts. Similarly, Schneider (*Apostelgeschichte,* 1.329), who views the blessing brought by Jesus (v 26) as the fulfillment of the blessing promised to Abraham (v 25); cf. Hamm, "Sign," 177.

[85] Or: "blessing you by turning each (of you) from your sins." The verb ἀποστρέφω may be either transitive or intransitive here (see BAG, 99–100; BDF, p. 162; Schneider, *Apostelgeschichte,* 1.329 n. 124).

[86] So, e.g., Acts 2:38; 3:19; 5:31.

[87] Luke cites Gen 22:18; 26:4. The prophecy of Isaiah 49:6 and the promise to Abraham thus converge: the mission "to the end of the earth" brings to fruition the promise given to Abraham ("all the families of the earth").

[88] The language of Acts 15:14 is significant. Concerning the first inclusion of Gentiles

Peter's speech in Acts 3:12-26, therefore, explains the first healing sign of the apostles' activity (3:1-10) and then uses that explanation (the healing power of the name of the resurrected Jesus) as a springboard for the summons to repentance. Verses 19-26 proceed to define the consequences of acceptance and repudiation of that summons. Positive response places the repentant among the ranks of God's people who enjoy the blessing of God, in fulfillment of the covenant with Abraham. Negative response places the intransigent outside the boundaries of God's covenant people. Luke has Peter in this sermon establish the paradigm which will govern the ensuing narrative.[89] The promise to Israel is indeed fulfilled in the course of Luke-Acts, but not without redefinition. Israel is restored even as it is divided.

2. Eschatology in Acts 3:19-26

The second half of Peter's speech in Acts 3 reveals a great deal about the weight and function of eschatological expectation in Luke-Acts. Verses 19-26 indicate that the determinative moment for one's end-time fortunes comes when one responds to the Christian preaching of Jesus and repentance (cf. Luke 24:47).[90] Yet, the expectation of God's ultimate action, with the return of Jesus, remains intact (v 21). Between present response to the mission claim and the future "sending" (parousia) of Jesus there stretches out a period during which God's restoration of Israel—indeed, of all things—is accomplished. Although Jesus is detained in heaven during this process of restoration (which effects God's promise announced through the prophets), he continues to be active through his commissioned apostles.[91] When people listen to Jesus' apostles, they in fact heed Jesus himself, the Mosaic prophet who is the centerpiece in God's saving of his people. The delay of the parousia, therefore, has as its cause the will of God, and as its motive the extension to all people of the mission call to repentance. This

---

in the church (Cornelius), James remarks: "Simeon related how God at the first visited for the purpose of taking out of the Gentiles a people for his name." As the Amos citation in 15:16-17 also indicates, the worldwide mission is a process whereby the people of God takes definitive form, encompassing both Jews and Gentiles. On 15:14, see N. A. Dahl, " 'A People for His Name' (Acts XV.14)," *NTS* 4 (1957) 319-27; J. Dupont, "Un Peuple d'entre les Nations (Actes 15.14)," *NTS* 31 (1985) 321-35.

[89] Culminating in Paul's confrontation with the Jews of Rome in Acts 28:17-31. Schneider (*Apostelgeschichte*, 1.328) notes the connection between Acts 3:22-23 and 28:28. See the discussion in the next section

[90] Cf. the discussion of Luke's "inaugurated eschatology" in Kurz ("Role," 312-13). See also Feiler, "Prophet," 49: the identification of Jesus (by virtue of God's vindication in resurrection/ascension) as the one through whom God's blessing is constituted "makes the present the crucial moment of decision for the Jews. Repentance results in participation in the blessing. Rejection results in being cut off from God's people."

[91] The motifs of "Spirit" and "name" also point to Jesus' activity despite his residence in heaven. See G. W. MacRae, "Whom Heaven Must Receive Until the Time," *Int* 27 (1973) 151-65.

mission affords, at the same time, the final opportunity to participate in the blessing which God promised to Abraham and now fulfills for believing Israel.[92]

In order to establish this reading of the function of eschatological expectation in Acts 3:19-26, I will first address a set of exegetical difficulties which represent a formidable obstacle for all interpretations of this passage. These difficulties revolve around the meaning of the expressions καιροὶ ἀναψύξεως and ἄχρι χρόνων ἀποκαταστάσεως πάντων ὧν ἐλάλησεν ὁ θεός — expressions at once as crucial to Luke's viewpoint as they are problematic. Only after justifying my reading of the meaning of this language will my presentation of the eschatological view of Acts 3:19-26 have persuasive power.

a. The Meaning of the Expressions καιροὶ ἀναψύξεως *and* ἄχρι χρόνων ἀποκαταστάσεως πάντων ὧν ἐλάλησεν ὁ θεός *in Acts 3:20-21*

The literature on the terms καιροὶ ἀναψύξεως and χρόνοι ἀποκαταστάσεως is extensive.[93] The chief issue is the temporal reference of each expression.[94] It has been argued that both the καιροί and the χρόνοι denote the eschatological future, the age of salvation.[95] Others have regarded both terms as descriptive of the present time of mission which precedes the future sending of Jesus.[96] Lane assigned the καιροί and χρόνοι to different eras, claiming that the καιροὶ ἀναψύξεως characterize the present as a new period of the Spirit, in which some of the "earmarks of the consummation" are actualized, yet which remains distinct from

[92] And, of course, the nations (Gentiles), as scripture had foretold.

[93] Among the most important studies are: Oepke, "ἀποκαθίστημι, ἀποκατάστασις," *TDNT* 1, 387-93; W. L. Lane, "Times of Refreshment: A Study of Eschatological Periodization in Judaism and Christianity" (Cambridge: Harvard University Th.D dissertation, 1962); Hamm, "Sign," 157-86; Hahn, "Problem," 144-48; Lohfink, "Christologie," 230-32, 238-40; Mussner, "Idee"; J. Parker, *The Concept of Apokatastasis in Acts* (Austin: Schola, 1978); and Feiler, "Prophet," 47-107, especially 58-61, 80-90. It should be noted that Parker's work (*Concept*) is essentially an elaboration of the brief article by Mussner ("Idee"). Unfortunately, Farrell ("Perspective") gives Acts 3:19-21 scant attention (pp. 185-86).

[94] Cf. Feiler, "Prophet," 80. In the following discussion, I am indebted to the sketch provided by Feiler (80-90).

[95] See, e.g., Haenchen, *Acts,* 208; Conzelmann, *Apostelgeschichte,* 40; Marshall, *Acts,* 93; Zehnle, *Pentecost,* 58-59; Lohfink, "Christologie," 230-31, 238-40. Lohfink does perceive a certain transmutation, however, when Luke introduced these terms borrowed from Jewish apocalyptic into his salvation-historical scheme.

[96] See, e.g., Hamm, "Sign," 158-59, 162-76; Kurz, "Role," 309-13; Cadbury, *Beginnings,* 4.37; Feiler, "Prophet," 90. Hamm places emphasis on the present process of restoration, yet acknowledges that the restoration of all things awaits the *"end* of these days" ("Sign," 176). He views (158-59) "times of refreshment" as "a way of describing conversion in apocalyptic language." Mussner ("Idee," 293-96) may also be assigned to this category, although he stresses the association of these two expressions with the end-time. His point is that, in Luke's narrative, the end-time has already arrived.

the future consummation, the χρόνοι ἀποκαταστάσεως.[97] Finally, Lane's temporal assignments have been reversed, with the καιροὶ ἀναψύξεως depicting the age of salvation subsequent to the parousia, and the χρόνοι ἀποκαταστάσεως denoting the period that leads up to the parousia.[98]

I. "Times and Seasons"

The first step toward a solution of the puzzle is to recognize the way in which Luke employs temporal expressions.[99] Luke's habit of juxtaposing singular and plural words for time, in relation to the eschaton, has already received comment.[100] In such instances, the term in the plural refers to a period of time preceding the event cast into the singular. For example, the "days" precede the "day" in Luke 17:26-27, 28-31; and the "last days" lead up to the "day of the Lord" in Acts 2:17-20.[101] In general, the plural terms ἡμέραι, καιροί, and χρόνοι point in Luke-Acts to a period of some duration. The analogous uses of καιροί in Luke 21:24, Acts 14:17 and 17:26 support the view that the expression "seasons of refreshment" refers not to the end-time blessings of the kingdom, but rather to a span of time leading up to the sending (parousia) of Jesus (3:20b). Similarly, the "times of restoration" (v 21) would denote a period that unfolds during Jesus' heavenly sojourn, a period that will find its consummation when Jesus returns. This preliminary finding must now be buttressed by detailed consideration of the background and meaning of the nouns ἀνάψυξις and ἀποκατάστασις.

II. "Repent, so that seasons of refreshment may come. . . ."

The noun ἀνάψυξις occurs only once in the LXX, at Exod 8:15. Here it points to the respite experienced by Pharaoh when the plagues ceased.[102] This passage

---

[97] "Refreshment," 171-72, 177-80. In Lane's view, the experience of the Spirit in the Jerusalem community marks the beginning of a new period in the eschatological timetable. "Seasons of refreshing" unfold until the parousia, at which time the restoration of all things commences. Lane's interpretation hinges on Symmachus' translation of Isa 32:15, in which the LXX image of the descent of the Spirit from on high is replaced with the descent of ἀνάψυξις (see "Refreshment," 164).

[98] See, e.g., Parker, *Concept,* 31, 37; Schille, *Apostelgeschichte,* 128-30. Parker concludes that "seasons of refreshing" refers to the future messianic salvation because the phrase is linked to the sending of the Christ in v 20 (*Concept,* 31).

[99] See especially Kurz, "Role," 309-10.

[100] See chapter two, section C.3.

[101] Cf. also Luke 21: ὁ καιρός (v 8; = τὸ τέλος, v 9) and "that day" (v 34), juxtaposed with "days" (v 6), "days of retribution" (v 22), and "times of the Gentiles" (v 24). Kurz ("Role," 310) terms this juxtaposition of singular and plural a "deliberate Lukan pattern."

[102] The noun ἀναψυχή does occur in the LXX in Ps 65:12; Hos 12:8-9; Jer 30:26. The verb ἀναψύχω appears in 2 Tim 1:16, and in the LXX at Exod 23:12; 31:17; Judg 15:19; 1 Kgdms 16:23; 2 Kgdms 16:14; Ps 38:14; 2 Macc 4:46; 13:11. The verb (whether used transitively or intransitively) refers to the act of refreshing or reviving. Cf. Lane, "Refreshment," 143-75; Feiler, "Prophet," 58; C. K. Barrett, "Faith and Eschatology in Acts 3," in

is of little help in pinpointing the meaning of the phrase in Acts 3:20, although it does suggest that ἀνάψυξις need not have eschatological import.[103] Indeed, such a meaning would be unusual for the noun.[104] Aquila's translation of Isa 28:12 employs ἀνάψυξις to refer to refreshment as the present experience of people *if* they listen to God![105] In the Greco-Roman literature generally, the noun ἀνάψυξις means "rest" or "respite."[106] The phrase "seasons of refreshment" in Acts 3:20, then, refers to the rest or refreshment experienced as a result of the forgiveness (v 19b) that accompanies repentance (v 19a). Only if the content of v 20b ("and that he may send the Christ appointed for you, Jesus") is allowed to determine the range of meaning for "seasons of refreshment" does an eschatological frame of reference suggest itself![107]

The goal of the summons to repentance (v 19a) is the erasure of sins (v 19b), and the intended result[108] is the experience, beginning in the present context of the church's mission, of respite or refreshment from God ("from the face of the Lord"; v 20a). This "blessing" (cf. the language of v 26) is contingent upon the act of repentance. Verse 20b rounds out the picture of the intended result of repentance: the "Christ appointed for you" may be sent. It is not that the parousia is contingent upon the repentance of Israel; rather, the "Christ appointed for you" will indeed be sent (for their benefit) when the Jews repent of their earlier rejection and execution of their Christ![109]

Glaube und Eschatologie, ed. E. Grässer and O. Merk (Tübingen: J. C. B. Mohr, 1985) 1–17, 11–13.

[103] Cf. also the use of "time of refreshment" in the Acts of John 22, where the present opportunity for healing is in view.

[104] It should be noted that Symmachus uses the noun ἀνάψυξις in his translation of Isa 32:15, a verse that describes the (eschatological) cessation of a time of desolation in the land. The LXX speaks here of the descent of the Spirit, Symmachus of the descent of "refreshment." See Lane, "Refreshment," 164–69.

[105] Cf. Lane, "Refreshment," 158–60.

[106] See, e.g., Philo, *De Abrah.,* 152; Galen, *San. Tuend.,* iii. 7; Hippocrates, *De Fracturis,* 25. For a more extensive listing, consult LSJ, 127.

[107] Cf. Barrett, "Faith," 12: "καιροὶ ἀναψύξεως does not suggest the final messianic deliverance brought about by the coming of the Messiah. It does suggest moments of relief during the time men spend in waiting for that blessed day."

[108] As Barrett points out ("Faith," 9) it is not clear whether the ὅπως-clause of 3:20 is dependent on the first purpose clause of v 19 ("so that your sins may be erased") or on the preceding imperatives ("repent and turn!"). Given the close connection between repentance and forgiveness of sins in Luke-Acts, it is perhaps not essential to make a choice. Barrett elects to follow the sequence of expressions: "First come repentance and turning; next, as the immediate consequence, the blotting out of sins; and then, as the consequence of the blotting out of sins, the coming of καιροὶ ἀναψύξεως and the sending of the Messiah" (p. 9).

[109] So also Feiler, "Prophet," 60; Lohfink, "Christologie," 236; Schneider, *Apostelgeschichte,* 1.326.

III. ". . .until the times of the restoration/fulfillment of all that God spoke . . . ."

The first detail to be examined is the force of the preposition ἄχρι. Luke employs this preposition with a plural object only in Acts 3:21 and 20:6. The latter instance is instructive for the exegesis of 3:21:

> But, after the days of unleavened bread, we sailed away from Philippi and came to them in Troas after five days (ἄχρι ἡμερῶν πέντε); there we remained for seven days.

Here ἄχρι ἡμερῶν πέντε must denote the length of time which was necessary for the journey to Troas; the sentence therefore speaks of an arrival at the *completion* of a specified period of time.[110] The phrase ἄχρι χρόνων ἀποκαταστάσεως in 3:21, accordingly, has in view a return of Jesus after the completion of the times of restoration:[111] "Him heaven must receive *until after* the times of the restoration of all. . . ." Jesus resides in heaven, as enthroned King and Lord, during the time of restoration.[112]

The second detail to be addressed is identification of the antecedent of the relative pronoun ὧν (v 21). Although χρόνων is not without its advocates,[113] the

---

[110] In agreement with Kurz ("Role," 311) and Feiler, ("Prophet," 85–86).

[111] Legitimate objections may be raised against this argument that is based on the usage of ἄχρι with a plural object and on the durative quality in Luke-Acts of plural nouns of time. First, it is hazardous to place too much weight on the analogous use of ἄχρι with the genitive plural in Acts 20:6, for one instance scarcely suffices to establish Luke's literary proclivities. Second, the observation that plural temporal terms indicate duration is compatible with the view that the preposition ἄχρι reaches to the beginning, not the completion, of this period of restoration. In fact, such a meaning would be consistent with (one interpretation of) the expression "one of the days of the Son of man" (Luke 17:22). That is, Luke may, after all, expect a period of some duration after the parousia, a period during which the universal restoration is accomplished. Even if this alternative analysis were correct, it would not substantially alter the lines of interpretation of Acts 3:19–21. There is other evidence in the narrative (see the discussion below) that a process of restoration is already underway; accordingly, the weight would fall on the πάντα of restoration as still future (and subsequent to Jesus' return.) At the inception of a future time of *final* restoration, this approach would urge, Jesus will return. Nevertheless, this alternative understanding of Luke's expectation for the end-time does not accord well with other elements of Luke's presentation. Jesus' parousia is depicted elsewhere (e.g., Luke 17:22–37) in terms of decisive eschatological separation, as the culmination of a set of earth-shaking events of cosmic scope (Luke 21:25–27; cf. Acts 2:17–21), and as the redemption of believers (Luke 21:28; cf. Acts 2:21) — but not as the inauguration of an era of restoration patterned after Elijah expectations.

[112] Which is, therefore, equivalent to God's subjection of the Lord Jesus' enemies (Ps 109:1 LXX, cited in Acts 2:35). When God has effected all that was announced through the prophets — and when he has subjugated all Jesus' enemies — *then* Jesus will return at his parousia.

[113] See, e.g., Bauernfeind, *Apostelgeschichte*, 69. Other works are cited by Lohfink, "Christologie," 238 n. 59.

majority of commentators have opted for πάντων.[114] Does the verse speak of an era of universal restoration which God had foretold through the prophets (χρόνων as antecedent), or does it refer to the restoration (= fulfillment?) of everything announced by the prophets (πάντων as antecedent)? Feiler adduces three considerations that support the latter reading. First, Luke commonly uses πᾶς with a relative clause.[115] Second, the word πάντων is the nearest possible antecedent.[116] Third, the relative pronoun has taken the genitive case by attraction. Since attraction occurs only when the relative clause is essential to complete the meaning of the antecedent, the antecedent must be πάντων.[117] To these observations a fourth may be added. The expression "all the things that God spoke" has a close parallel in Luke 24:25 and corresponds to the fundamental Lukan prophecy/fulfillment pattern.[118] I conclude, then, that verse 21 pictures the detainment of Jesus in heaven during the times of the ἀποκατάστασις of all the things that God had spoken through the mouths of his holy prophets.

But what precisely is that ἀποκατάστασις? The noun ἀποκατάστασις does not appear in the LXX. However, Josephus uses it to denote the return from exile[119] and Philo uses it to refer to the redemption from Egypt[120] and to jubilee restoration of inheritances.[121] The Epistle of Aristeas speaks of the return of Jewish emissaries to Jerusalem with this word (123).[122] The prevalent sense of ἀποκατάστασις is "restitution" or "return" or "restoration," whether to an original condition or to a previous location.[123] This meaning of the noun ἀποκατάστασις in Acts 3:21 is supported by the presence of the verb ἀποκαθίστημι in 1:6: the disciples ask Jesus whether now is the time of God's restoring the kingdom to Israel. This verb became a technical term in the Old Testament for the political restoration of Israel by God.[124] Not only the terms "restore" and "restoration"

---

[114] So, e.g., Oepke, *TDNT* 1, 391; Haenchen, *Acts,* 208; Lohfink, "Christologie," 238; Schneider, *Apostelgeschichte,* 1.327 n. 109; Parker, *Concept,* 31; Feiler, "Prophet," 86–87.

[115] Feiler, "Prophet," 86–87 n. 55. Examples of πάντων (or πασῶν, Luke 19:37) with ὧν are: Luke 3:19; 19:37; Acts 1:1; 10:39; 22:10; 24:8; 26:2.

[116] Ibid.

[117] Ibid. The relative clause is necessary to complete πάντων but not χρόνων, which is qualified by its own genitive ἀποκαταστάσεως. See H. W. Smyth, *Greek Grammar* (Cambridge: Harvard, 1956) 567, par. 2524.

[118] Cf. Luke 18:31; 21:22; 24:44; Acts 13:29; 24:14. Lohfink ("Christologie," 238) concludes from these data that the problem of the antecedent of ὧν in Acts 3:21 has now been finally settled in favor of πάντων.

[119] *Antiquities* 11, 63.

[120] *Rerum Divinarum Heres,* 293.

[121] *De Decalogo,* 164.

[122] These references are conveniently gathered in Parker, *Concept,* 2.

[123] Cf. Diog. Laert. 7, 59, where ἀποκατάστασις has to do with the Stoic cyclical view of nature. In secular documents, the restitution may apply to health or property. In the sphere of astronomy, the return of the constellations to their original position is in view. See Oepke, *TDNT* 1, 389–90.

[124] See, e.g., in the LXX Ps 16:5; Jer 15:19; 16:15; 23:8; 24:6; Ezek 16:55; 17:23; Hos

(Acts 1:6; 3:21), but also several larger features of Luke's story indicate that a process of Israel's restoration is underway. The Davidic king is enthroned (Luke 1:32–33; Acts 2:30–36). The twelve are reconstituted, so that they may judge the twelve tribes of Israel (Acts 1:15–26; cf. Luke 22:28–30). Further, the inclusion of Gentiles in the people of God is tied to the rebuilding of the "fallen booth of David" (Acts 15:14–18).[125] The narrative of Luke-Acts tells of the process whereby Israel's restoration is effected, but in such a way that the nations take their place, too. The restoration of all things (Acts 3:21) does not negate the question of Israel's restoration (1:6), yet it does represent a particular interpretation of it (in light of Isa 49:6). The parousia does not await a reconstitution of national Israel, but rather the conclusion of a mission to the "end of the earth" which brings the claim of Jesus' kingship and Lordship to all people. After this mission has accomplished the divine design for it, the end-time sending of the Messiah Jesus will occur.

It would be mistaken to deny this "restoration" nuance in Luke's use of ἀποκατάστασις in Acts 3:21.[126] Nevertheless, the combination of ἀποκατάστασις with prophecies inspired by God (taking πάντων as the antecedent of ὧν) yields an aporia. The statement should concern the restoration of all things — a *restoration about* which God had spoken through the prophets — not the restoration of things prophesied. This rough edge leads Feiler to conclude that "fulfillment," not "restoration," is the meaning of ἀποκατάστασις here: "In relation to prophecy, ἀποκατάστασις means "establishment of what was predicted" rather than "restoration of an earlier condition.""[127] I suggest that Luke has merged the motifs of

---

11:11. The verb ἀποκαθίστημι occurs 48 times in the Old Testament, with reference to healing (Jer 15:19; Exod 4:7; Lev 13:16; Job 5:18), but particularly with reference to Israel's restoration to the land (restoration of the temple: 2 Macc 11:25). Especially important, of course, is the characterization of Elijah's work as a "restoring" (Mal 3:22–23 LXX; Sir 48:10; cf. Mark 9:11–13).

[125] For a more extensive discussion of restoration motifs in Luke-Acts, see Mussner, "Idee"; and Parker, *Concept*. On restoration eschatology in general, and in relation to the activity of Jesus, see now E. P. Sanders, *Jesus and Judaism* (Philadelphia: Fortress, 1985) 77–119.

[126] Feiler ("Prophet," 89) appears to err in this direction. For example, passages which Feiler (following F. F. Bruce, *Acts,* 112) adduces to support the meaning "fulfillment" or "realization" (Ps 16:5; Job 8:6; 2 Macc 12:39; 15:20) tend to work against his view. See the discussion in Barrett, "Faith," 14–15.

[127] Feiler, "Prophet," 89. Oepke's handling of the problem is instructive: "For the concept of restoration, which is so strong in the term, does not strictly refer to the content of the prophetic promise, but to the relations of which it speaks. These are restored, i.e., brought back to the integrity of creation, while the promise itself is established or fulfilled. *The difficulty arises from, but is also resolved in, the fact that the two thoughts set out in the translation are linked in pregnant brevity*" (*TDNT* 1, 391; emphasis mine). While the importing of the notion of creation is not warranted by the text (cf. also Lohfink, "Christologie," 239 n. 61), Oepke's observation that exegetical difficulty stems from the

restoration and prophecy/fulfillment in this verse, and that the resulting compact construction requires some such expansion as ". . . until the times of the restoration of all things, fulfilling what God has spoken through the mouths of his holy prophets from an age long past."

In sum, both "seasons of refreshment" and "times of restoration/fulfillment" refer to aspects of the present era of mission, which leads up to the final sending of Jesus (the parousia). The process of Israel's restoration, in fulfillment of ancient promise, is now underway — and moves out beyond the bounds of Israel to the nations (also in fulfillment of scriptural promise). When this process is completed, God will again send his Christ (the eschaton). The sense of vv 19–21, therefore, is:

> Repent, therefore, and return, in order that your sins may be blotted out, so that seasons of refreshing may (now in the era of the worldwide mission) come upon you, and so that he may send (at the parousia, and for your benefit) the Christ appointed for you, Jesus (whom you have rejected and killed), whom heaven must (continue to) receive during the(se) times of the restoration of all things about which God spoke through the mouths of his holy prophets from of old.

b. The Present Time in Which Response to Jesus is Demanded and Given is the Determinative Moment for Eschatology

Now that the most troublesome pieces of the puzzle have been assembled, it is appropriate to present my reading of the function of eschatology in Acts 3:19–26. In the first place, this passage heightens the role played by the present mission of the church in relation to the end-time. Verses 22–23 in particular define the negative consequences that accompany rejection of the Christian preaching (which is to be identified with the voice of Jesus, the Mosaic prophet). Those who fail to respond in repentance and faith are rooted out of God's covenant people. There is no hint of a future second chance; the time of ignorance (Acts 3:17; cf. 17:30–31) is at an end, and no excuse remains. The outcome of one's response to the apostolic mission is irrevocable and final, for salvation resides in "no other name" (4:10–12). Acts 3:22–23, therefore, gives the flip side of 2:21. Salvation is assured for all who call upon Jesus as Lord;

---

compactness of the formulations is a clue to understanding the passage. Likewise, Lohfink ("Christologie," 238–39) sees the blending of two concepts: *Vorstellung* as fulfillment (of prophecy; this is Lukan); and *Vorstellung* of the end-time age of salvation, the world restored (this nuance derives from the apocalyptic realm from which Luke borrowed the term). Lohfink's treatment points to the possibility that the noun ἀποκατάστασις bears different meanings at the levels of tradition and redaction ("restoration," then "fulfillment"). However, the evidence of restoration motifs in the narrative as a whole suggests that Luke was not oblivious to this connotation of the term. The multivalence of the word has resulted, instead, from the compact construction and from Luke's correlation of the "restoration" motif with his basic prophecy/fulfillment pattern.

exclusion from the people of God's salvation is certain for all who repudiate Jesus![128]

Concrete hopes for the end of history remain intact and important in Luke-Acts.[129] Nevertheless, Luke casts the spotlight on the present life of those who would experience the eschaton as blessing rather than judgment.[130] Luke 12:35-48 summoned Luke's readers to a vigilant and faithful way of life. Luke 17:20-18:8 identified the present confrontation with Jesus' claim as the decisive encounter with the kingdom (17:20-21). It warned against a manner of life in the present that would call forth judgment on the "day of the Son of man" (17:26-30), for life immersed in daily routines and not oriented eschatologically will not equip one to survive the perils of the eschaton (17:31-35). The burning question at the return of Jesus will be, "Is there any faith on earth?" (18:8b). Since the parousia's arrival is not susceptible to prediction, the question about persevering faith is not just a question for the future; it is primarily a challenge to faith today. Acts 1:6-8 deflects attention away from the timing of the End and toward the present task of mission under the power of the Spirit. Acts 2:17-21 and 3:19-26 show what is to be gained and lost during the period of mission to the "end of the earth."

God's blessing includes the forgiveness of sins, and this benefit accrues to the repentant beginning now (vv 19-20, 26). So the covenant promise to Abraham comes to fruition; the blessing that accompanies repentance is granted to "all the families of the earth" (v 25). Yet, interest is not reduced to the fate of the individual. The final phase of Israel's history as the people of God has been launched. The restoration of Israel — kingship, twelve tribes, Spirit-enabled obedience to Torah, incorporation of the Gentiles — is well on the road toward completion. At the culmination of this process of restoration, God's final act in the eschatological drama will occur with the sending (parousia) of the Son of man/Christ. That end-time expectation serves to highlight the ultimate significance of what is happening in and around the church in the present.

---

[128] For the best recent treatment of the "soteriological imperative" contained in Acts 3:22-23, see Feiler, "Prophet," 47-107.

[129] In this passage, specific reference is made to Jesus' return as Christ (v 20) at the completion of the "times of restoration" (v 21).

[130] Cf. E. Schweizer, *The Good News According to Luke,* tr. D. E. Green (Atlanta: John Knox, 1984) 323, 328: "The danger then is flight into a fantasy world that once more refuses to take seriously the world and the time remaining before the expected end. If we want to avoid [this danger], we must follow Luke in holding fast to expectation of a consummating final act of God but placing the major emphasis on human conduct in the interim, as determined by this final act . . ." (328). Cf. also Fitzmyer's slogan: "from *eschaton* to *sēmeron*" (*Luke,* 1.234). I will later argue (see below, chapter 4) that it is not simply the fact of the final judgment but also its timing that gives shape to Luke's correlation between end-time and present situation.

c. The Function of Parousia Delay

The character of the present has much — everything — to do with the outcome of things at the eschaton. Therefore, the delay in the parousia — not explicitly expressed, yet presupposed in 3:19-26 ("whom heaven must receive until. . .") — appears in a fresh light. This passage explains the delay even as it defines its function.[131] During the resultant interim period, the worldwide mission, pursuant to the mandate of Acts 1:8 and Luke 24:46-48, attains its goal. People everywhere, Jews and non-Jews alike, are summoned to listen in repentance and faith to Jesus (by heeding the preaching of his followers). So they ensure their participation in the salvation from God,[132] and so the promise to Abraham that stands at the beginning of Israel's story finds fulfillment at that story's end. In other words, the postponement of the eschaton has as its corollary the extension of access to salvation (with the opportunity comes the either-or result) to all people. Delay makes possible the mission.

At the same time, the cause (source) of the delay is transparent: the parousia is held back by divine decree. The returning Christ remains in heaven by the will of God (δεῖ) until the process of restoration of everything spoken by God is completed. Integral to those words of promise is the prophecy of Gentile inclusion in the people of God. Only when the mission among Gentiles attains its terminus (the "end of the earth") will God send his Christ. Parousia delay, then, far from being a reason for discouragement or complacency, is given by God for the sake of the church's mission activity. Acts itself takes the reader to the threshold of the mission focused on the Gentiles (28:28). Accordingly, while the End is not to be expected at any point in the story, beyond the narrative lies an era of mission (primarily among Gentiles) which reaches to Luke's own time. Luke and his readers stand on the far side of this worldwide mission, hence closer (by an undefined interval)[133] to the end of the process of restoration which

---

[131] Schnackenburg ("Aussagen," 258) also detects the delay motif in Acts 3:19-21.

[132] Luke does not imply that repentance will hasten the parousia (against Bruce, "Speeches," 53-68, 68). The emphasis of Acts 3:19-20 is not on the parousia as contingent upon repentance, but rather on repentance as the condition of participation in the blessings of God.

[133] In addition to the absence of any specific indication of the timing of the parousia in this passage, the necessity of a "restoration of *all things*" prior to the eschaton rules out any possibility of calculation. Cf. Parker (*Concept,* 32), who suggests that Acts 3:19-21 does not address the subject of delay or imminence, asserting only the certainty of the parousia. "The text simply states that Jesus' admission to heaven until his parousia corresponds to the will of God, and that he is not returning again until his parousia" (32). Similarly, Feiler ("Prophet," 61): this passage "emphasizes not the interval until the parousia — neither its imminence nor its delay — but only the certainty of the parousia as a blessing for those who repent." Although the motif of delay is not explicitly expressed here, I do see it as presupposed. Others who ascribe a role to parousia delay in Acts 3:19-21 are Lohfink, "Christologie," 237; Schneider, *Parusiegleichnisse,* 87-89; Schneider, *Apostelgeschichte,* 1.327; Haenchen, *Acts,* 208; Schnackenburg, "Aussagen," 258.

culminates in the parousia. The Acts narrative takes the reader well on the way toward the eschaton, but the end-time events remain a matter of expectation.

Within the story, Peter's speech (together with the following events which it provokes) affords Jerusalem Jews their (final) opportunity to take their place within the covenant people who experience the salvation of God. For Luke's readers, these verses stress the importance of penitent faith, and the urgency of the church's mission.[134] Jesus' return is certain — though unpredictable — but Luke places the focus on the urgent business of the interim. Eschatological expectation serves to heighten the urgency of the church's activity in the present.

EXCURSUS 5: TRADITION AND COMPOSITION IN ACTS 3:12-26

The problem of tradition and composition in Acts 3:12-26, especially vv 19-21, is a vexed one, and has prompted diverse proposals. O. Bauernfeind discerned in 3:19-25 a Jewish Elijah tradition which had been slightly Christianized before Luke inserted it into its present context.[135] Bauernfeind called attention to several features of Peter's speech that suggest the presence of pre-Lukan tradition. First, the speech takes a surprising turn, when the call to repentance (v 19) is followed by a return to the christological kerygma. Second, the expression "Repent, so that God may send the Messiah" (vv 19-20) is peculiar in early Christian literature. Third, the theme of resurrection remains undeveloped after v 15.[136] Fourth, the reference to God's *end-time* sending of Jesus (v 20) is without parallel elsewhere in the New Testament. Fifth, v 21 bypasses the usual terminology of session at the right hand to describe Jesus' present status in heaven. Sixth, the expressions καιροὶ ἀναψύξεως and χρόνοι ἀποκαταστάσεως are unparalleled in Luke-Acts.[137] Bauernfeind was impressed, at the same time, by the verbal correspondences between Acts 3:19-21 and the Elijah traditions preserved in Mal 3:22-23 LXX and Sir 48:10 (notably, the combination of the motifs of "sending" and "restoration"). Bauernfeind concluded that Acts 3:19-25 stems from Jewish circles that expected Elijah's return as a messianic figure. Only the substitution of "Jesus" for "Elijah" at the close

---

[134] Cf. A. L. Moore (*The Parousia in the New Testament* [Leiden: Brill, 1970] 148): " . . . the promise of the Parousia standing here at the outset of the church's life and work serves as a constant reminder that the history being narrated is to come to an end, that the opportunity for mission is temporary, and therefore that the missionary task of the church is urgent, forbidding idle wistfulness and lethargic sorrow."

[135] *Die Apostelgeschichte* (Leipzig: Deichertsche, 1939) 62, 66-68. Lohfink ("Christologie," 223-25) provides a convenient summary of Bauernfeind's argument. Bauernfeind updates his own hypothesis in "Tradition und Komposition in dem Apokatastasisspruch Apostelgeschichte 3,20F.," in *Abraham unser Vater*," ed. O. Betz, M. Hengel, and P. Schmidt (Leiden: Brill, 1963) 13-23.

[136] However, note the recurrence of the motif of God's "raising up" Jesus in vv 22, 26 (cf. O'Toole, "Observations").

[137] Bauernfeind, *Apostelgeschichte*, 65-66.

of v 20 was necessary to Christianize this Jewish material![138] Needless to say, such a proposal leaves little space for Lukan composition in vv 19–26![139]

Although Wilckens follows Bauernfeind's general proposal, he reduces the scope of the pre-Lukan tradition to Acts 3:20–21a![140] To the evidence marshalled by Bauernfeind, Wilckens is therefore able to add the observation that vv 20–21 interrupt the flow of thought from v 19 to v 22 and stand out—in terminology and content—as an insertion![141] But Lohfink takes an even larger step than Wilckens in the direction of Lukan composition; he reduces the extent of the pre-Lukan tradition to the vanishing point. Noting the abundance of Lukan vocabulary and stylistic features even in 3:19–21 (apart from the half-verse 3:20a), Lohfink concludes that Luke has composed the entire passage, incorporating the notion, borrowed from Jewish apocalyptic, that "times of refreshment would come from the face of the Lord."[142] In typical Lukan fashion, the author has used a "mosaic-technique," composing vv 19–21 out of elements borrowed from the Old Testament, Jewish apocalyptic, and Christian mission and liturgy![143] It is the apocalyptic element that prevails, as Luke gives this portion of the speech a "Jewish coloring" for its Jewish audience![144]

In an equally careful analysis of the passage, F. Hahn, like Lohfink, finds insufficient evidence of a pre-Christian, Jewish origin of the traditions in 3:19–21![145] Hahn contends that Lukan and non-Lukan features are tightly

---

[138] Ibid., 67.

[139] Bauernfeind does concede the possibility that 3:19 has been formulated by Luke to introduce vv 20–25 (Ibid., 66–67). The hypothesis of J. A. T. Robinson ("The Most Primitive Christology of All?," *JTS* 7 [1956] 177–89)—namely, that embedded within Acts 3:12–26 is a primitive Christian tradition which spoke of Jesus as only Christ-elect until the parousia (p. 181)—is bolder even than Bauernfeind's. The two approaches agree on the minimal extent of Lukan conceptuality and language in (at least portions of) Peter's speech. A similar verdict is reached by Zehnle, *Pentecost,* 47–53, 71–94. Zehnle perceives Acts 3:12–26 as replete with primitive (and non-Lukan) features; indeed, "the discourse of Acts 3 is the most primitive and undeveloped christological statement in the New Testament" (94). Like Robinson, Zehnle fails to see Lukan theology in Acts 3:12–26 because he has misread the role played by the speech in Luke's narrative as a whole.

[140] *Missionsreden,* 153–56.

[141] Ibid., 43; cf. 154.

[142] "Christologie," 227–41. Lohfink presents the best summary of the recent debate on tradition and redaction in 3:19–21 (pp. 223–27), and the clearest discussion of the details of vocabulary and style (227–39). Schille (*Apostelgeschichte,* 129) assumes that Lohfink's analysis provides the answer to the question concerning early tradition in this passage. Schneider (*Apostelgeschichte,* 1.324–27) follows Lohfink's tradition/redaction findings and details of his interpretation of vv 19–21.

[143] "Christologie," 240.

[144] Ibid.

[145] "Problem," 148–49. Especially useful is Hahn's discussion of the methodological difficulties in discriminating between tradition and redaction in Acts (pp. 129–35).

interwoven in vv 19–21; a tidy separation of tradition and redaction is, therefore, impossible![146] Nevertheless, the accumulation of Lukan *hapax legomena* indicates that Luke has indeed taken over traditional material. Behind vv 19–21 lies an early Christian tradition shaped in the context of mission preaching. Although a precise determination of the language of the tradition is not possible, the critical content of the tradition—both eschatologically[147] and christologically[148]—is discernible![149]

What conclusions may be reached on the problem of tradition and composition in Acts 3:12–26? First, it is appropriate to narrow the focus to vv 19–21, for the evidence of pre-Lukan tradition is concentrated in these verses![150] Second, it is clear that eschatological expressions not typical of Luke appear (specifically, καιροὶ ἀναψύξεως and χρόνοι ἀποκαταστάσεως)![151] Nonetheless, the evidence of Lukan composition is far more weighty. The combination of μετανοέω and ἐπιστρέφω (v 19), and the connection between repentance and forgiveness of sins (v 19, though with the unusual word ἐξαλειφθῆναι), are attested elsewhere in Luke![152] Although the successive final clauses of vv 19–20 are striking (and suggest the possibility that one—likely the clause introduced by ὅπως ἄν [v 20]—stems from tradition), Luke uses both constructions elsewhere![153] The use of "Christ" as the equivalent of "the Messiah," and the term προκεχειρισμένον (v 20), are also typical of Luke. The relative clause introduced by ὅν (v 21) is characteristic of Luke's style in the speeches of Acts![154] Both χρόνων and

[146] In large measure, Hahn agrees with Haenchen (*Acts*, 204–12) and Lohfink on the Lukan character of the passage, in its present form ("Problem," 139–40).

[147] That is, the linking of repentance and the effecting of eschatological salvation.

[148] That is, the view that Jesus' decisive messianic activity lies in the future.

[149] Hahn, "Problem," 150–51.

[150] This is not to say that the arguments of Robinson ("Primitive") and Zehnle (*Pentecost*, 47–53, 71–94), among others, concerning the archaic christological titles in Acts 3:12–26 as a whole (παῖς; δίκαιος, and ἅγιος; ἀρχηγὸς τῆς ζωῆς) are to be dismissed. Nevertheless, the strong evidence of Lukan composition throughout this section sets "Lukan archaizing" alongside "archaic tradition" as an equally attractive hypothesis (cf. Schneider, *Apostelgeschichte*, 1.316). In any case, if Luke has incorporated early traditions here, he has thoroughly reworked them to fit them into his narrative. He has made them "his own."

[151] Even here, caution is necessary, however. The juxtaposition of the terms καιροί and χρόνοι is by no means limited to this passage in the Lukan corpus (cf. Acts 1:7).

[152] The verbs μετανοέω and ἐπιστρέφω are found together in Luke 17:3–4 and Acts 26:20. On the linking of repentance and forgiveness of sins, see, e.g., Luke 24:47; Acts 2:38; 5:30–32; 26:18. Cf. Schneider, *Apostelgeschichte*, 1.323 nn. 81, 83.

[153] For εἰς + τό + the infinitive, see Luke 4:29 (A C); 5:17; Acts 7:19. (If πρός + τό + the infinitive is the correct reading in 3:19 [ℵ B], Luke 18:1 is analogous.) For ὅπως ἄν, see Luke 2:35; Acts 15:17 (from Amos citation). The only other New Testament occurrence of ὅπως with ἄν in a final clause is Rom 3:4 (= Ps 50:6 LXX). Cf. Schneider, *Apostelgeschichte*, 1.324 n. 85; Lohfink, "Christologie," 229–30.

[154] Cf. Acts 2:24, 36; 3:13, 15; 4:10; 5:30; 10:39; 13:37. Note also the presence of μέν

ἀποκαταστάσεως (v 21) echo the language of Acts 1:6–7: ἀποκαθιστάνεις and χρόνῳ (χρόνους ἢ καιρούς), and the formulation of v 21b is nearly identical to that of Luke 1:70.[155] To be sure, the use of ἀποστέλλω with reference to Jesus' parousia is without parallel in Luke-Acts. However, the verb itself is a favorite one of Luke, and when, as here, he accents the *divine* action in the return of Jesus, it is difficult to think of a better choice.[156] The language used of Jesus' detainment in heaven is certainly unusual for Luke (v 21), yet δεῖ is characteristic of Luke, and the imagery is consonant with the function of Jesus' ascension in Acts.

In sum, there is sufficient evidence of Luke's compositional activity in Acts 3:19–21 to render probable the view that—whatever source material he may have incorporated—Luke has composed this part of Peter's speech. Even as the surrounding verses (vv 12–16 with an eye backward to the healing of 3:1–10; vv 22–26 with an eye ahead to the ensuing mission) not only accord with but also serve to define the fundamental patterns of the larger narrative, so vv 19–21 fit well into Luke's story.[157] They express not unassimilated primitive eschatological notions but an eschatological perspective with which Luke agrees.[158] Because of the method adopted for this study,[159] it is not necessary to offer a precise tradition/redaction reconstruction for this passage. The discussion has shown that Luke—the peculiarity of his formulations notwithstanding—probably makes eschatological statements expressive of his own viewpoint, and does not reproduce a primitive eschatology standing in tension with his own conception.[160]

---

uncompleted by δέ (Acts 3:21; cf. Acts 1:1; 3:13, 21; 21:39; 27:21; 28:22). See Lohfink, "Christologie," 236–37; Schneider, *Apostelgeschichte,* 1.324 n. 86.

[155] For a more detailed analysis, see Lohfink, "Christologie," 227–39.

[156] Rightly noted by Lohfink ("Christologie," 234; cf. Schnackenburg, "Aussagen," 258), who calls attention to the prevalent theocentric formulations in the speeches of Acts. It should also be mentioned that Hamm ("Sign," 183–84) argues that the "sending" of Jesus alluded to in 3:20 refers not to the parousia but rather to the mission carried out by the apostles.

[157] The prominent role played here by the appeal for repentance, and its beneficial results, the fixing by God of a period during which the mission unfolds (cf. Acts 1:6–8), and the establishment of God's will foretold by the prophets from ancient times all cohere with fundamental Lukan motifs.

[158] Cf. the attempt by Kurz ("Test") to demonstrate that, far from transmitting a primitive christology which conflicts with his own prevalent view, Luke in Acts 3:19–26 thoroughly assimilates "whatever sources or traditions he had to his own theological framework" (309).

[159] See chapter one above.

[160] For the opposite view, see F. F. Bruce, "The Speeches in Acts—Thirty Years Later," in *Reconciliation and Hope,* ed. R. Banks (Grand Rapids: Eerdmans, 1975) 53–68, 68.

D. THE HOPE OF ISRAEL AND ESCHATOLOGICAL FULFILLMENT: THE ENDING OF ACTS (ACTS 28:17-31)

The "hope of Israel" gives to Luke's narrative its point of departure and its destination. Luke 1-2 portrayed the advent of John and Jesus as the inauguration of a new era of fulfillment for Israel. Jesus stepped onto the stage of history as the one who would fulfill definitively the hopes of Israel: he would be enthroned as the Messiah-King descended from David, in fulfillment of the promise to David (Luke 1:32-33; Acts 2:30-36); through him salvation and forgiveness would come to God's people, in fulfillment of the covenant with Abraham (Luke 1:68-75; 2:30; Acts 3:25-26). Nevertheless, Luke tells the story of a final division within Israel even as he narrates the fulfillment of Israel's hope. God's people gather in repentance and faith around the crucified Messiah, but many in Israel (notably the leaders of the people) refuse the agent of their redemption and so come to be expelled from the people of God. (This division is prophesied by Simeon in Luke 2:34-35, and the paradigm is established in Acts 3:22-23.) Yet, there is also evidence of hope extinguished. Jesus announces that the holy city, whose redemption is the object of the hope of pious Israel at the beginning of the story (Luke 2:38; cf. 2:25), will meet destruction because it has rejected the agent of its redemption (Luke 19:41-44; 21:20-24). And the identity of Israel appears to undergo radical redefinition through the incorporation of Gentiles into the people of promise, although, on closer inspection, one finds this surprising turn to be itself the fulfillment of the scriptural agenda promised to Israel (Luke 2:32; 24:47; Acts 3:25; 13:47; 15:14-18).

The hope of Israel is at stake in the course of events narrated in Luke-Acts. The history of God's people enters here its final chapter. At the outset of this exegetical inquiry, I asserted that "there can be no Christian eschaton that does not satisfactorily—and definitively—address these Jewish expectations."[161] What resolution does Luke offer in his concluding episode (Acts 28:17-31)? What place does Luke reserve for the hope of Israel in his picture of the end-time? After analyzing the literary function of Paul's confrontation with Roman Jews in relation to the defense speeches of Paul, I will examine the function of the Isaiah citation (28:26-27) in order to prepare for a concluding discussion of "Israel and the eschaton" in Luke-Acts.

1. The Irony of Paul's Apology before the Roman Jews

Acts 28:17-22 culminates a series of apologies (Acts 21-26) in which Paul refutes charges[162] that he is a renegade Jew who has incited fellow Jews to

---

[161] See the discussion of Luke 1:30-33 in chapter two, section A.

[162] The preceding apologies appear in 22:1-21; 23:1-7; 24:10-21; 25:10-11; 26:2-23. P. Schubert ("The Final Cycle of Speeches in the Book of Acts," *JBL* 87 [1968] 1-16) has observed that chapters 21-28 form an "ascending climax" (10); cf. C. B. Puskas, "The Conclusion of Luke-Acts: An Investigation of the Literary Function and Theological

abandon their Torah. Countering accusations that he is apostate,[163] Paul exposes the irony of his imprisonment at the instigation of the authorities at Jerusalem: it was precisely because of the "hope of Israel" that Paul had become a prisoner (28:20)![164] Paul's first conversation with prominent Roman Jews provides a retrospective summary of the course of Paul's trial and self-defense (chapters 21–28). Luke gives to Paul the last word in his own defense: "I am innocent [v 19] and have done nothing against my people [v 17]." Luke has spared no detail[165] to establish Paul's standing as a law-abiding, devout Jew of Pharisaic pedigree![166]

Significance of Acts 28:16–31" (St. Louis: St. Louis University Ph.D. dissertation, 1980) 36–77. For further discussion of the function of Acts 28:17–22 in relation to the arrest and trials of Paul, see Dupont, "La Conclusion des Actes et son rapport à l'ensemble de l'ouvrage de Luc," in Les Actes des Apôtres: Tradition, rédaction, théologie, ed. J. Kremer (Leuven: University, 1979) 359–404, 380–83. It is crucial to note that the entire narrative of Acts 21:1–28:16, not just the speeches of Paul, serves to defend Paul and his mission among Gentiles. On the apologetic effect of 27:1–28:16, see, e.g., P. Pokorny, "Die Romfahrt des Paulus und der antike Roman," ZNW 64 (1973) 233–44; G. B. Miles and G. Trompf, "Luke and Antiphon: The Theology of Acts 27–28 in the Light of Pagan Beliefs about Divine Retribution, Pollution, and Shipwreck," HTR 69 (1976) 259–67; S. M. Praeder, "Acts 27:1–28:16: Sea Voyages in Ancient Literature and the Theology of Luke-Acts," CBQ 46 (1984) 683–706.

[163] Though these accusations have not preceded Paul to his Jewish audience! This literary device enables Luke to color the episode as a mission situation (cf. Haenchen, Acts, 727–30).

[164] This claim picks up a recurring theme of Paul's defense speeches (Acts 23:6; 24:15–16; 26:6–7): he stood accused by the Jewish leaders for nothing other than his affirmation of Israel's hope (specifically its realization in the resurrection).

[165] Decisive pronouncement of Paul's innocence by Agrippa (26:32); survival of shipwreck (27:21–44; cf. 28:4) and of contact with a venomous viper (28:3–6); the unhindered preaching activity of Paul at Rome (28:30–31). God's verdict on Paul and his mission is, of course, self-evident (e.g., 22:6–21; 23:11; 26:12–18), even without these corroborating details.

[166] The prominent role played in the last half of Acts by apology on behalf of Paul suggests that Luke's setting included attacks directed against Paul either by the synagogue or by Jewish Christians who viewed Paul as unfaithful to Torah. By defending Paul, Luke, as spokesperson for the Gentile churches for which Paul was the founding father, defended at the same time the Gentile Christianity indebted to Paul. In order to paint the church as an attractive option for Jews and for Gentiles associated with the synagogue (proselytes and "God-fearers"), Luke must counter charges that Paul (hence the churches stemming from him) had abandoned the Torah of Israel. On the contrary, Paul—in contrast to his Jewish antagonists—accepts the promise that both law and prophets held out to Israel (24:14–15). For a suggestive attempt to correlate the apology for Paul with the setting of Luke-Acts, see N. A. Dahl ("The Purpose of Luke-Acts," in Jesus in the Memory of the Early Church [Minneapolis: Augsburg, 1976] 87–98, 94–97); cf. Adams ("Suffering," 298–305).

Acts 28:18 establishes Paul's innocence in the eyes of the Roman authorities.[167] Verses 19 and 20 spell out the irony of Paul's situation. He has appealed to Caesar only in self-defense against the opposition[168] of "the Jews" — not because he has any accusation to raise against his own nation (v 19). The leaders of his own people have not refrained, however, from accusing Paul.[169] Ironically (v 20), Paul stands accused because of his affirmation of the hope of Israel. Acts 26:6–8 (cf. 23:6; 24:21) defines the object of that hope as resurrection of the dead:

> And now I stand on trial for [my] hope in the promise made by God to our fathers, to which our twelve tribes hope — as they serve in earnest night and day — to attain. Concerning this hope I am being accused by the Jews, O King. Why is it deemed unbelievable by you (plural) that God raises the dead?

Because Paul, like Luke's Peter before him (Acts 2:30–36) believes such hope to be fulfilled in Jesus' resurrection (cf. also 13:33–37),[170] the crux of the debate is this: Paul sees in Jesus the decisive fulfillment of the hope of Israel; his Jewish opponents reject this claim.[171]

This is all news to the leading Jews of Rome, however (v 21). Indeed, they are eager to hear[172] Paul's thoughts from his own mouth (v 22). Luke thereby sets the stage for the final mission proclamation of his story (vv 23–31). These Jewish listeners will face the challenge of a genuine "hearing" of the message.

2. "To the Gentiles": The Function of the Isaiah Quotation in Acts 28:26–27

Even as Paul's apology before the leaders of the Jewish community at Rome (Acts 28:17–22) completes a series of speeches defending Paul's status as a faithful Jew, so also the second meeting of Paul with Roman Jews (in larger numbers, vv 23–28; cf. the similar pattern in Acts 13:44) culminates a series of encounters in which rejection of the Christian proclamation by diaspora Jews leads Paul to a mission among Gentiles (13:44–48; 18:4–6; cf. 19:8–10). Paul's activity in the capital of the empire thereby follows the same pattern as his

---

[167] This detail does not exactly match the foregoing narrative; however, it does bring Paul into parallel with Jesus (cf. Acts 13:28), so underscoring — for the reader — Paul's innocence. Cf. Puskas, "Conclusion," 49.

[168] The participle ἀντιλεγόντων echoes Simeon's prophecy (Luke 2:34); cf. also Acts 13:45.

[169] Apart from its use in Acts 28:19, where Paul does not accuse, the verb κατηγορέω appears repeatedly in Acts 21–26 as the Jewish leaders accuse Paul of being an enemy of Judaism (22:30; 24:2, 8, 13, 19; 25:5, 11, 16).

[170] Which, together with the ascension, constitutes Jesus' accession to the throne, thus fulfilling Luke 1:32–33.

[171] The Sadducees because they deny resurrection faith *per se*, the Pharisees because they fail to recognize the fruition of their expectation in the person of Jesus.

[172] The repetition of the verb ἀκούω in this passage is a key to a proper reading of it; cf. also Dupont, "Conclusion," 372–76, and see the discussion below.

mission in Asia Minor and Greece. There he preached first among the Jews (and Gentiles associated with the synagogue). When his message elicited a divided response among the Jews, with some being persuaded and others opposing Paul forcefully, he turned to the Gentiles. Twice Paul declared to his Jewish antagonists the rationale for this move:

> It was necessary for the word of God to be spoken to you first; since you spurn it and judge yourselves unworthy of eternal life, behold, we turn to the Gentiles. For so the Lord commanded us: "I appointed you to [be] a light of [the] Gentiles, so that you may bring salvation to the end of the earth" (13:46–47)![173]

> Your blood is on your [own] heads; I am innocent. From now on I will go to the Gentiles (18:6)![174]

While it is inaccurate to say that the Gentile mission (or even Paul's Gentile mission) in Acts is the consequence of rejection of Christian preaching by the Jews![175] the programmatic force of these passages is unmistakable. Through them Luke justifies Paul's activity among the Gentiles: he was compelled by God's will, scriptural prophecy, and Jewish resistance to take up a Gentile-centered mission. Thereby Luke places Gentile believers alongside believing Jews — Jews who refused the Christian preaching have been rooted out of the people — as the inheritors of the promise and hope of Israel. In neither case (13:46–47; 18:6) is final transition to an exclusively Gentile mission involved, for Paul resumes his work among the Jewish people in his next stop![176] The final episode of Acts stands alone, however, both because of its climactic position in the narrative and

---

[173] Note the way in which the quotation from Isaiah 49:6 picks up the mandate/promise of Acts 1:8. This link probably accounts for the unusual introduction of the citation ("so the Lord commanded us"). In this instance, Luke depicts the motive of Jewish hostility to Paul as jealousy at Paul's success among the Jews (and others!) of Pisidian Antioch (13:45).

[174] Here opposition to Paul on the part of Corinthian Jews appears to stem directly from repudiation of the claim that Jesus is the Messiah (18:5).

[175] For several reasons: (1) As Jervell has correctly argued ("Divided"), the initial success of the Jewish mission (most striking in the Jerusalem narrative) points to a process of Israel's restoration, in which Gentiles, too, take their place (cf. Acts 15:14–18); (2) scriptural promise plays a fundamental role (e.g., Luke 24:44–47; Acts 1:8; 13:47; 15:14–18), as does direct divine intervention, particularly in the Cornelius episode (cf. Acts 10:3–6, 9–16, 19–20, 22, 44–45; 11:15–18); (3) never is Jewish reaction to the message one of univocal rejection, even when the opposition to Paul escalates in the diaspora mission (see, e.g., 17:1–9; 18:5–8; 19:8–10); (4) conversions among the Gentiles characteristically begin with Paul's activity in the synagogue (e.g., 13:44; 14:1; 17:4, 12; 18:4). See further Dupont, "Conclusion," 403; Feiler, "Prophet," 105. Feiler remarks: "while Jewish obduracy is a catalyst for Paul's mission, it is neither the mission's primary cause nor the basis for the offer of salvation to the Gentiles."

[176] In the Lukan scheme, however, there is finality to the soteriological consequences of rejection of the Christian claim, for those disbelieving Jews (see the discussion above, section C.1. of this chapter).

because of the impressive length of the scriptural indictment applied by Paul against his Jewish audience.

After an all-day session in which Paul has addressed to a sizable gathering of Roman Jews the standard Christian proclamation (28:23),[177] the outcome is a split verdict (v 24). Some are persuaded; others disbelieve.[178] Paul has the last word, however; he aims at his divided Jewish audience, just prior to their departure,[179] the stern rebuke of Isaiah 6:9-10:[180]

Go to this people and say,
  "In hearing, listen and do not understand;
  And in looking, see and do not perceive."
    For the heart of this people became dull,
    And they listened with ears hard [of hearing],
    And they closed their eyes,
  Lest they should see with their eyes,
    And hear with their ears,
    And understand with their hearts,
      And return, and I heal them (vv 26-27).[181]

This appeal to scripture serves as a comment on Paul's mixed success among the Jews, indeed (by virtue of the citation's climactic position in the narrative) as an interpretive gloss on the entire mission program of the church. The failure of adherents of the "Way" to win over the Jews *en masse,* or even in substantial numbers outside Jerusalem, does not cast doubt on the legitimacy of Christian faith as the heir and fulfillment of the history of God's people Israel. On the contrary, in rejecting the completion of their heritage, those Jews who have refused to acknowledge Jesus as Messiah and Lord unwittingly confirm the

[177] Summarized with the rubrics of the "kingdom of God" and the testimony of scripture "concerning Jesus."

[178] Both the antithetical parallelism between ἐπείθοντο and ἠπίστουν and the analogy of Acts 17:4 suggest that ἐπείθοντο here denotes conversion to Christian faith on the part of a segment of Paul's audience.

[179] Note the aorist participle εἰπόντος (v 25). By presenting the (chronologically prior) last statement of Paul *after* the narration of the Jews' departure, Luke casts the spotlight on the Isaiah quotation.

[180] Luke follows closely the text of the LXX. The alteration in the first line may conform the prophecy to Paul's mission career: Luke's version reads "go to this people and say," rather than "go and say to this people." If so (and this may over-interpret the difference), the quotation interprets not only the immediate occasion, but also the whole mission activity of Paul among "this people." The climactic position of the passage also favors such a reading.

[181] Reading ἐπιστρέψωσιν (the future indicative ἐπιστρέφουσιν is attested in A E Ψ 048 81 and other mss.) and ἰάσομαι (the aorist subjunctive ἰάσωμαι appears in E 33 81 2464 and other mss.), and taking both "return" and "heal" as governed by the introductory μήποτε.

prophecies buried in their own treasured scripture (cf. also Acts 13:27)[182] When Paul announces (for the third time) that God's salvation has been sent to the Gentiles (v 28), this declaration does not constitute a final rejection of the Jews nor a final turn away from the Jewish mission—Paul's unresponsive Jewish listeners have, by their rejection of the proclamation, already ensured their own rejection, and Roman Jews are apparently included among Paul's listeners after this meeting[183]—but rather an acknowledgment that a period of mission focused on non-Jews, and a church increasingly dominated by non-Jews, is the future of the church. Yet, this church remains rooted in the Judaism whose completion it represents.

The repetition of the verb ἀκούω in this passage substantiates this view of the function of the Isaiah quotation. In response to Paul's intitial self-defense, the ranking Jews ask to hear (ἀκοῦσαι) from Paul what is on his mind. When they do listen to his message, it provokes a mixed response among them, prompting Paul to direct the Isaiah citation against them![184] In a fashion consistent with their ancestors, the Jews of Paul's audience have listened (cf. v 22), yet without hearing (understanding). By contrast, the Gentiles—to whom this saving message has also been sent—*will hear* (v 28). Peter's speech in Acts 3 defined the consequences of failure to hear Jesus, the prophet like Moses (3:22-23): exclusion from God's people. The ironic reversal implicit in the conclusion of Acts thus becomes transparent. Gentiles, who will in large numbers continue[185] to respond positively to the Christian mission, now form part of the people of God, while many Jews—by refusing to hear—now stand outside the sphere of fulfilled promise. The process of Israel's restoration is indeed well underway (cf. Acts 1:6-8), and with it the hope of Israel has entered the era of determinative fulfillment. However, as the Amos citation in Acts 15:16-18 also indicates, that

---

[182] The climax of the speech by Stephen in Acts 7 carries a similar punch (especially 7:51-53). Stephen explicitly places his listeners in solidarity with their "fathers"; a similar identification must be assumed in the case of Paul as well. That is, Paul appeals to Isaiah not simply to indict "your fathers" (28:25), but also to locate his unbelieving hearers within "this people" who have lost capacity to perceive God's word and action.

[183] According to Acts 28:30, Paul received "all" who came to him; there is no exclusion of Jews; cf. Brawley, "Paul," 132; Feiler, "Prophet," 105. For the opposite view, see Gnilka, *Verstockung,* 130 n. 3; Sanders, "Salvation," 108-09.

[184] If ἐπείθοντο in v 24 carries the connotation of conversion, then the quotation does not really serve as a blanket accusation but has as its target those in Paul's audience who fail to perceive.

[185] Although Luke does not emphasize mass conversions among the Gentiles as he does in the case of the Jews (Acts 2:41; 4:4; 6:7; 21:20; but cf. 13:48; 14:1; 17:4; 18:8), he does indicate that Paul's activity among the people—including Gentiles—of Corinth (18:11) and Ephesus (19:10) continued for an extended period. If Luke writes from the vantage point of a church of the Gentile mission, whose Jewish pedigree is subject to question (from outside) or to amnesia (within), then it will serve Luke more effectively to accent the conversion of Jews than to highlight the inclusion of masses of Gentiles (an obvious fact of history in Luke's own time).

restoration/fulfillment encompasses faithful Gentiles alongside faithful Jews. Nevertheless, nothing is amiss, nothing revolutionary. All these developments correspond to the plan of God, announced to Israel in ancient scripture.

The rejection of Jesus by the Jewish leaders at Jerusalem was a direct cause of the destruction of Jerusalem and its temple![186] However, that culpable repudiation of Jesus was not irreversible, from a soteriological point of view![187] The apostolic mission to Israel, beginning at Jerusalem, affords the opportunity for life-giving repentance. Nevertheless, wherever the message of Jesus' apostles is spurned, Jesus himself—and therefore the God of Israel—stands rejected![188] The result is exclusion from the people of God.

Acts 28:17-31 brings the reader to the dawn of a new era![189] Yet, this is so only from within the story. The predominantly Gentile church, indebted to the career of Paul, is now a datum of history—and there Luke's own church is situated. In this sense, the final episode of Acts is no program for the future of the church and its mission, but, instead, an attempt to explain the past![190] Non-Jews have, in accordance with scriptural mandate, come to participate in the salvation promised to Israel, even as large numbers of Jews have refused to acknowledge the claim that the Jewish story finds its culmination here![191] Through his two-volume work, Luke would have his community embrace its solidarity with Israel—ironically, at the same time, denying the same privilege and prerogative to unbelieving Israel.

[186] See Luke 19:41-44, where the demise of Jerusalem is portrayed as the result of the city's failure to recognize the time of its (divine) visitation by Jesus. Of course, the first cause of both Jerusalem's rejection of Jesus and the city's destruction is the will of God, expressed in scripture (see, e.g., Luke 21:22).

[187] As the call to repentance and offer of forgiveness in Acts (2:36, 38; 3:17, 19; cf. 5:30-31) make clear.

[188] Cf. Luke 10:16, a formulation unique to Luke.

[189] Not in the sense that the Gentile-centered mission is launched only now, but rather that the center of gravity has shifted—decisively—from Jewish to Gentile mission. Such a shift occurs at the beginning (Acts 13:46-47), in the middle (18:6; 19:8-10), and now at the climax of Paul's career.

[190] Similarly, Franklin (Christ, 115): "This is less a programme for the future than a justification of what has happened. . . . As such, Paul's final statement is not a rejection of the Jews. Rather it is a commentary in the light of Scripture upon a situation which has arisen out of the Jewish refusal of the gospel and its ready acceptance by the Gentiles."

[191] I discern the thrust of the final passage of Acts as a justification—from scripture, mediated through Paul—of the Gentile Christianity of Luke's day in view of its Jewish roots. The positive declaration of Acts 28:28—not the indictment of obdurate Jews (vv 26-27)—is the goal of the passage. This reading of Acts 28:17-31 accords with the view that the "all" of v 30 includes both Jews and Gentiles (see above, note 183). Paul's open, unhindered preaching at Rome (vv 30-31) not only brings Luke's narrative to a triumphant conclusion, but also places a question mark beside the thesis that Luke's emphasis in his final episode is the final rejection of the Jews.

3. Israel and Eschaton

The view is occasionally advanced that Luke expected the restoration of political Israel, or the conversion of Israel *en masse,* at (or before) the eschaton, despite the bleak present![192] According to Chance, several features of Luke-Acts indicate that Luke still held to a future hope for the Jews and Jerusalem. First, Acts 28 does not necessarily depict a final rejection of the Jews, for some believed even here![193] Second, the prophecy of Luke 13:35b ("I tell you, you will certainly not see me until you say, 'Blessed is the one who comes in the name of the Lord'") is not necesssarily fulfilled in 19:38. At some point in the future, Jerusalem will herald the triumphant coming of Jesus![194] Third, Acts 3:19–21 asserts that the Jews' repentance must precede the End![195] Fourth, Luke 21:24c may imply a future restoration of Jerusalem, for it speaks of the limited duration of Gentile domination of Jerusalem, and many Jewish texts portray the restoration of the temple following its desolation![196] Finally, Luke 21:28 envisages the redemption of the Jews![197]

If this thesis could be maintained, then my exegesis of Acts 28:17–31 would be undermined, and my presentation of Luke's eschatological perspective would require significant modification. Luke would, on this view, regard as unfulfilled significant aspects of Israel's hope which I have perceived as fulfilled (with some redefinition). And Luke would uphold a set of expectations for the end-time which I have omitted.

Nevertheless, the case for such an end-time restoration of Israel cannot be sustained. In the first place, Acts 28 may not narrate a final rejection of the Jews![198] but that does not mean that Luke expected a future conversion of Israel in his future. The literary and social settings of the narrative are not to be equated: a continued mission among Jews in Paul's future (Luke's past) is not the same thing as a restoration of Israel in Luke's future. Second, the close verbal correspondence between Luke 13:35c and 19:38 indicates that the former prophecy is, after all, fulfilled in Jesus' entry into Jerusalem, even if it is "the whole crowd of disciples" that utters the acclamation (19:37). Jesus' prophecy in 13:35 would, in fact, be disconfirmed by the subsequent narrative if 19:38 were not the realization of 13:35. Jerusalem *has* seen Jesus (the Jerusalem ministry) before an end-time acclamation of Jesus as the one "who comes in the name of

---

[192] See especially Wainright, "Restoration;" Tiede, *Prophecy;* Chance, "Jerusalem," 379–87.

[193] "Jerusalem," 380–82.

[194] Ibid., 382–83.

[195] Ibid., 383.

[196] Ibid., 385. Chance lists (p. 298) several texts which identify Jerusalem as the locus of the restored people of God: Isa 35:8–10; 4 Ezra 13:12–13, 39–40; Bar 5:5–9; PsSol 11:5–7; 4 Q Ps 37,III: 10–11; Pes. de Rab. Kah. 20:7; b B Bat. 75b.

[197] Ibid., 385–86.

[198] Indeed, I have not endorsed this position in my study.

the Lord." Third, my analysis of Acts 3:19–26 has already shown that vv 19–21 do not affirm that the Jews' repentance must precede the End. Participation of Jews in the blessings (including those of the end-time) promised by God is, on the other hand, contingent upon repentance. According to 3:19–21, the eschaton awaits not the repentance of all Israel but the completion of the "restoration/fulfillment of all things spoken by God through the prophets." Fourth, while Luke 21:24c limits the duration of Gentile subjugation of Jerusalem, the text proceeds (vv 25–27) not to the restoration of the city but to the cosmic signs immediately preceding the parousia of the Son of man. Abundant parallels in Jewish texts are important evidence of the range of possibilities open to Luke but should not blind one to the data Luke has actually given us. Fifth, the assurance given by Jesus in Luke 21:28 (". . . lift your heads, because your redemption is close at hand") is addressed not to the Jews, but rather to Luke's community![199] We are left, then, with no passages in Luke-Acts where any hint of Israel's future restoration is to be detected. It is all the more significant, therefore, that, when citing Joel 3:1–5 LXX (Acts 2:17–21), Luke omits that part of the prophecy which localized salvation in Jerusalem and Zion.

Finally, the burden of Luke's entire narrative works against this understanding of the place of Israel at the eschaton. Luke has told the story of the coronation of Israel's King, of the consolidation of new leadership over the twelve tribes of Israel, of the fulfillment of the covenant-promise to Abraham, and of the realization of Israel's God-given task of bearing light to the Gentiles. And all these emblems of the fulfillment of Israel's hope find their place in relation to Jesus Messiah, and the early church's proclamation of him. This *is* the definitive process of Israel's restoration! For Luke to add a supplement in which, at the end of time, the temple is rebuilt, Jerusalem and political Israel established, and the nation brought to repentance and faith, would contradict the force of Luke's whole narrative. Both scriptural prophecy (Isa 6:8–9; Deut 18:15/Lev 23:29) and Spirit-inspired prophecy at the outset of the story (Luke 2:34–35) envisaged severance of a portion of ethnic Israel from the salvation for which it longed. Accordingly, the fulfillment of Israel's hope occurs through the Messiah-King Jesus and the mission mandated by him. Israel's restoration, which forms one component of the restoration of all things preceding the end-time return of Jesus, is well underway, and is—in Luke's own time—being advanced via the mission among Gentiles. The consummation of history awaits the completion of this process—not, however, a "third chance" for unrepentant, unbelieving Israel.

I am suggesting that Luke does not expect anything different for Israel at the eschaton from what he has related in his two-volume writing. The crucial moment for eschatology is the present time of response to Jesus, of the summons

---

[199] The second plural of Luke 21:27 cannot be considered in isolation from Luke's use of personal pronouns in the discourse as a whole. Luke consistently casts his Markan source into the second plural, and vv 12–19 make clear that the message of the eschatological discourse has as its target the Christian community addressed by Luke.

to repentance and to a faithful, vigilant manner of life. The eschatological outcome will be true to the pattern dictated by history.

A word remains to be said in critique of the thesis that Paul's mission at Rome symbolizes the completion of the mission program announced in Acts 1:8. According to this reading, the final episode of Acts is "eschatologically charged," for the world-wide mission has attained its destination.[200] The conclusion of Acts, therefore, brings the reader to the verge of the End. This interpretation meets with two telling objections. The weight of the evidence opposes the assumption that "end of the earth" (Acts 1:8; cf. 13:47) is a cipher for Rome.[201] Moreover, such an approach to the ending of Acts fails to square the literary setting of Acts with the eschatological discourse of Luke 21.[202]

The final episode of Acts does not bring the reader to the edge of the climax of history, for beyond the ending of Acts lies the destruction of Jerusalem (which Luke distinguishes from the end-time!) and a continuing world mission which reaches to Luke's own time. In *that* situation, imminent expectation of world-shaking, end-time events of cosmic proportion, accompanied by the return of Jesus, does become appropriate. God's dealings with his people Israel will soon come to a climax. But Israel's place in the eschaton will bring no surprises to discerning readers of Luke's story.

---

[200] See above all Smith, "History," 894, 897–98; cf. Mattill, *Last,* 54; Farrell, "Perspective," 274–75.

[201] See note 23 of this chapter.

[202] See Excursus 3 above.

4
Conclusion

This study has examined the eschatological perspective of Luke-Acts in relation to the situation that prompted Luke's literary project. I have singled out eschatology as a significant aspect of Luke's literary purpose and setting. Not only the extent of eschatological materials in the Lukan corpus (and not only the preoccupations of previous scholars!), but also the care with which Luke has handled these traditions confirms the value of such an approach to Luke-Acts.

Yet I acknowledge that my probe has been restricted to one facet of a many-sided crystal. Luke's expectation for the end-time is only one dimension (though an important one) of his theological perspective (or, from another angle, of his world view). The treatment of eschatological themes in Luke-Acts does not reflect the author's only—or indeed primary—purpose in writing. Luke's situation was far more complex than any picture of a crisis focused on eschatology would suggest. In fact, my discussion of eschatology and situation has already pointed to the larger question of Israel as a pressing problem confronting the Christian communities known to Luke. Luke's era witnessed the movement of the "Way" out beyond the synagogue, yet Christian groups continued to claim for themselves the scripture, heritage, and promise—the past *and* the future—of Israel. In such a setting, the legitimacy of the church, increasingly composed of non-Jews, as the heir of Israel's hope, was something requiring demonstration. Luke's narrative, from beginning (Luke 1-2) to end (Acts 28:17-31), grounded that task of legitimation in the continuity of God's saving activity in the history of his people.

Though not the only issue facing Luke and his community(ies), the status and character of end-expectation were live questions, and Luke answers them in the way he tells his story. The baseline, as Luke sees it,[1] is the unpredictability of the parousia. No one knows—or can know—the timing of the End. Chronology remains a matter of the freedom and prerogative of God (Luke 12:35-48; Acts 1:6-8). Yet ignorance of the "when" is countered by certainty of the "that."[2] Jesus will return suddenly, and his appearance will signal universal, inescapable, and

---

[1] The motif of the parousia's unpredictability is, of course, part of the pre-Lukan tradition. However, he elaborates the theme in his own manner (cf. especially Acts 1:6-8).

[2] Luke 12:35-48; 17:22-37; 18:8b; Acts 3:19-21. My formulation follows the treatment of this theme in Acts 1:6-11.

final division (Luke 17:22-37). Redemption will greet the faithful (21:28), but consternation, chaos, and destruction will overtake all others (17:26-37; 21:25-26). Immediately before Jesus' return, cosmic and heavenly portents will alert the discerning (believers whose expectancy is informed by Jesus' teaching [Luke 21:25-32] and by scripture [Acts 2:17-21]) that their deliverance is at hand (Luke 21:28, 29-31).

Luke has incorporated delay into his eschatological scenario (Luke 12:35-48; 19:11-27; 21:5-36; Acts 1:6-8). In fact, as Conzelmann rightly observed, delay is a dominant theme in Luke's handling of traditions concerning the end-time. However, the function of delay in Luke-Acts becomes transparent only when we distinguish the literary and social settings of the document. Luke wrote at a time when delay and duration were data of history. The End had not yet materialized—during Jesus' ministry, following his resurrection and ascension, during the first decades of the church's worldwide mission, or at the destruction of Jerusalem. If Luke is to maintain the credibility of imminent hope in his own situation, then he must show delay and duration to have been the "orders of the day" throughout his narrative. Delay, therefore, serves for Luke the opposite function to that identified by Conzelmann. Delay does not oppose but undergirds expectation of an imminent End in Luke's own situation.

Both the contours of the entire narrative and details of Lukan redaction (e.g., Luke 19:11; 21:12) reflect Luke's concern to assimilate delay and duration into the eschatological program. Yet this was not a theoretical exercise. Rather, in adopting and adapting the traditions that had come to him, Luke addressed the prevailing ethos of Christian communities known to him. He witnessed a loss of urgency in mission activity (cf. Acts 1:6-11), complacency in execution of assigned responsibilities (Luke 12:35-48), and a "business as usual" orientation to life (17:26-30) that no longer reckoned with Jesus' return. And faith itself— eschatological faith oriented toward Jesus' return—found the experience of delay to be a threat (Luke 18:8b). Not delay *per se,* but delay-and-duration as the occasion for irresponsible conduct, oblivious to the eschaton, is the background against which Luke's shaping of eschatological traditions is to be understood. Luke sought to reinforce living eschatological faith, all the while summoning his readers to vigilant, faithful service.

As Fitzmyer has noted,[3] Luke's paraenetic interest shifts the center of gravity away from the eschaton toward the sēmeron. Luke emphasizes the definitive quality of the present; one's response to Jesus' claims (= the claims of the kingdom, Luke 17:20-21; the claims of the prophet like Moses, Acts 3:22-23), and a life of fidelity and vigilance during the time preceding the End (Luke 12:35-48; 17:22-37),[4] provide the criteria for end-time destiny. Nevertheless, Luke has not, as Fitzmyer claims,[5] dulled the edge of eschatology to

---

[3] See *Luke,* 1.234.

[4] Cf. also my discussion of Acts 2:17-21 and 3:19-26 in chapter 3 above (sections B.2.c. and C.2.b.).

[5] *Luke,* 1.235.

make of it a paraenetic device. The eschaton is not "swallowed up" in the sēmeron. Only because Luke continues to expect a sudden return of Jesus (and soon!) does his appeal for an alert, faithful manner of living have motivating force.[6] And because the future of Israel and of all nations — not just the salvation of the individual believer — is at stake in the eschatological climax (e.g., Luke 21:24, 25-26, 34-36; Acts 1:6-8; 3:19-26), hope of God's future victory is not absorbed into the "today" of repentance, faith, and faithfulness. Eschatology is not in Luke's hands reduced to the future of individual believers (important as that is for Luke).[7]

My sketch of Luke's eschatological perspective and situation places him in continuity with much that had preceded him. "Q" and Mark before him — and Matthew alongside him — had adjusted eschatological expectations in view of delay, yet without abandoning eschatological faith, and had summoned believers to preparedness. Luke was less of an innovator (in the realm of eschatology) than Conzelmann and Grässer suspected. Nevertheless, Luke has presided over a marriage of salvation history and living end-expectation that is without parallel in early Christian literature, particularly in its historical sketch of the status of the promises and hopes of Israel. Further, Luke's insistence on correlating eschatological claims with one's present manner of life — otherwise put, Luke's concern to correlate eschatology and situation — represents a distinctive (though of course not unique[8]) feature of his eschatological view. The focus of my project (though couched in terms of historical and exegetical inquiry) thereby stands in continuity with Luke's own presentation.

---

[6] Cf. Schnackenburg ("Aussagen," 261-62): only because Luke takes the parousia seriously as a future event does his appeal for constant readiness carry weight. Schnackenburg correctly recognizes Luke's insistence on the "Tatsächlichkeit" of the parousia, but fails to discern the role still played by imminent hope in Luke's perspective.

[7] So also Schnackenburg ("Aussagen," 264-65): despite the inroads made by "individual eschatology" in Luke's theology, he does not abandon the "universal-cosmic perspective."

[8] Matthew, too, forcefully addresses "ecclesiological" concerns with eschatological statements (see, e.g., G. Bornkamm, "End-Expectation and Church in Matthew," in Bornkamm, G. Barth, and H. J. Held, *Tradition and Interpretation in Matthew* [Philadelphia: Westminster, 1963] 15-51).

Bibliography

I. Texts, Translations, and Reference Works

Aland, K. *Synopsis Quattuor Evangeliorum.* 10th ed. Stuttgart: Deutsche Bibelstiftung, 1978.

————. (ed.) *Vollständige Konkordanz zum griechischen Neuen Testament.*

Bauer, W., Arndt, W., and Gingrich, F. W. *A Greek-English Lexicon of the New Testament and Other Early Christian Literature.* 4th ed. Chicago: University, 1957.

Biblia Hebraica. 7th ed. Edited by R. Kittel. Stuttgart: Württembergische Bibelanstalt, 1963.

Blass, F. and Debrunner, A. *A Greek Grammar of the New Testament and Other Early Christian Literature.* Translated and revised by R. W. Funk. Chicago: University, 1961.

Charlesworth, J. H. *The Old Testament Pseudepigrapha.* 2 volumes. Garden City: Doubleday, 1983, 1985.

Danby, H. *The Mishnah.* London: Oxford University, 1933.

Greek New Testament. Edited by K. Aland, M. Black, C. M. Martini, B. M. Metzger, and A. Wikgren. 2nd ed. New York: American Bible Society, 1968.

Hatch, E. and Redpath, H. *A Concordance to the Septuagint.* Oxford: Clarendon, 1897.

Hennecke, E. and Schneemelcher, W. (ed.) *New Testament Apocrypha.* 2 volumes. English translation edited by R. McL. Wilson. Philadelphia: Westminster, 1965.

Interpreter's Dictionary of the Bible. 4 volumes. Nashville: Abingdon, 1962. Supplementary Volume, 1976.

Josephus. Loeb Classical Library. 9 volumes. Edited by H. Thackeray, R. Marcus, A. Wikgren, and L. H. Feldman. Cambridge: Harvard, 1926–65.

Kittel, R. and Friedrich, G. (eds.) *Theological Dictionary of the New Testament.* 10 volumes. Grand Rapids: Eerdmans, 1964–76.

Liddell, H. G. and Scott, R. *A Greek Lexicon.* 9th ed. Oxford: Clarendon, 1961.

Lohse, E. *Die Texte aus Qumran.* Darmstadt, 1964.

Metzger, B. M. *A Textual Commentary on the Greek New Testament.* New York: United Bible Societies, 1971.

Moulton, W. F. and Geden, A. S. *A Concordance to the Greek New Testament.*

Nag Hammadi Library in English. Edited by J. M. Robinson. San Francisco: Harper and Row, 1977.

Novum Testamentum Graece. Edited by E. Nestle, K. Aland, et al. 26th ed. Stuttgart: Deutsche Bibelstiftung, 1979.

Old Testament in Greek. Edited by H. B. Swete. 3 volumes. Cambridge: University, 1930, 1930, 1934.

Philo. Loeb Classical Library. 10 volumes. Edited by F. H. Colson and G. H. Whitaker. Cambridge: Harvard, 1929–43.

Schürer, E. *The History of the Jewish People in the Age of Jesus Christ.* 2 volumes. Revised and edited by G. Vermes, F. Millar, and M. Black. Edinburgh: T. & T. Clark, 1973, 1979.

Septuaginta. Edited by A. Rahlfs. Stuttgart, 1965.

Smyth, H. W. *Greek Grammar.* Revised by G. M. Messing. Cambridge: Harvard, 1956.

Turner, N. *A Grammar of New Testament Greek.* Volume 3: Syntax. Edinburgh: T. & T. Clark, 1963.

Vermes, G. *The Dead Sea Scrolls in English.* 2nd ed. New York: Penguin, 1975.

II. Commentaries and Studies

Aalen, S. " 'Reign' and 'House' in the Kingdom of God in the Gospels." *NTS* 8 (1961–62) 215–40.

———. "St. Luke's Gospel and the Last Chapters of I Enoch." *NTS* 13 (1966–67) 1–13.

Adams, D. R. "The Suffering of Paul and the Dynamics of Luke-Acts." New Haven: Yale University Ph.D. Dissertation, 1979.

Albertz, R. "Die 'Antrittspredigt' Jesu im Lukasevangelium auf ihrem alttestamentlichen Hintergrund." *ZNW* 74 (1983) 182–206.

Allen, P. "The Meaning of ἐντός." *ExpTim* 49 (1937) 476–77.

———. "Luke 17,21." *ExpTim* 50 (1938) 233–35.

Arai, S. "Individual- und Gemeindeethik bei Lukas." *Ann Japan Bib Inst* 9 (1983) 88–127.

Argyle, A. W. "The Theory of an Aramaic Source in Acts 2,14–40." *JTS* N.S. 4 (1953) 213–14.

Aune, D. E. "The Significance of the Delay of the Parousia for Early Christianity." In *Current Issues in Biblical and Patristic Interpretation*. Edited by G. F. Hawthorne. Grand Rapids: Eerdmans, 1975. Pp. 87-109.

Barnard, L. W. "Justin Martyr's Eschatology." *VC* 19 (1965) 86-98.

Barrett, C. K. *Luke the Historian in Recent Study*. London: Epworth, 1961.

———. "Stephen and the Son of Man." In *Apophoreta: Festschrift für Ernst Haenchen*. Berlin: Töpelmann, 1964. Pp. 32-38.

———. "Faith and Eschatology in Acts 3." In *Glaube und Eschatologie: Festschrift für Werner Georg Kümmel zum 80. Geburtstag*. Edited by E. Grässer and O. Merk. Tübingen: J. C. B. Mohr, 1985. Pp. 1-17.

Bartsch, H. W. "Parusieerwartung und Osterbotschaft." *EvT* 7 (1947-48) 115-26.

———. "Zum Problem der Parusieverzögerung bei den Synoptikern." *EvT* 19 (1959) 116-31.

———. *Wachtet aber zu jeder Zeit! Entwurf einer Auslegung des Lukasevangeliums*. Hamburg-Bergstedt: H. Reich, 1963.

———. "Early Christian Eschatology in the Synoptic Gospels." *NTS* 11 (1964-65) 387-97.

Bauernfeind, O. *Die Apostelgeschichte*. Leipzig: Deichert, 1939.

———. "Tradition und Komposition in dem Apokatastasisspruch Apostelgeschichte 3,20f." In *Abraham unser Vater*. Edited by O. Betz et al. Leiden: Brill, 1963. Pp. 13-23.

———. "πόλεμος." *TDNT* 6. Pp. 502-15.

Berger, K. "Das Canticum Simeonis (Lk 2:29-32)." *NovT* 27 (1985) 27-39.

Berger, P. and Luckmann, T. *The Social Construction of Reality*. Garden City: Doubleday, 1966.

Berger, P. *The Sacred Canopy*. Garden City: Doubleday, 1967.

Betz, O. "The Kerygma of Luke." *Int* 22 (1968) 131-46.

Bösen, W. *Jesusmahl, Eucharistisches Mahl, Endzeitmahl: Ein Beitrag zur Theologie des Lukas*. Stuttgart: Katholisches Bibelwerk, 1980.

Boor, W. de. *Die Apostelgeschichte*. Wuppertal: Brockhaus, 1965.

Borgen, P. "Eschatology and Heilsgeschichte in Luke-Acts." Madison, NJ: Drew University Ph.D. Dissertation, 1956.

———. "From Paul to Luke. Observations toward Clarification of the Theology of Luke-Acts." *CBQ* 31 (1969) 168-82.

Bovon, F. "Israel, die Kirche und die Völker im lukanischen Doppelwerk." *TL* 108 (1983) 403-14.

———. " 'Schon hat der heilige Geist durch den Propheten Jesaja zu euren Vatern gesprochen' (Acts 28 25)." *ZNW* 75 (1984) 226-32.

———. *Luc le théologien: vingt-cinq ans de recherches (1950-1975)*. Neuchatel/Paris: Delachaux & Niestlé, 1978.

Bowker, J. W. "Speeches in Acts: A Study in Proem and Yelammedenu Form." *NTS* 14 (1967-68) 96-111.

Braumann, G. "Das Mittel der Zeit, Erwägungen zur Theologie des Lukasevangeliums." *ZNW* 54 (1963) 117-45.

———. "Die lukanische Interpretation der Zerstörung Jerusalems." *NovT* 6 (1963) 120-27.

Brawley, R. L. "The Pharisees in Luke-Acts: Luke's Address to the Jews and His Irenic Purpose." Princeton: Princeton Theological Seminary Ph.D. Dissertation, 1978.

———. "Paul in Acts: Lucan Apology and Conciliation." In *Luke-Acts: New Perspectives*. Edited by C. H. Talbert. New York: Crossroad, 1984. Pp. 129-47.

Brodie, T. L. "A New Temple and a New Law. The Unity and Chronicler-based Nature of Luke 1:1-4:22a." *JSNT* 5 (1979) 21-45.

Brown, R. E. *The Birth of the Messiah*. Garden City: Doubleday, 1979.

Brown, S. *Apostasy and Perseverance in the Theology of Luke*. Rome: Biblical Institute, 1969.

———. "Precis of Eckhard Plümacher, Lukas als hellenistischer Schriftsteller." SBL 1974 *Seminar Papers*. Edited by G. MacRae. Cambridge: SBL, 1974. Pp. 103-13.

———. "The Role of the Prologues in Determining the Purpose of Luke-Acts." In *Perspectives on Luke-Acts*. Edited by C. H. Talbert. Danville: Association of Baptist Professors of Religion, 1978. Pp. 99-111.

Bruce, F. F. *Commentary on the Book of Acts*. Grand Rapids: Eerdmans, 1954.

———. "The Speeches in Acts—Thirty Years After." In *Reconciliation and Hope*. Edited by R. Banks. Grand Rapids: Eerdmans, 1975. Pp. 53-68.

Buchanan, G. W. "Eschatology and the 'End of Days.' " *JNES* 20 (1961) 188-93.

Büchsel, F. "λύτρωσις, ἀπολύτρωσις." *TDNT* 4. Pp. 351-56.

———. "γενεά." *TDNT* 1. Pp. 662-63.

Bultmann, R. *The History of the Synoptic Tradition*. Translated by J. Marsh. Rev. ed. New York: Harper and Row, 1976.

———. *Theology of the New Testament*. 2 volumes. Translated by K. Grobel. London: SCM, 1952, 1955.

———. *The Presence of Eternity: History and Eschatology*. New York: Harper, 1957.

Cadbury, H. J. *The Making of Luke-Acts*. New York: Macmillan, 1927.

——. *The Book of Acts in History.* London, 1955.

——. "Acts and Eschatology." In *The Background of the New Testament and Its Eschatology.* Edited by W. D. Davies and D. Daube. Cambridge: University, 1964. Pp. 300–21.

——. "Lukan Expressions of Time." *JBL* 82 (1963) 272–78.

Catchpole, D. R. "The Son of Man's Search for Faith (Luke XVIII 8b)." *NovT* 19 (1977) 81–104.

Cerfaux, L. "Citations scripturaires et tradition textuelle dans le Livre des Actes." In *Aux sources de la Tradition chrétienne. Mélanges offerts a M. Maurice Goguel.* Neuchatel: Delachaux & Niestlé, 1950. Pp. 43–51.

Chance, J. B. "Jerusalem and the Temple in Luke-Acts in the Context of Lucan Eschatology." Durham: Duke University Ph.D. Dissertation, 1984.

Clarke, A. K. and Collie, N. E. W. "A Comment on Luke xii 41–58." *JTS* (1916) 299–301.

Clarke, W. K. L. "The Use of the Septuagint in Acts." In *The Beginnings of Christianity.* Vol. 2. Edited by F. J. Foakes Jackson and K. Lake. London: Macmillan, 1922. Pp. 66–105.

Conzelmann, H. "Zur Lukasanalyse." *ZTK* 49 (1952) 16–33.

——. *The Theology of St. Luke.* Translated by G. Buswell. New York: Harper and Row, 1961.

——. *Die Apostelgeschichte.* Tübingen: J. C. B. Mohr, 1963.

——. "Present and Future in the Synoptic Tradition." *JTC* 5 (1968) 26–44.

Cosgrove, C. H. "The Divine ΔEI in Luke-Acts." *NovT* 26 (1984) 168–90.

Cotter, A. C. "The Eschatological Discourse." *CBQ* 1 (1939) 125–32.

Cranfield, C. E. B. "The Parable of the Unjust Judge and the Eschatology of Luke-Acts." *SJT* 16 (1963) 297–301.

Crawford, B. S. "Near Expectation in the Sayings of Jesus." Nashville: Vanderbilt University Ph.D. Dissertation, 1978.

——. "Near Expectation in the Sayings of Jesus." *JBL* 101 (1982) 225–44.

Creed, J. M. *The Gospel According to St. Luke.* London: Macmillan, 1930.

Crockett, L. C. "The Old Testament in the Gospel of Luke." Brown University Ph.D. Dissertation, 1966.

Dahl, N. A. "'A People for His Name' (Acts XV.14)." *NTS* 4 (1957) 319–27.

——. "Eschatology and History in Light of the Qumran Texts." In *The Crucified Messiah and Other Essays.* Minneapolis: Augsburg, 1974. Pp. 129–45.

——. "The Story of Abraham in Luke-Acts." In *Jesus in the Memory of the Early Church.* Minneapolis: Augsburg, 1976. Pp. 66–86.

————. "The Purpose of Luke-Acts." In *Jesus in the Memory of the Early Church.* Minneapolis: Ausburg, 1976. Pp. 87–98.

Danker, F. W. *Jesus and the New Age According to St. Luke.* St. Louis: Clayton, 1972.

Davies, P. "The Ending of Acts." *ExpTim* 94 (1983) 334–35.

Delling, G. "Das letzte Wort der Apg." *NovT* 15 (1973) 193–204.

————. "ἡμέρα." *TDNT* 2. Pp. 947–953.

————. "καιρός." *TDNT* 3. Pp. 455–62.

————. "πίμπλημι; πλήρης, πληρόω." *TDNT* 6. Pp. 128–34, 283–98.

————. "τέλος." *TDNT* 8. Pp. 49–57.

Deterding, P. E. "Eschatological and Eucharistic Motifs in Luke 12:35–40." *Concordia Journal* 5 (1979) 85–94.

Dibelius, M. *Studies in the Acts of the Apostles.* Translated by M. Ling. Edited by H. Greeven. London: SCM, 1956.

Dodd, C. H. "The Fall of Jerusalem and the Abomination of Desolation." *JRS* 37 (1947) 47–54. Reprinted in *More New Testament Studies.* Manchester: University, 1968. Pp. 69–83.

————. *According to the Scriptures: The Sub-Structure of New Testament Theology.* Digswell Place: Nisbet, 1952.

Doeve, J. W. *Jewish Hermeneutics in the Synoptic Gospels and Acts.* Assen, Netherlands: Koninklijke, 1954.

Drury, J. *Tradition and Design in Luke's Gospel: A Study in Early Christian Historiography.* London: Darton, Longman & Todd, 1976.

Dubois, J.-D. "La figure d'Elie dans la perspective lucanienne." *RHPR* 53 (1973) 155–76.

Dupont, J. *The Sources of the Book of Acts.* Translated by K. Pond. London: Darton, Longman & Todd, 1964.

————. "La Parabole du Figuier qui Bourgeonne." *RB* 75 (1968) 526–48.

————. "La Parabole du Maître Qui Rentre dans la Nuit (Mc 13,34–36)." In *Mélanges Bibliques.* Edited by A. Descamps. Gembloux: Duculot, 1970. Pp. 89–116.

————. "L'après-mort dans l'oeuvre de Luc." *RTL* 3 (1972) 3–21.

————. "Individuelle Eschatologie." In *Orientierung an Jesus.* Edited by P. Hoffmann. Freiburg: Herder, 1973. Pp. 37–47.

————. "Les discours de Pierre dans les Actes et le chapitre XXIV de l'évangile de Luc." In *L'Evangile de Luc: Problèmes littéraires et théologiques.* Edited by F. Neirynck. Bibliotheca Ephemeridum Theologicarum Lovaniensium XXXII, 1973. Pp. 329–74.

——. "La conclusion des Actes et son rapport à l'ensemble d' l'ouvrage de Luc." In *Les Actes des Apôtres: Traditions, rédaction, théologie.* Edited by J. Kremer. Leuven: University, 1979. Pp. 359-404.

——. *The Salvation of the Gentiles: Studies in the Acts of the Apostles.* Translated by J. R. Keating. New York: Paulist, 1979.

Easton, B. S. *The Purpose of Acts.* London: SPCK, 1936.

——. "Luke 17,20-21: An Exegetical Study." *AJT* 16 (1912) 275-83.

Edwards, R. A. "The Eschatological Correlative as a Gattung in the New Testament." *ZNW* 60 (1969) 9-19.

——. "The Redaction of Luke." *JR* 49 (1969) 392-405.

Egelkraut, H. L. *Jesus' Mission to Jerusalem: A Redaction Critical Study of the Travel Narrative in the Gospel of Luke, Lk 9:51-19:48.* Bern/Frankfurt: Lang, 1976.

Ellis, E. E. "Present and Future Eschatology in Luke." *NTS* 12 (1965-66) 27-41.

——. "Midrashic Features in the Speeches of Acts." In *Mélanges Bibliques.* Hommage au R. P. B. Rigaux. Gembloux: Duculot, 1970. Pp. 303-12.

——. *Eschatology in Luke.* Philadelphia: Fortress, 1972.

——. "La fonction de l'eschatologie dans l'évangile de Luc." In *L'Evangile de Luc: Problèmes littéraires et théologiques.* Edited by F. Neirynck. Bibliotheca Ephemeridum Theologicarum Lovaniensium XXXII, 1973. Pp. 141-55.

Epp, E. J. "The 'Ignorance Motif' in Acts and Anti-Judaic Tendencies in Codex Bezae." *HTR* 55 (1962) 51-62.

——. *The Theological Tendency of Codex Bezae Cantabrigiensis in Acts.* Cambridge: University, 1966.

Ernst, J. *Herr der Geschichte: Perspektiven der lukanische Eschatologie.* Stuttgart: Katholisches Bibelwerk, 1978.

Evans, C. A. "The Prophetic Setting of the Pentecost Sermon." *ZNW* 74 (1983) 148-50.

Evans, C. F. " 'Speeches' in Acts." In *Mélanges Bibliques.* Edited by A. Descamps. Gembloux: Duculot, 1970. Pp. 287-302.

Farrell, H. "The Eschatological Perspective of Luke-Acts." Boston: Boston University Ph.D. Dissertation, 1972.

Farris, S. *The Hymns of Luke's Infancy Narratives.* Sheffield: JSOT, 1985.

Feiler, P. F. "Jesus the Prophet: The Lucan Portrayal of Jesus as the Prophet Like Moses." Princeton: Princeton Theological Seminary Ph.D. Dissertation, 1986.

Ferraro, G. "Kairoi anpsyxeōs. Annotazioni su Atti 3,20." *RevistB* 23 (1975) 67-78.

Festinger, L., Riecken, H. W., and Schachter, S. *When Prophecy Fails.* Minneapolis: University of Minnesota, 1956.

Feuillet, A. "La double venue du Règne de Dieu et du Fils de l'homme en Luc XVII,20–XVIII,8. Recherches sur l'eschatologie des Synoptiques." *RevThom* 81 (1981) 5–33.

————. "Le discours de Jésus sur la ruine du Temple, d'après Marc XIII et Luc XXI,5–36." *RB* 55 (1948) 481–502 and 56 (1949) 61–92.

Fitzmyer, J. A. *The Gospel According to Luke.* 2 volumes. Garden City: Doubleday, 1981, 1985.

————. "David, 'Being Therefore a Prophet . . .' (Acts 2:30)." *CBQ* 34 (1972) 332–39.

Flender, H. *St. Luke: Theologian of Redemptive History.* Translated by R. Fuller and I. Fuller. Philadelphia: Fortress, 1967.

Flückiger, F. "Luk.21,20–24 und die Zerstörung Jerusalems." *TZ* 28 (1972) 385–90.

Flusser, D. "Salvation Present and Future." *Types of Redemption.* Studies in the History of Religions, vol. 18. Edited by R. J. Zwi Werblowsky and C. J. Bleeker. Leiden: Brill, 1970. Pp. 46–61.

Foakes Jackson, F. J. "The Kingdom of God in Acts and the 'City of God.' " *HTR* 12 (1919) 193–200.

Foakes Jackson, F. J. and Lake, K. *The Beginnings of Christianity.* 5 volumes. London, 1920–33.

Francis, F. O. "Eschatology and History in Luke-Acts." *JAAR* 37 (1969) 49–63.

Franklin, E. "The Ascension and the Eschatology of Luke Acts." *SJT* 23 (1970) 191–200.

————. *Christ the Lord: A Study in the Purpose and Theology of Luke-Acts.* Philadelphia: Fortress, 1975.

Fuchs, A. *Sprachliche Untersuchungen zu Matthaeus und Lukas: Ein Beitrag zur Quellenkritik.* Rome: Biblical Institute, 1971.

Gaston, L. *No Stone on Another.* Leiden: Brill, 1970.

————. "The Lukan Birth Narratives in Tradition and Redaction." SBL 1976 *Seminar Papers.* Edited by G. W. MacRae. Missoula: Scholars, 1976. Pp. 209–17.

Gause, R. H. "The Lukan Transfiguration Account: Luke's Pre-Crucifixion Presentation of the Exalted Lord in the Glory of the Kingdom of God." Atlanta: Emory University Ph.D. Dissertation, 1975.

Gaventa, B. R. "The Eschatology of Luke-Acts Revisited." *Encounter* 43 (1982) 27–42.

Geiger, R. *Die lukanischen Endzeitreden.* Bern: Herbert Lang, 1973.

George, A. "Israel dans l'oeuvre de Luc." *RB* 75 (1968) 481–525.

——. *Etudes sur l'oeuvre de Luc.* Paris: Gabalda, 1978.

——. "L'attente du maître qui vient. Lc 12,32–48." *AsSeign* 50 (1974) 66–76.

——. "La parabole du juge qui fait attendre le jugement. Lc. 18,1–8." *AsSeign* 60 (1975) 68–79.

Giblin, C. H. "Complementarity of Symbolic Event and Discourse in Acts 2,1–40." *Studia Evangelica.* Texte und Untersuchungen, 112. Pp. 189–96.

Giles, K. "Present-Future Eschatology in the Book of Acts." *Reformed Theological Review* 40 (1981) 65–71.

——. "Present-Future Eschatology in the Book of Acts." *Reformed Theological Review* 41 (1982) 11–18.

Gnilka, J. *Die Verstockung Israels. Isaias 6,9–10 in der Theologie der Synoptiker.* Munich: Kösel, 1961.

——. "Der Missionsauftrag des Herrn nach Mt 28 und Apg 1." *BibLeb* 9 (1968) 1–9.

Goodenough, E. R. "The Perspective of Acts." In *Studies in Luke-Acts.* Edited by L. E. Keck and J. L. Martyn. Nashville: Abingdon, 1966. Pp. 51–59.

Goppelt, L. *Theology of the New Testament.* 2 volumes. Translated by J. E. Alsup. Edited by J. Roloff. Grand Rapids: Eerdmans, 1981, 1982.

Gourgues, M. "Lecture christologique du Psaume CX et fête de la Pentecôte." *RB* 83 (1976) 5–24.

Grässer, E. *Das Problem der Parusieverzögerung in den Synoptischen Evangelien und in der Apostelgeschichte.* Berlin: Töpelmann, 1957.

——. "Die Apostelgeschichte in der Forschung der Gegenwart." *TRu* 26 (1960) 93–167.

——. "Die Parusieerwartung in der Apostelgeschichte." In *Les Actes des Apôtres: traditions, rédaction, théologie.* Edited by J. Kremer. Leuven: University, 1979. Pp. 99–127.

——. "Acta-Forschung seit 1960." *TRu* 41 (1976) 259–90 and *TRu* 42 (1977) 1–68.

Greene, G. R. "The Portrayal of Jesus as Prophet in Luke-Acts." Southern Baptist Theological Seminary Ph.D. Dissertation, 1975.

Griffiths, J. G. "ἐντός." *ExpTim* 63 (1951) 30–31.

Grundmann, W. "δεῖ." *TDNT* 2. Pp. 21–25.

——. "δύναμαι, δύναμις." *TDNT* 2. Pp. 284–317.

——. *Das Evangelium nach Lukas.* Berlin: Evangelische, 1961.

Guthrie, D. *The Apostles.* Grand Rapids: Eerdmans, 1975.

Haacker, K. "Das Bekenntnis des Paulus zur Hoffnung Israels nach der Apostelgeschichte des Lukas." *NTS* 31 (1985) 437-51.

Haenchen, E. "Schriftzitate und Textüberlieferung in der Apg." *ZTK* 51 (1954).

———. *The Acts of the Apostles.* Translated by B. Noble and G. Shinn. Revised by R. McL. Wilson. Philadelphia: Westminster, 1971.

Hahn, F. "Das Problem alter christologischer Überlieferungen in der Apostelgeschichte unter besonderer Berücksichtigung von Act 3,19-21." In *Les Actes des Apôtres: traditions, rédaction, théologie.* Edited by J. Kremer. Leuven: University, 1979. Pp. 129-54.

Hamm, M. D. "This Sign of Healing." St. Louis: St. Louis University Ph.D. Dissertation, 1975.

———. "Acts 3:12-26: Peter's Speech and the Healing of the Man Born Lame." *Perspectives in Religious Studies* 11 (1984) 199-217.

Hanson, R. P. C. *The Acts.* Oxford: Clarendon, 1967.

Harris, J. R. "A Lacuna in the Text of the Acts of the Apostles." *ExpTim* 36 (1924-25) 173-75.

Hartman, L. "A Linguistic Examination of Luke 21,13." *Coniectanea Neotestamentica* 19 (1963) 57-75.

———. *Prophecy Interpreted. The Formation of Some Jewish Apocalyptic Texts and of the Eschatological Discourse, Mark 13 Par.* Lund, 1966.

———. "The Functions of Some So-Called Apocalyptic Timetables." *NTS* 22 (1975-76) 1-14.

Hiers, R. H. "Eschatology and Methodology." *JBL* 85 (1966) 170-84.

———. "Why Will They Not Say, 'Lo, Here!' or 'There!'?" *JAAR* 35 (1967) 379-84.

———. "The Problem of the Delay of the Parousia in Luke-Acts." *NTS* 20 (1974) 145-55.

Hill, D. "The Spirit and the Church's Witness: Observations on Acts 1:6-8." *IrBibStud* 6 (1984) 16-26.

Holtz, T. *Untersuchungen über die alttestamentlichen Zitate bei Lukas.* Texte und Untersuchungen, 104. Berlin: Akademie, 1968.

Hubbard, B. J. "The Role of Commissioning Accounts in Acts." In *Perspectives on Luke-Acts.* Edited by C. H. Talbert. Danville: Association of Baptist Professors of Religion, 1978. Pp. 187-98.

———. "Luke, Josephus, and Rome: A Comparative Approach to the Lukan Sitz im Leben." SBL 1979 *Seminar Papers.* Vol. 1. Edited by P. J. Achtemeier. Missoula: Scholars, 1979. Pp. 59-68.

Jeremias, J. "παράδεισος" *TDNT* 5. Pp. 765-73.

Jervell, J. *Luke and the People of God.* Minneapolis: Augsburg, 1972.

————. *The Unknown Paul: Essays on Luke-Acts and Early Christian History.* Minneapolis: Augsburg, 1984.

Johnson, E. E. "A Study of 'Basileia Tou Theou' in the Gospel of Luke." Dallas: Dallas Theological Seminary Ph.D. Dissertation, 1968.

Johnson, L. T. *The Literary Function of Possessions in Luke-Acts.* Missoula: Scholars, 1977.

————. "On Finding the Lukan Community: A Cautious Cautionary Essay." In *SBL 1979 Seminar Papers.* Vol. 1. Edited by P. J. Achtemeier. Missoula: Scholars, 1979. Pp. 87–100.

————. "The Lukan Kingship Parable." *NovT* 24 (1982) 139–59.

Jones, C. P. M. "The Epistle to the Hebrews and the Lucan Writings." In *Studies in the Gospels: Essays in Memory of R. H. Lightfoot.* Edited by D. E. Nineham. Oxford: Blackwell, 1955. Pp. 113–43.

Joüon, P. "La Parabole du Portier qui doit veiller (Marc,XIII,33–37) et la Parabole des Serviteurs qui doivent veiller (Luc,XII,35–40)." *RSR* (1940) 365–68.

Judge, E. A. *The Social Pattern of the Christian Groups in the First Century.* London: Tyndale, 1960.

Juel, D. "Social Dimensions of Exegesis: The Use of Psalm 16 in Acts 2." *CBQ* 43 (1981) 543–56.

————. *Luke-Acts: The Promise of History.* Atlanta: John Knox, 1983.

Käsemann, E. "The Problem of the Historical Jesus." In *Essays on New Testament Themes.* London: SCM, 1964. Pp. 15–47.

Kaestli, J.-D. *L'Eschatologie dans l'Oeuvre de Luc.* Genève: Labor et Fides, 1969.

Karris, R. J. "The Lukan Sitz-im-Leben: Methodology and Prospects." SBL 1976 *Seminar Papers.* Edited by G. MacRae. Missoula: Scholars, 1976. Pp. 219–33.

————. "Poor and Rich: The Lukan Sitz im Leben." In *Perspectives on Luke-Acts.* Edited by C. H. Talbert. Danville: Association of Baptist Professors of Religion, 1978. Pp. 112–25.

————. "Windows and Mirrors: Literary Criticism and Luke's Sitz im Leben." In *SBL 1979 Seminar Papers.* Vol. 1. Edited by P. J. Achtemeier. Missoula: Scholars, 1979. Pp. 47–58.

————. "Missionary Communities: A New Paradigm for the Study of Luke-Acts." *CBQ* 41 (1979) 80–97.

Keck, F. *Die öffentliche Abschiedsrede Jesu in Lk 20,25–21,36.* Stuttgart: Katholisches Bibelwerk, 1976.

Keck, L. E. "On the Ethos of Early Christians." *JAAR* 42 (1974) 435–52.

Kerrigan, A. "The 'Sensus Plenior' of Joel,III,1-5 in Act.,II,14-36." In *Sacra Pagina.* Edited by J. Coppens, A. Descamps, and E. Massaux. Paris: Miscellanea Biblica, 1959. Pp. 259-313.

Kesich, V. "Resurrection, Ascension, and the Giving of the Spirit." *GOTR* 25 (1980) 249-60.

Kilgallen, J. J. "The Unity of Peter's Pentecost Speech." *Bible Today* 82 (1976) 650-56.

Kilpatrick, G. D. "Some Quotations in Acts." In *Les Actes des Apôtres: traditions, rédaction, théologie.* Edited by J. Kremer. Leuven: University, 1979. Pp. 81-97.

Klein, G. "Die Prüfung der Zeit (Lukas 12,54-56)." *ZTK* 61 (1964) 373-90.

———. "Eschatologie" (IV, Neues Testament). *TRE* 10 (1982) 270-99.

Klein, H. "Zur Frage nach dem Abfassungsort der Lukasschriften." *EvT* 32 (1972) 467-77.

Klijn, A. F. J. "In Search of the Original Text of Acts." In *Studies in Luke-Acts.* Edited by L. E. Keck and J. L. Martyn. Nashville: Abingdon, 1966. Pp. 103-10.

Knoch, O. "Die eschatologische Frage, ihre Entwicklung und ihr gegenwärter Stand." *BZ* N.F. 6 (1962) 112-20.

Kodell, J. "Luke's Use of LAOS, 'People,' Especially in the Jerusalem Narrative (Lk 19,28-24,53)." *CBQ* 31 (1969) 327-43.

———. "The Theology of Luke in Recent Study." *BTB* 1 (1971) 115-44.

Kränkl, E. *Jesus der Knecht Gottes. Die heilsgeschichtliche Stellung Jesu in den Reden der Apostelgeschichte.* Regensburg: Pustet, 1972.

Kraybill, D. B. and Sweetland, D. M. "Possessions in Luke-Acts: A Sociological Perspective." *Perspectives in Religious Studies* 10 (1983) 215-39.

Kümmel, W. G. *Promise and Fulfillment.* Translated by D. M. Barton. London: SCM, 1957.

———. "Futurische und präsentische Eschatologie im ältesten Urchristentum." *NTS* 5 (1958-59) 113-26.

———. *Introduction to the New Testament.* Translated by A. J. Mattill. London: SCM, 1966, 1975[2].

———. "Luc en accusation dans la theologie contemporaine." In *L'Evangile de Luc: Problèmes littéraires et théologiques.* Edited by F. Neirynck. Bibliotheca Ephemeridum Theologicarum Lovaniensium XXXII. Pp. 93-109.

Kürzinger, J. *Die Apostelgeschichte.* 2 volumes. Düsseldorf: Patmos, 1966, 1970.

Kurz, W. S. "Acts 3,19-26 as a Test of the Role of Eschatology in Lukan Christology." In SBL 1977 *Seminar Papers.* Edited by P. J. Achtemeier. Missoula: Scholars, 1977. Pp. 309-23.

Ladouceur, D. "Hellenistic Preconceptions of Shipwreck and Pollution as a Context for Acts 27-28." *HTR* 73 (1980) 435-49.

Lagrange, M. J. "L'Avènement du Fils de l'homme." *RB* 3 (1906) 382-411.

Lake, K. and Cadbury, H. J. *The Acts of the Apostles.* Vol. 4 of *The Beginnings of Christianity.* Edited by F. J. Foakes Jackson and K. Lake. London: Macmillan, 1933.

Lane, W. L. "Times of Refreshment: A Study of Eschatological Periodization in Judaism and Christianity." Cambridge: Harvard Divinity School Th.D. Dissertation, 1962.

———. "Times of Refreshment: A Study of Eschatological Periodization in Judaism and Christianity." Precis of dissertation. *HTR* 56 (1963) 88-89.

Lauras, A. "Le commentaire patristique de Lc. 21,25-33." *Studia Patristica* 7. Texte und Untersuchungen, 92. Pp. 503-15.

Laurentin, R. *Structure et Théologie de Luc I-II.* Paris: Gabalda, 1957.

LaVerdiere, E. A. "The Ascension of the Risen Lord." *Bible Today* 95 (1978) 1553-59.

LaVerdiere, E. A. and Thompson, W. G. "New Testament Communities in Transition." *TS* 37 (1976) 567-97.

Legrand, L. "The Structure of Acts 2: The Integral Dimensions of the Charismatic Movement according to Luke." *IndTS* 19 (1982) 193-209.

Levine, L. I. *Caesarea under Roman Rule.* Leiden: Brill, 1975.

Lindars, B. *New Testament Apologetic: The Doctrinal Significance of the Old Testament Quotations.* Philadelphia: Westminster, 1961.

Lövestam, E. "Der Rettungsappell in Apostelgeschichte 2,40." *ASTI* 12 (1983) 84-92.

Lohfink, G. "Christologie und Geschichtsbild in Apg 3,19-21." *BZ* N.F. 13 (1969) 223-41.

———. *Die Sammlung Israels: Eine Untersuchung zur lukanischen Ekklesiologie.* Munich: Kösel, 1975.

———. *Die Himmelfahrt Jesu.* Munich: Kösel, 1971.

Lohse, E. "Lukas als Theologe der Heilsgeschichte." *EvT* 14 (1954) 256-75.

Lucchesi, E. "Précédents non Bibliques à l' Expression Néotestamentaire: 'Les Temps et les Moments.' " *JTS* 28 (1977) 537-40.

Lührmann, D. "Noah und Lot (Lk 17,26-29) — ein Nachtrag." *ZNW* 63 (1972) 130-32.

Lygre, J. G. "Exaltation: Considered with Reference to the Resurrection and Ascension in Luke-Acts." Princeton: Princeton Theological Seminary Ph.D. Dissertation, 1975.

MacNeill, H. L. "The *Sitz im Leben* of Luke 1 5–2 20." *JBL* 65 (1946) 123–30.

MacRae, G. W. "Whom Heaven Must Receive Until the Time." *Int* 27 (1973) 151–65.

Maddox, R. *The Purpose of Luke-Acts*. Edinburgh: T. & T. Clark, 1982.

Mahoney, M. "Luke 21:14–15: Editorial Rewriting or Authenticity?" *ITQ* 47 (1980) 220–38.

Mangatt, G. "The Pentecostal Gift of the Spirit." *Biblehashyam* 2 (1976) 227–39, 300–14.

Mannheim, K. *Ideology and Utopia*. Translated by L. Wirth and E. Shils. New York: Harcourt Brace Jovanovich, 1936.

Marshall, I. H. *Commentary on Luke*. Grand Rapids: Eerdmans, 1978.

———. *Luke: Historian and Theologian*. Grand Rapids: Zondervan, 1970.

———. "The Significance of Pentecost." *SJT* 30 (1977) 347–69.

Martini, C. M. "L'esclusione dalla communità del popolo di Dio e il nuovo Israele secondo Atti 3,23." *Biblica* 50 (1969) 1–14.

Martyn, J. L. *History and Theology in the Fourth Gospel*. 2nd ed. Nashville: Abingdon, 1979.

Mattill, A. J. "Naherwartung, Fernerwartung, and the Purpose of Luke-Acts: Weymouth Reconsidered." *CBQ* 34 (1972) 276–93.

———. *Luke and the Last Things*. Dillsboro: Western North Carolina, 1979.

Meeks, W. A. *The First Urban Christians*. New Haven: Yale University, 1983.

Meeks, W. A. and Wilken, R. L. *Jews and Christians in Antioch in the First Four Centuries of the Common Era*. Missoula: Scholars, 1978.

Meinertz, M. "'Dieses Geschlecht' im Neuen Testament." *BZ* 1 (1957) 283–89.

Ménard, J.-E. "PAIS THEOU as Messianic Title in the Book of Acts." *CBQ* 19 (1957) 83–92.

Merk, O. "Das Reich Gottes in den lukanischen Schriften." In *Jesus und Paulus*. Edited by E. E. Ellis and E. Grässer. Göttingen: Vandenhoeck and Ruprecht, 1975. Pp. 201–20.

Miles, G. B. and Trompf, G. "Luke and Antiphon: The Theology of Acts 27–28 in the Light of Pagan Beliefs about Divine Retribution, Pollution, and Shipwreck." *HTR* 69 (1976) 259–67.

Minear, P. S. "Luke's Use of the Birth Stories." In *Studies in Luke-Acts*. Edited by L. E. Keck and J. L. Martyn. Nashville: Abingdon, 1966. Pp. 111–30.

Moessner, D. P. "Luke 9:1–50: Luke's Preview of the Journey of the Prophet Like Moses of Deuteronomy." *JBL* 102 (1983) 575–605.

Moore, A. L. *The Parousia in the New Testament*. Leiden: Brill, 1966.

Moule, C. F. D. "The Ascension—Acts i.9." *ExpTim* 68 (1956–57) 205–09.

——. "The Influence of Circumstance on the Use of Eschatological Terms." *JTS* N.S. 15 (1964) 1–15.

Munck, J. *The Acts of the Apostles.* Revised by W. F. Albright and C. S. Mann. Garden City: Doubleday, 1967.

Mussner, F. "In den letzten Tagen." *BZ* N.F. 5 (1961) 263–65.

——. "Die Idee der Apokatastasis in der Apostelgeschichte." In *Lex Tua Veritas.* Edited by H. Gross and F. Mussner. Trier: Paulinus, 1961. Pp. 293–306.

——. "Wann kommt das Reich Gottes?" *BZ* N.F. 6 (1962) 107–11.

——. "Die Gemeinde des Lukasprologs." *SUNT* 6–7 (1981–82) 113–30.

Nicol, W. "Tradition and Redaction in Luke 21." *Neotestamentica* 7 (1973) 61–71.

Noack, B. *Das Gottesreich bei Lukas: Eine Studie zur Luk. 17,20–24.* Uppsala: Gleerup, 1948.

O'Dea, T. F. *The Sociology of Religion.* Englewood Cliffs: Prentice-Hall, 1966.

——. *Sociology and the Study of Religion: Theory, Research, and Interpretation.* New York: Basic, 1970.

Oepke, A. "πάρειμι, παρουσία." *TDNT* 5. Pp. 858–71.

——. "ἀποκαθίστημι, ἀποκατάστασις." *TDNT* 1, 387–93.

Oliver, H. H. "The Lucan Birth Stories and the Purpose of Luke-Acts." *NTS* 10 (1963–64) 202–26.

O'Neill, J. C. "The Use of KYRIOS in the Book of Acts." *SJT* 8 (1955) 155–74.

——. *The Theology of Acts in Its Historical Setting.* London: SPCK, 1961.

O'Reilly, L. "Chiastic Structure in Ac 1–7." *ProcIrBibAs* 7 (1983) 87–103.

O'Toole, R. F. "Why Did Luke Write Acts (Lk-Acts)?" *BTB* 7 (1977) 66–76.

——. "Luke's Understanding of Jesus' Resurrection—Ascension—Exaltation." *BTB* 10 (1979) 106–14.

——. "Some Observations on ANISTĒMI, 'I Raise,' in Acts 3:22,26." *Science et Esprit* 31 (1979) 85–92.

——. "Acts 2:30 and the Davidic Covenant of Pentecost." *JBL* 102 (1983) 245–58.

——. *The Unity of Luke's Theology: An Analysis of Luke-Acts.* Wilmington: Glazier, 1984.

Owen, H. P. "Stephen's Vision in Acts 7:55–56." *NTS* 1 (1955) 224–26.

Parker, J. *The Concept of Apokatastasis in Acts.* Austin: Schola, 1978.

Parker, P. "The 'Former Treatise' and the Date of Acts." *JBL* 84 (1965) 52–58.

Pérez, A. "Deráš Lucano de Mc 13 a la luz de su 'Teología del Reino': Lc 21,5–36." *EstBib* 39 (1981) 285–313.

Perrot, C. "Essai sur le Discours Eschatologique." *RSR* 47 (1959) 481–514.

Plümacher, E. *Lukas als hellenistischer Schriftsteller.* Göttingen: Vandenhoeck and Ruprecht, 1972.

――――. "Die Apostelgeschichte als historische Monographie." In *Les Actes des Apôtres: traditions, rédaction, théologie.* Edited by J. Kremer. Leuven: University, 1979. Pp. 457–66.

――――. "Acta-Forschung 1974–1982." *TRu* 48 (1983) 1–56 and *TRu* 49 (1984) 105–69.

Plummer, A. *A Critical and Exegetical Commentary on the Gospel According to St. Luke.* 5th ed. Edinburgh: T. & T. Clark, 1922.

Pokorny, P. "Die Romfahrt des Paulus und der antike Roman." *ZNW* 64 (1973) 233–44.

Preisker, H. "ἐγγύς, ἐγγίζω." *TDNT* 2. Pp. 330–32.

Proctor, K. S. "Luke 17.20,21." *Bible Translator* 33 (1982) 245.

Puskas, C. B. "The Conclusion of Luke-Acts: An Investigation of the Literary Function and Theological Significance of Acts 28:16–31." St. Louis: St. Louis University Ph.D. Dissertation, 1980.

Rasco, E. *La Teologia de Lucas: Origen, Desarrollo, Orientaciones.* Rome: Universita Gregoriana, 1976.

Reicke, B. "Synoptic Prophecies on the Destruction of Jerusalem." In *Studies in New Testament and Other Early Christian Literature.* Edited by D. E. Aune. Leiden: Brill, 1972. Pp. 121–34.

Rese, M. *Alttestamentliche Motive in der Christologie des Lukas.* Studien zum Neuen Testament 1. Gütersloher, 1969.

――――. "Die Funktion der alttestamentlichen Zitate und Anspielungen in den Reden der Apostelgeschichte." In *Les Actes des Apôtres: traditions, rédaction, théologie.* Edited by J. Kremer. Leuven: University, 1979. Pp. 61–79.

――――. "Neuere Lukas-Arbeiten." *TL* 106 (1981) 225–37.

Richard, E. "Luke―Writer, Theologian, Historian: Research and Orientation of the 1970's." *BTB* 13 (1983) 3–15.

Ridderbos, H. N. *The Speeches of Peter in the Acts of the Apostles.* London: Tyndale, 1962.

Riesenfeld, H. "παρατήρησις." *TDNT* 8. Pp. 148–51.

――――. "Gudsriket ― här eller där, mitt ibland människor eller inom dem? Till Luk 17:20–21." *Svensk Exegetisk Årsbok* 47 (1982) 93–101.

Roark, D. M. "The Great Eschatological Discourse." *NovT* 7 (1964) 123–27.

Roberts, C. H. "The Kingdom of Heaven (Lk. XVII.21)." *HTR* 41 (1948) 1–8.

Robertson, R. *The Sociological Interpretation of Religion.* New York: Schocken, 1970.

Robinson, J. A. T. "The Most Primitive Christology of All?" *JTS* 7 (1956) 177-89.

Robinson, W. C. *Der Weg des Herrn.* Hamburg: H. Reich, 1964.

Ropes, J. H. *The Text of Acts.* Vol. 3 of *The Beginnings of Christianity.* Edited by F. J. Foakes Jackson and K. Lake. London: Macmillan, 1926.

Rostovtzeff, M. *The Social and Economic History of the Roman Empire.* 2nd ed. revised by P. M. Fraser. Oxford: University, 1957.

Rüstow, A. "ENTOC YMWN ECTIN, zur Deutung von Lc 17 20-21." *ZNW* 51 (1960) 197-224.

Russ, H.-E. *Urkirche auf dem Weg in die Welt: Ein Kommentar zur Apostelgeschichte.* Würzburg: Arena, 1967.

Ryoo, S. W. "The Lukan Birth Narratives and the Theological Unity and Purpose of Luke-Acts." Boston: Boston University Th.D. Dissertation, 1969.

Sabourin, L. "The Eschatology of Luke." *BTB* 12 (1982) 73-76.

Salas, A. *Discurso Escatologico Prelucano: Estudio de Lc. XXI,20-36.* Biblioteca La Ciudad de Dios, Monasterio de al Escorial, 1967.

———. "Los signos cósmicos de Lc. XXI,25-28, a la luz del concepto biblico 'dia de Yahve.'" *La Ciudad de Dios* 180 (1967) 43-85.

Sanders, E. P. *Jesus and Judaism.* Philadelphia: Fortress, 1985.

Sanders, J. T. "The Parable of the Pounds and Lucan Anti-Semitism." *TS* 42 (1981) 660-68.

———. "The Salvation of the Jews in Luke-Acts." In *Luke-Acts: New Perspectives.* Edited by C. H. Talbert. New York: Crossroad, 1984. Pp. 104-28.

Schenk, W. "Naherwartung und Parusieverzögerung: Die urchristliche Eschatologie als Problem der Forschung." *Theologische Versuche* 4 (1972) 47-69.

Schille, G. *Die Apostelgeschichte des Lukas.* Berlin: Evangelsiche, 1983.

Schlier, H. "Jesu Himmelfahrt nach dem lukanischen Schriften." In *Besinnung auf das Neue Testament.* Freiburg: Herder, 1964. Pp. 227-41.

Schlosser, J. "Les Jours de Noé et de Lot. A propos de Luc, XVII,26-30." *RB* 80 (1973) 13-36.

Schmeichel, W. "Christian Prophecy in Lukan Thought: Luke 4:16-30." In SBL 1976 *Seminar Papers.* Edited by G. MacRae. Missoula: Scholars, 1976. Pp. 293-304.

Schmidt, K. L. "βασιλεία." *TDNT* 1. Pp. 574-93.

Schmitt, J. "L'Eglise de Jérusalem ou la 'Restauration' d'Israel d'apres cinq premiers chapitres des Actes." *RevScRel* 27 (1953) 209-18.

Schnackenburg, R. "Zur Frage: Heilsgeschichte und Eschatologie im Neuen Testament." *BZ* N.F. 4 (1960) 116–25.

——. "Der eschatologische Abschnitt Lk 17,20–37." In *Mélanges Bibliques.* Edited by A. Descamps. Gembloux: Duculot, 1970. Pp. 213–34.

——. "Die lukanische Eschatologie im Lichte von Aussagen der Apostelgeschichte." In *Glaube und Eschatologie: Festschrift für Werner Georg Kümmel zum 80. Geburtstag.* Edited by E. Grässer and O. Merk. Tübingen: J. C. B. Mohr, 1985. Pp. 1–17.

Schneider, G. *Parusiegleichnisse im Lukas-Evangelium.* Stuttgart: Katholisches Bibelwerk, 1975.

——. *Die Apostelgeschichte.* 2 volumes. Freiburg: Herder, 1980.

——. "Anbruch des Heils und Hoffnung auf Vollendung bei Jesus, Paulus und Lukas." In *Lukas, Theologe der Heilsgeschichte: Aufsätze zum lukanischen Doppelwerk.* Bonn: Peter Hanstein. 1985. Pp. 35–60.

Schrenk, G. "ἐκδίκησις." *TDNT* 2. Pp. 445–46.

Schubert, P. "The Structure and Significance of Luke 24." In *Neutestamentliche Studien für Rudolf Bultmann.* Edited by W. Eltester. Berlin: Töpelmann, 1954. Pp. 165–86.

——. "The Final Cycle of Speeches in the Book of Acts." *JBL* 87 (1968) 1–16.

Schweitzer, A. *The Quest of the Historical Jesus.* New York, 1956³.

Schweizer, E. "πνεῦμα." *TDNT* 6. Pp. 396–455.

——. "Concerning the Speeches in Acts." In *Studies in Luke-Acts.* Edited by L. E. Keck and J. L. Martyn. Nashville: Abingdon, 1966. Pp. 208–16.

——. *The Good News According to Luke.* Translated by D. E. Green. Atlanta: John Knox, 1984.

Scobie, C. H. H. "The Use of Source Material in the Speeches of Acts III and VII." *NTS* 25 (1979) 399–421.

Seccombe, D. P. *Possessions and the Poor in Luke-Acts.* Linz: Studien zum Neuen Testament und seiner Umwelt, B, Band 6, 1982.

Sledd, A. "The Interpretation of Lk 17,21." *ExpTim* 50 (1938) 235–36.

Sleeper, C. F. "Pentecost and Resurrection." *JBL* 84 (1965) 389–99.

Smalley, S. S. "The Delay of the Parousia." *JBL* 83 (1964) 41–54.

——. "Spirit, Kingdom, and Prayer in Luke-Acts." *NovT* 15 (1973) 59–71.

Smith, R. H. "The Eschatology of Acts and Contemporary Exegesis." *CTM* 29 (1958) 641–63.

——. "History and Eschatology in Luke-Acts." *CTM* 29 (1958) 881–901.

Sneed, R. "The Kingdom of God Is within You." *CBQ* 24 (1962) 363–82.

——. "The Kingdom's Coming: Luke 17,20–21." Catholic University of America S.T.D. Dissertation, 1962.

Stählin, G. *Die Apostelgeschichte.* 12th ed. Göttingen: Vandenhoeck and Ruprecht, 1968.

Stegemann, W. *The Gospel and the Poor.* Translated by D. Elliott. Philadelphia: Fortress, 1984.

Stempvoort, P. A. van. "The Interpretation of the Ascension in Luke and Acts." *NTS* 5 (1958–59) 30–42.

Stowers, S. "The Synagogue in the Theology of Acts." *RestQ* 17 (1974) 129–43.

Stravinskas, P. M. J. "The Role of the Spirit in Acts 1 and 2." *Bible Today* 18 (1980) 263–68.

Strobel, A. "In dieser Nacht (Luk 17,34)." *ZTK* 58 (1961) 16–29.

——. "Die Passa-Erwartung als urchristliches Problem in Lc 17 20f." *ZNW* 49 (1958) 157–95.

——. "A. Merx über Lc 17,20f." *ZNW* 51 (1960) 133–34.

——. "Zu Lk 17,20f." *BZ* N.F. 7 (1963) 111–13.

Sweetland, D. M. "The Lord's Supper and the Lukan Community." *BTB* 13 (1983) 23–27.

——. "Discipleship and Persecution: A Study of Luke 12:1–12." *Biblica* 65 (1984) 61–80.

Talbert, C. H. "II Peter and the Delay of the Parousia." *VC* 20 (1966) 137–45.

——. "The Redaction Critical Quest for Luke the Theologian." In *Jesus and Man's Hope.* Edited by D. G. Buttrick. Pittsburgh, 1970. Pp. 171–222.

——. *Literary Patterns, Theological Themes, and the Genre of Luke-Acts.* Missoula: Scholars, 1974.

——. "Shifting Sands: The Recent Study of the Gospel of Luke." *Int* 30 (1976) 381–95.

——. *What Is a Gospel?* Philadelphia: Fortress, 1977.

——. "Promise and Fulfillment in Lucan Theology." In *Luke-Acts: New Perspectives.* Edited by C. H. Talbert. New York: Crossroad, 1984. Pp. 91–103.

Tannehill, R. C. "The Composition of Acts 3–5: Narrative Development and Echo Effect." In SBL 1984 *Seminar Papers.* Edited by K. H. Richards. Chico: Scholars, 1984. Pp. 217–40.

——. "Israel in Luke-Acts: A Tragic Story." *JBL* 104 (1985) 69–85.

Tatum, W. B. "The Epoch of Israel: Luke I-II and the Theological Plan of Luke-Acts." *NTS* 13 (1966–67) 184–95.

188 ESCHATOLOGY AND SITUATION IN LUKE-ACTS

Taylor, V. "A Cry from the Siege: A Suggestion Regarding a Non-Marcan Oracle Embedded in Lk. XXI 20-36." *JTS* 26 (1924-25) 136-44.

Thompson, J. W. "The Gentile Mission as an Eschatological Necessity." *RestQ* 14 (1971) 18-27.

Thornton, T. C. G. "To the end of the earth: Acts 1:8." *ExpTim* 89 (1978) 374-75.

Tiede, D. L. *Prophecy and History in Luke-Acts.* Philadelphia: Fortress, 1980.

———. "The Exaltation of Jesus and the Restoration of Israel in Acts 1." In SBL 1985 *Seminar Papers.* Edited by K. H. Richards. Atlanta: Scholars, 1985. Pp. 369-75.

———. "Ac 1:6-8 and the Theo-Political Claim of Christian Witness." *WordWorld* 1 (1981) 41-51.

Trompf, G. W. "On Why Luke Declined to Recount the Death of Paul: Acts 27-28 and Beyond." In *Luke-Acts: New Perspectives.* Edited by C. H. Talbert. New York: Crossroad, 1984. Pp. 225-39.

Tyson, J. B. "The Problem of Food in Acts: A Study of Literary Patterns with Particular Reference to Acts 6:1-7." In SBL 1979 *Seminar Papers.* Edited by P. J. Achtemeier. Missoula: Scholars, 1979. Pp. 69-85.

———. "The Jewish Public in Luke-Acts." *NTS* 30 (1984) 574-83."

Unnik, W. C. van. " 'Acts' the Confirmation of the Gospel." *NovT* 4 (1960) 26-59.

———. "Der Ausdruck 'ΕΩΣ 'ΕΣΧΑΤΟΥ ΤΗΣ ΓΗΣ (Apostelgeschichte 1:8) und sein alttestamentlicher Hintergrund." *Studia Biblica et Semitica.* T.C. Vriezen dedicata. Wageningen: Veenman and Zonen, 1966. Pp. 335-49.

———. "Luke's Second Book and the Rules of Hellenistic Historiography." In *Les Actes des Apôtres: traditions, rédaction, théologie.* Edited by J. Kremer. Leuven: University, 1979. Pp. 37-60.

Vielhauer, P. "On the 'Paulinism' of Acts." In *Studies in Luke-Acts.* Edited by L. E. Keck and J. L. Martyn. Nashville: Abingdon, 1966. Pp. 33-50.

———. "Das Benedictus des Zacharias (Luk. 1,68-79)." *ZTK* 49 (1952) 255-72.

Völkel, M. "Zur Deutung des 'Reiches Gottes' bei Lukas." *ZNW* 65 (1974) 57-70.

Voss, G. " 'Zum Herrn und Messias gemacht hat Gott diesen Jesus' (Apg 2,36)." *BibLeb* 8 (1967) 236-48.

Waard, J. de. "The Quotation from Deuteronomy in Acts 3.22,23 and the Palestinian Text: Additional Arguments." *Biblica* 52 (1971) 537-40.

Wainright, A. W. "Luke and the Restoration of the Kingdom to Israel." *ExpTim* 89 (1977) 76-79.

Weinert, F. D. "The Parable of the Throne Claimant (Luke 19:12,14-15a,27) Reconsidered." *CBQ* 39 (1977) 505-14.

Weiser, A. "Von der Predigt Jesu zur Erwartung der Parusie überlieferungsge-schichtliches zum Gleichnis vom Türhüter." *BibLeb* 12 (1971) 25-31.

Werner, M. *The Formation of Christian Dogma.* London: Adam and Charles Black, 1957.

Wilckens, U. *Die Missionsreden der Apostelgeschichte.* Neukirchen: Neukir-chener, 1961, 1974³.

Wilcox, M. *The Semitisms of Acts.* Oxford: Clarendon, 1965.

Wilder, A. N. "Eschatological Imagery and Earthly Circumstance." *NTS* 5 (1958-59) 229-45.

Williams, C. S. C. *The Acts of the Apostles.* London: Adam and Charles Black, 1957.

Wilson, B. R. "A Typology of Sects in a Dynamic and Comparative Perspective." In *Archives de Sociologie de Religion* 16 (1963) 49-63.

Wilson, S. G. "Lukan Eschatology." *NTS* 15 (1969-70) 330-47.

———. "The Ascension: A Critique and an Interpretation." *ZNW* 59 (1968) 269-81.

———. *The Gentiles and the Gentile Mission in Luke-Acts.* Cambridge: Univer-sity, 1973.

Zehnle, R. F. *Peter's Pentecost Discourse.* Nashville: Abingdon, 1971.

Zmijewski, J. *Die Eschatologiereden des Lukas-Evangeliums.* Bonn: Peter Hanstein, 1972.

———. "Die Eschatologiereden Lk 21 und Lk 17." *BibLeb* 14 (1973) 30-40.

Indexes

ANCIENT AUTHORS BY PASSAGE